An Arabian Son's Journey

Adel Alsuhaimi

AABB PRESS

Copyright © 2021 Adel Alsuhaimi
All rights reserved.

No part of this publication may be reproduced, stored in or introduced into a retrieval system, or transmitted, in any form, or by any means (electronic, mechanical, photocopying, recording, or otherwise), without the prior permission of the publisher except in the case of brief quotations embodied in critical articles and review.

Requests for permission should be directed
to adel.alsuhaimi@outlook.com.

Book Cover and Interior Design by Monkey C Media
Edited by Barbara Desantis
Photo credits listed at back of book

First Edition
Printed in the United States of America

ISBNs: 978-1-7359769-1-4 (hardcover)
978-1-7359769-0-7 (trade paperback)
978-1-7359769-2-1 (ebook)

Library of Congress Control Number: 2020925214

This book is dedicated to
my father Abdulaziz,
my mother Madawi,
my grandfather Abdulrahman,
my grandmother Nourah,
and my brother Basim.

God rest their souls in peace.

CONTENTS

Introduction 1
   The Promise 1
Chapter 1 14
   Al Khalouj, A Poet's Call for Arms 14
   History of Early Unayzah 23
Chapter 2 34
   A Journey of a lifetime 34
   History Of The Alsuhaimi Family 49
Chapter 3 55
   The Great War 55
   The Ottoman Empire and the Arabian Peninsula 57
   Captain William Shakespear 61
   The Treaty of Darin 63
   The "Sick Man of Europe" 66
   Blockade of seaports in the Eastern Arabian region 66
   The McMahon-Hussein Correspondence and the
      Arab Revolt 67
   The Sykes-Picot Agreement 68
   Help from Lawrence of Arabia 73
   The Balfour Declaration 76
   Britain's Role in the Creation of Saudi Arabia 78
Chapter 4 82
   The Majestic Deserts of Arabia 82

Chapter 5 99
   A Family Loss 99
   The Uqair Seaport 102
   The Motive for the Kuwaiti Merchants' Decision 107
   Jubail: The Birthplace of Alsuhaimi Business 116
   The History of Jubail 117

Chapter 6 119
   Life in Jubail and a Unique Friendship 119

Chapter 7 134
   Security and Political Uncertainty in Jubail; the need to
      explore trade sources farther out 134
   The Wise Arbiter of Jubail 148

Chapter 8 152
   The Dream 152
   The Road to Black Gold 156
   The Anglo-Persian Oil Company 157
   Gulf Oil Corporation 157
   Iraq Petroleum Company (IPC) 157
   SoCal 159
   Saudi ARAMCO 159
   The Battle for Oil in Iraq 160
   Major Frank Holmes, Father of Oil 166
   Bahrain 167
   Kuwait 169
   Arabian Oil and Jack Philby 170
   Discovery of oil in Dammam 174
   Britain and Saudi Arabia: The ending of the colonial
      relationship 183

Chapter 9 184
   WWII and Oil Supremacy 184
   Saleh's Reunion 190
   An Investment Worth Its Weight 195

Chapter 10 .... **201**
    The Boomtown of Dammam 201
Chapter 11 .... **220**
    A Thriving Business; Time to Hand Over Reigns
        to Abdulaziz 220
Epilogue **231**
    The Grand Sons; Adel, Brothers and Cousins 231
    Youth Unemployment and Labor Rights......................... 235
    Education 237
    Political Instability 238
    Economy... 239
    Women's Rights 239
    Environment... 240
    Healthcare 241
    The Need for Accountability... 242
    Saudi Arabia Vision 2030 243
Acknowledgments.. **245**
Photo Credits **247**

INTRODUCTION

The Promise

All my life I lived with my family in the Eastern province of Saudi Arabia on the Al Hasa Gulf[1] coast, in the capitol city of Dammam. My father, Abdulaziz, and my mother, Madhawi, had migrated there in 1952, four years before I was born, traveling the sixty miles south from their small fishing village of Jubail where the scent of sea wafted in from shore. Named for the small mountain to the northeast that once rose from the sea but now lies beneath it, Jubail has its roots in antiquity. Some claim the Phoenicians inhabited it as early as 3000 BC.

My father treasured his memories of growing up there, and often when the family gathered in our living room, he dragged out the faded sepia photographs of his Jubaili friends for me and my siblings to see, along with, of course, some rather awkward photos of

---

1 Al Hasa Gulf was named after one of the largest oasis in the Arabian Peninsula, and is also known as the Arabian Gulf as well as the Persian Gulf. "According to historian and map specialist Sami Al-Maghlouth, Italian sailors in Venice in 1693, had named the Arabian Gulf the 'Al-Ahsa Gulf.' It had various other names in the past determined by those who controlled the area. Islamic maps had documented the area as the 'Bahrain Gulf.' The 'Gulf of Basra' was used under the Ottoman Empire, and was renamed the Arabian Gulf after the end of the British occupation." Arab News, Travel, "Arabian Gulf formerly named Al-Ahsa Gulf"; Arab News, Sultan Al-Sughair, August 19, 2015; <http://www.arabnews.com/travel/news/793561>

Adel Alsuhaimi

Abdulaziz A.R. Alsuhaimi, 1959, Dammam.

our much younger selves. My father wasn't a talkative man, his taciturn manner often frustrating my mother who had always appreciated the fine art of conversation. That never fazed my father though, who seemed oblivious to her desire to have him converse with the family. Somehow he found a way to let others do the talking while he kept working on whatever needed to be done. Pragmatic comes to mind when I think of him, industrious too, and yes, taciturn. He'd rather strain his body doing push-ups for three days straight than carry on a conversation for five minutes. I suppose this was what motivated him to want to record the stories his father had told him. Since he was never going to give us an oral account, he needed a written one if we were to ever learn about our family's history.

I'd soon learn that it meant more than a family keepsake to him; it was his deepest wish to bequeath to his children and grandchildren and all his future generations a permanent record of the history of my paternal grandfather, Abdulrahman Alsuhaimi. He held on to that dream for his entire life.

I was a senior in Dammam High School (1970-73) when my father, Abdulaziz, first mentioned the idea. He thought it would be useful to have a printed collection of the anecdotes and photographs to document his father's early life. It was important to him that the future generations learned not only about their roots but how they came to live such a privileged life, one that can be traced back to his father's journey that began in 1915 at the age of sixteen when he traveled by camel from Unayzah in the heart of the peninsula and across uncharted Arabian territory through the Great Nefud Desert to the pearling cities of Basra and Kuwait and the small Gulf village

Semm Yubah

of Jubail, before finally settling in Dammam where the discovery of black gold would transform everyone's life. The subject had surfaced frequently after that, especially when Father met with his brothers and childhood friends from Jubail, and reminisced about the good old days. Or when Father was teaching me how to drive.

Driving lessons were conducted in his 1964 9-seater Land-Rover Defender on our farm at the outskirts of Dammam. He rounded up all of the children after school on Thursday afternoons and together we set off for our farm in the desert. (At the time Friday was considered Saudi Arabia's official weekend and our only day off. On October 16th, 1975, the weekend was expanded to include both Thursday and Friday but it wasn't until 2013 when King Abdullah issued a royal decree did the nation's weekend shift to Friday and Saturday to keep it in synch with its neighbors.) We looked forward to those excursions when we got the chance to swim in the pool at our farm, a special treat for children growing up in a harsh desert climate. As soon as we arrived, but before

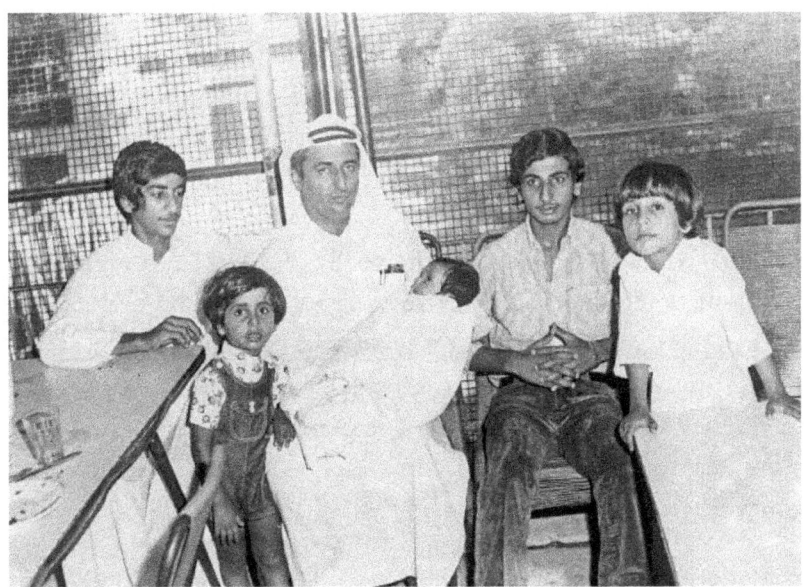

Father Abdulaziz (center) & sons, left to right: Mosaad, Fahad, Yousef, Adel, and Basim, in Lebanon, 1973.

anyone was allowed to go for a swim, we motored out to the nearby dunes where I could safely practice my driving far from the city traffic and any pedestrians. I drove in the wide open expanse of desert but Father still sat vigilant in the front passenger seat, ready to assume control of the car as I shifted gears and negotiated the pedals and steering wheel. During those driving lessons, the subject of Jubail always came up and the importance of recording on paper my grandfather's story. I suppose it was the wide sweep of desert wilderness—beguiling and ominous at the same time—that evoked his early memories of growing up so close to it and recalled his father's great passion for a time and place long gone, but I wouldn't really understand the depth of his desire to have a written account of his father's life until much later.

It was my Father's wish that I study in the United States to get a better education, and when I graduated high school in 1973, he sent me to school in the northwest. (It was no small coincidence that the American school was also located near his cousin's home.) After a semester abroad, I found the disparity between the two cultures overwhelming. The liberal atmosphere of young Americans in the early seventies was too challenging and confusing for an eighteen-year-old Arab boy raised in a conservative environment. Still, I waited until I completed my first year before I returned home to Saudi Arabia to enroll in Dhahran's King Fahd University of Petroleum and Minerals, and in 1978 graduated with a Bachelor of Science degree. After earning my MBA, I worked the next few years as a lecturer of Economics and Operations Management. During this time my father kept mentioning his desire to write his father's story but he never got around to it, and in 1980 I had little time to help, having just embarked on a career within the family business and was also in the midst of wedding preparations for my marriage. Still, it was then that I had made the pledge to my father. I was in

Semm Yubah

my mid-twenties then but I told him I would set aside everything and write my grandfather's story—one day.

I remember where we were when I first promised him. It was his habit to stay late in his office in Dammam long after his staff had left, the perfect time for me to sit with him and catch up any business or family matters. Every day at work's end I poured us some English Breakfast tea, dropped a few mint leaves into each cup to steep, and padded to his office for a chat before going home.

Piles of papers, catalogs, and folders obscured his desk and office floor, every available inch of space covered, including the top of his two large safes. He hated throwing anything out and kept unnecessary duplicates of everything, creating endless stacks of paper. Ironically, he rarely misplaced a document. Still, my brothers and I repeatedly cleaned out his office, sifting through mountains of paper, organizing documents, making the stacks much smaller and more manageable, only for the paper to pile up again days later. That afternoon his office looked as cluttered as usual, and as he sipped the tea I'd given him, he spoke in his typical shorthand. At first I had difficulty understanding his clipped sentences but I had years of learning how to interpret his measured speech. A yes, no, or fine, accompanied with a nod and a grin, or what in Arabic we call "a Red Eye" (of anger), spoke volumes of what our beloved father meant. My siblings and I usually understood and did whatever he needed. That day was no different. He didn't say much, but I understood when he said, *Yubah* (the Arabic word for father) and saw his face cloud. Although he never articulated his emotions, his respect and adoration for his father had always been apparent, and that day the look in his eyes told me he desperately wanted to keep his father's story from fading into oblivion.

I was the eldest son in the family and eldest grandchild, and first to achieve an undergraduate and a Master's degree, accomplishments that made my father very proud. My younger brothers had succeeded, too, in earning their degrees in the States but not until much later in the 1990's, and it fell to me as the eldest to fulfill my father's dream.

It wasn't until December of 2013, my father in his eighties, gravely ill and bed-confined, that I renewed that promise. We were in the family compound in Dammam. In Saudi Arabia families generally live together or at least near each other, and my family has been fortunate enough to own a large compound of several acres, with each of my five brothers having his own home there. My father had lived in the largest one. (My five married sisters live in their own homes within their husband's family compound.)

My father's house contained a spacious living room with wall-to-wall French windows with a clear view of the palms outside. Here is where his bed had been set up during his final days, chairs placed all around him. Since we all lived within the compound, at no time was he alone, one or all of us were always there to keep him company.

That day as I kept vigil at his bedside, he drifted in and out of sleep, and the sound of rain rapping at the windows beckoned. I couldn't help but be captivated by the palms playing with the wind, their fronds wet and gleaming in the fractured light, a surreal landscape to any native of the Arabian desert. It brought to mind a story my father often told me—my grandfather, a young boy on the back of a camel battling the desert rain—and I thought about my failure to fulfill my father's dream. When he roused

Father Abdulaziz at home reception, in Dammam, 2010.

I renewed my vow, promising him I'd record the story of my paternal grandfather, Abdulrahman, and my great-grandfather, Saleh, and keep alive the tale of how a 16-year-old boy on the

Semm Yubah

Arabian Peninsula in 1915, separated from family and home, became a man, how the journey began with him accompanying his father by camel caravan through a merciless desert for the sake of their family's welfare, and how a few years later he was left on his own to make his way in the world. It was a journey that would forever change the course of his life, and alter the destiny of future generations of his family.

The Saudi Arabia of my grandfather's early youth, of course, was nothing like the country I grew up in, nothing like the modern country it is today, and nothing had existed then that even vaguely resembled a stable economy. The Arabian Peninsula was a vast unmapped territory without borders or boundaries, with no infrastructure, and whose most prominent feature were endless stretches of sun-bake desert. It was a poor country with a predominantly agricultural economy, and its immense and isolated and often ruthless terrain was primarily inhabited by Bedouins, the proud nomadic tribes of camel herders and shepherds whose claim to any particular parcel of land depended on the tribe's grazing areas and location of their hand-dug water wells. Whenever ownership came into dispute, they fought for control of their region's resources or roamed the desert in oppressive heat, migrating from oasis to oasis, crossing wind-swept dunes to mountain valleys, seeking verdant pastures and better places to trade their wares. With tenacity and endurance, they met the challenges of a cruel desert climate exacerbated by famines and drought. Many struggled to maintain even the basic necessities for their families. Tribal warfare became a common occurrence, often lasting decades and spanning generations, their finest Arab warriors battling to the end to gain authority over the land.

British explorer and travel writer Wilfred Thesiger, who had spent five years living with Arabia's Bedouins, claimed that "Without the Bedu my journey would have been a meaningless penance…The human spirit achieves an essential nobility under conditions of hardship…In their courage, endurance, good temper and generosity, the Bedu were infinitely superior to my race. Their spirit lit the desert like a flame."[2]

The Arabian Peninsula has a much longer history than that of the last few centuries, and dates back more than 100,000 years. Ancient civilizations such as Thamud, Sheba and Dilmun, have their roots there. The land had been much more hospitable then. "Enhanced monsoonal rainfall transformed the Arabian Peninsula into an area covered with lakes and rivers when humans lived there 85,000 years ago."[3] Imagine, the Al Nefud Desert was once "a grasslands teeming with wildlife alongside a freshwater lake."[4]

Standing between the Nile River Valley and Mesopotamia, the Arabian Peninsula had served as the crossroads of their worlds. Once, two historic superpowers, the Roman-Byzantine and Persian empires, ruled the region. But following the spread of Islam in the 7th century, the control and authority of these two empires fell to the Muslims under the second Caliph of the Rashidun Caliphate, Umar Ibn Al-Khattab[5], and for centuries afterward, Muslim-rule dominated. Later, this region, known as *Hejaz*, which comprises most of the western part of modern-day Saudi Arabia, emerged as a center of development and learning, and became a thriving hub for trade. It also contains the sacred

---

2 Michael Winn1981, Aramco World, accessed March 2016, <http://archive.aramcoworld.com/issue/198104/a.taste.for.freedom.htm>

3 Katy Scott, Inside The Middle East, CNN, accessed 10 June 2018, <https://www.cnn.com/2018/04/09/health/saudi-arabia-fossil-finger/index.html>

4 Will Dunham, SCIENCE & SPACE 2018, Reuters, accessed 10 June 2018, <https://www.reuters.com/article/us-science-finger/fossil-homo-sapiens-finger-from-saudi-desert-is-90000-years-old-idUSKBN1HG2YC>

5 The Rashidun Caliphate consisted of the first four Caliphs who led the Islamic empire after the death of the Prophet Muhammad (PBUH). Umar Ibn Al-Khattab, the 2nd Caliph, an expert Muslim jurist, was known for his pious and just nature, and was also called Al-Farooq, Arabic for "the one who distinguishes right and wrong."

cities of Makkah,[6] the birthplace of the prophet Muhammad (PBUH),[7] and Madinah,[8] home to the Prophet's Mosque, and continues to serve as the holiest sites of Islam and the pilgrimage destination for millions of Muslims worldwide fulfilling their religious obligation (*Hajj*)[9] to visit the holy city of Makkah once during their lifetime.

Decades would pass before the Arabia of my grandfather's youth began to even remotely resemble the more modern country it is today. In 1902 the charismatic twenty seven-year-old Abdulaziz Ibn Saud[10], a direct descendent of Muhammad Ibn Saud and the House of Saud (who had been in and out of power in central Arabia for more than 130 years[11]), rode into the desert with seventy of his clansmen and loyal Subaei tribesmen to restore the rule of the Al Saud family and recapture their ancestral home of Riyadh in central Arabia from their archrivals, Al Rasheeds. But it wouldn't

---

    6 Mecca is the original English transliteration of the Arabic name. In the 1980s, the Saudi Arabian government and others began promoting the transliteration Makkah (in full, Makkah al-Mukarramah), which more closely resembles the actual Arabic pronunciation. The spelling Makkah or Meccah is not new and has always been a common alternative. Mecca, New World Encyclopedia contributors, New World Encyclopedia, 2019, accessed 17 July 2019, <http://web.newworldencyclopedia.org/entry/Mecca> The Qur'an also refers to the city as both Makkah and Bakkah.
    7 PBUH stands for Peace and Blessings be upon Him, the English translation of the Arabic phrase, Sallallahu Alayhi Wa Sallam, and is used as a sign of respect for the Prophet.
    8 Medina is the English transliteration of the Arabic name, Maddinah.
    9 The greater Muslim pilgrimage to Makkah is called Hajj and takes place the last month of the year. All Muslims are expected to make the pilgrimage at least once during their lifetime if they can afford to do so. It is one of the Five Pillars of Islam.
    10 Abdulaziz Ibn Saud, usually known within the Arab world as Abdulaziz and in the West as Ibn Saud, was the first monarch and founder of Saudi Arabia. "Ibn" means "son of" in Arabic.
    11 The Al Saud family, ancestors of Abdulaziz Ibn Saud, had occupied a central authority within the region for the last 130 years. They first had attempted to establish a First Saudi State through the unification of the Arabian Peninsula in 1744, but it had been destroyed by the Ottomans' proxy—the Egyptian Army in 1818. In 1824, the Second Saudi State was established when the Al Saud family regained power but their rule was restricted to central Arabia, and throughout the 19th century they had been rivaled by the Al Rasheed family. By 1891, with Ottoman support, the Al Rasheeds successfully ousted the Al Saud family and forced them into exile to Kuwait until 1902.

Al Saud Dynasties

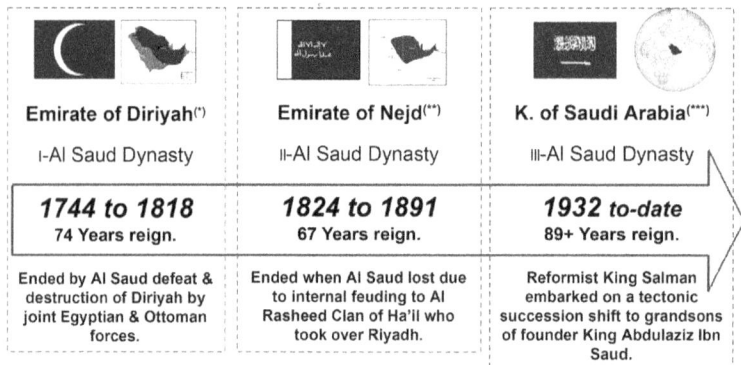

(*) http://en.wikipedia.org/wiki/Emirate_of_Diriyah
(**) http://en.wikipedia.org/wiki/Second_Saudi_State
(***) http://en.wikipedia.org/wiki/Saudi_Arabia

be for another twenty two years after that before they regained control of the holy cities of *Makkah* and *Madinah* (with the help of the British), and still more than a decade later before the country unified, and later the world's most sought after natural resource discovered, providing the people of Saudi Arabia with what is still considered their greatest natural blessing—the black gold of the middle east—oil. Of course the enormous revenues generated from oil has been a mixed blessing. Saudi Arabia's supply of oil and other energy sources are finite, and eventually our reserve will be depleted. Although Saudi Arabia has used these revenues since 1975 to help improve the country's infrastructure, much more needs to be done to ensure that future generations will benefit from the vast amount of wealth generated, and that it will be used for the betterment of all members of the society, not just an elite few. But I will discuss that in more detail in the Epilogue.

On September 23, 1932, Abdulaziz Ibn Saud had successfully united his dominions into the Kingdom of Saudi Arabia and declared himself its king, but it was only after oil was discovered in commercial quantities in 1938 (in Dammam's well #7, now called

Semm Yubah

The Prosperity Well), did its export lead to the transformation of the country and the development of its basic infrastructure: roads, schools, hospitals, and airports. During this time, the national oil company, Aramco, was established, which invested heavily in the country's production facilities—building plants and pipelines, housing communities and business centers—that promoted a modern Saudi Arabian economy.

In 1960, nearly three decades after its establishment, Saudi Arabia along with four other countries: Venezuela, Kuwait, Iraq, and Iran, founded the oil cartel, OPEC (Organization of the Petroleum Exporting Countries) to improve their bargaining leverage with the World Oil Super Majors and to ensure oil prices remained reasonable, stable and regulated in the international market. (The six largest non-state owned oil companies, formed during the consolidation of the oil industry during the mid-1990's were Exxon, Mobil, Total S.A., Royal Dutch Shell, British Petroleum, Chevron, and ConocoPhillips) Today, OPEC consists of 14 member countries.

Many years would pass before Saudi Arabia started making 5-year development plans that would be followed sequentially and become the motivating force behind a number of infrastructure development projects in the country.

During the 1973 oil crisis, oil prices skyrocketed, boosting Saudi Arabia's oil revenues and making it one of the fastest growing economies in the world. The government used the oil revenues for the improvement of the country's infrastructure and the development of its defense among other projects. Saudi Arabia's oil revenues peaked again during the outset of the 1980 Iran-Iraq War.

However, in many instances afterwards, Saudi Arabia faced a glut in production and an overall slump in oil prices, which resulted in a substantial decrease in the number of barrels of oil produced, and the price of oil dropped to one fifth of its original fee. Since then, Saudi Arabia has changed its oil policy by agreeing to adhere to an OPEC collective and binding production quota.

In this book I will further discuss the economic and political development of the Arabian Peninsula as well as its history as it pertains to my grandfather's life, but suffice it to say that the world of my grandfather as a young boy was dramatically different from the Saudi Arabia of today.

Eventually oil enabled many Saudis to go from the proverbial rags to riches, having helped them establish successful businesses and take advantage of the excellent infrastructure projects, government incentives and subsidies from the high oil revenues. Others achieved something far more valuable, a legacy of determination, diligence and integrity for their future generations to emulate. One such man was my paternal grandfather, the proud son of Unayzah: Abdulrahman Saleh Alsuhaimi.

Much time has passed since I've made that pledge to my father to

HRH Amir IBN Jiluwi (left), sits with Desco Chairman Abdulrahman Alsuhaimi (author's grandfater), and ARAMCO government relations official at Desco opening, December 13, 1965.

Semm Yubah

share my grandfather's story, life having intruded as it so often does with the demands of work and family. I am now sixty-two and a far cry from that young man learning to drive in the desert. Still I haven't forgotten my promise and believe this book fulfills the pledge I made so many years ago. I hope by telling my grandfather's story I will keep his spirit alive, and that our family and our future generations will understand how the boy from a small village became a man, and will appreciate the scope of Abdulrahman's accomplishments and the challenges he faced. I hope his story will demonstrate how his hard work and business acumen, his perseverance and sacrifices, as well as his generosity and compassion, not only translated into shaping the future of the Alsuhaimi family, providing them with continuous security and prosperity, but will explain how he played an important role in the development of the eastern province of Saudi Arabia.

But I also have a larger vision for this book. At a time when xenophobia is on the rise and the differences of "other" less tolerated, I hope this book successfully illustrates that my grandfather, a devout Muslim, was a man not unlike most men of a certain generation and age. That he had cared deeply for family and home, God and country, and had worked hard to provide and care for the people he loved. I hope by sharing my grandfather's story I will give readers a glimpse of what life was like for a boy growing up in the interior of the Arabian Peninsula in the early part of the 20th century, and they will see that dreams and hopes and desires are universal, and that family is held just as close to the heart, and perhaps my grandfather's story will help foster a greater understanding, appreciation and tolerance for the "other."

—Adel Abdulaziz Alsuhaimi, 2018

CHAPTER 1

Al Khalouj, A Poet's Call for Arms

It was winter in Dammam, Saudi Arabia, 1978, the sky blessed with clouds as we patiently awaited the arrival of rain to cleanse our dusty land after ten long, dry months. I had just returned from Kuwait and was on my semester break and had rushed over to my *Yubah's*,[12] eager to give him the gift I'd brought back with me. Whenever I entered his house, Indian incense burned in the background, and on that morning it infused his living room with the same sweet earthy aroma. It was especially potent during winter when he kept the windows shuttered and the coal fireplace lit.

As soon as my Grandfather stepped into the room, a familiar fragrance wafted toward me as if in an embrace. I inhaled the *Oud*, and felt pure joy. Indian *Oud* has been popular in the east for centuries. Arabs have long fragranced their skin and hair with the perfume concentrate derived from the agar tree and burned its dry wood to sweeten their house with its scent. Every morning my grandfather worked a small drop of its oil into his palms, and its pungent fragrance lingered like a flower's. Today, one whiff still

---

12 Yubah is Arabic slang for Grandfather.

Semm Yubah

conjures up images of my *Yubah*. I always felt it imbued him with a highly dignified and respectable air.

My grandfather was tall and lean, and looked especially regal in the traditional winter *thobe*, a tunic-styled, ankle-length garment worn by Arabian men. This one had been woven from wool and the same bluish gray of a Dusky Turtle Dove. His *Gutra*, the large square of crimson cotton he donned as a head scarf whenever he left the house, hung on the back of a door with his *Iqal*, the corded black band that held his *Gutra* in place. I shifted my weight trying to contain my excitement as he settled into his cushioned seat on the floor. I had been fortunate to find a recording of his favorite Arabian poem, *Al Khalooj*, performed by the famous Kuwaiti singer, Abdullah Fadalah, and that was accompanied by the *Rubaba*, the small one-string cello of his beloved Bedouins. He would be thrilled hearing it along with his favorite poem. I couldn't wait to see the look on his face.

My grandfather's love affair with poetry begun at an early age when he had lived in close proximity to the Bedouins, the desert nomads who wandered the Peninsula in search of water and grazing lands. Their songs and poems of glory and sorrow had regaled him as a boy. In the tribe's community, the poet held an honorary position as custodian of their history, connected them to their ancestors and anchored them to their past. A Bedouin poet possessed the uncanny ability to spontaneously describe in verse a recent tribal event or some crucial historical moment, recounting tales of victory and defeat, love and loss, all the tragedies and anguish accompanying war.

The famous Arabian poet, Muhammad Al Ouny, had written my grandfather's favorite, *Al Khalouj*,[13] (Arabic for the calf of the camel), around 1903, a year after the young, charismatic leader Abdulaziz Ibn Saud had reclaimed for the House of Saud the central Arabian city of Riyadh from his rival, Al Rasheed. (Ibn

---

13 Al Zamil 2008, Subaie Algalba Tribe website, accessed 20 September 2016. (Original poem and story in Arabic), <http://www.sobe3.com/vb/showthread.php?t=29039>

Adel Alsuhaimi

Mother Camel mourning her dead calf.

Saud would go on to consolidate the various Arabian tribes to form the kingdom of Saudi Arabia and proclaim himself their first king). Al Ouny had written the poem specifically to help garner support for Ibn Saud's cause.

Al Ouny hoped to appeal to those fierce warriors of the Qassim region (which included my grandfather's hometown of Unayzah, and the neighboring town of Buraydah, among others in central Arabia). Al Ouny believed his poem would tug at his countrymen's heartstrings prompting them to join Ibn Saud's forces in liberating the rest of their homeland from the hands of their rivals, Al Rasheed.

The poem recounts the story of a mother camel's anguish over losing her young calf at Kuwait's Al Sabah Palace.

> *A mother cries her heart out,*
> *Her tears and heartbeats break the silence of the desert.*
> *She urges anyone with a conscience to listen to her story,*
> *One that left her devastated, her soul lost.*
>
> *I begged her to stop grieving,*
> *She cried: my calf was fair-skinned, a shy babe, a unique beauty.*
> *But the envious with their prying eyes frightened him.*

Semm Yubah

Every year she returns to the same spot hoping to be reunited with her offspring only to be disappointed, and wails, realizing her calf will never return home to her.

The bereft mother camel represented the Qassim region (a sub region of Najd in central Arabia), and the dead calf symbolized Qassim's sons who had migrated far from their homes, most of them never returning to loved ones.

She is our mother, and all abandoned her and left.
I never seen such motherly devotion, and we forgot how she looked.
She sheltered us, kept us fed and warm,
Now she is naked and crying, and no one notices.

The poem had a dramatic impact on the community of Qassim immigrants who had long ago left their families.

Many will ask you for news and destination
Especially about what Najd faced after you left.
Tell them about Qassim and the other areas,
How all men were sent to save their beloved
But only your mother stayed behind grieving,
Crying for her sons, and no single soul to comfort her.
The invaders wreaked mayhem, but none of you cared.

Al Khalooj had evoked powerful feelings of remorse and guilt in Ibn Saud's fellow tribesmen, and achieved Al Ouny's goal: Ibn Saud's migrated subjects had returned home and joined him in his fight against his archrival, Al Rasheed.

To my grandfather, the poem paralleled his early life, and recalled his teenage years when he had left his own mother to travel with his father to foreign lands in search of work. My grandfather never saw his mother again and learned of her death long after the fact, which only complicated his grief. In early twentieth century Arabia, news had traveled slowly by camel from his hometown of Unayzah across desert and dunes, through small towns, to the northeast where he had migrated–Kuwait. How much time had transpired after her passing and when he learned of it, is anyone's guess. A variety of factors come into play: how long it took someone to compose a letter with the news and then find someone else to act as mail carrier, and how soon that person scheduled the trip to Kuwait. It also depended on the security of the route, tribal conflicts in the areas often hindering travel, and the weather of course, the weather was always an obstacle. If the carrier had traveled during springtime or summer he surely had to contend with the *shamals*, those ferocious northwesterly winds that produce blinding sandstorms. But from what I've pieced together from the various accounts of family members, she died almost three years after my grandfather had left home, around 1918, and it took possibly a few years after that, before he received news of her death.

It was this kind of tragic loss that Muhammad Al Ouny eloquently depicts in his poem about the grieving camel. More and more we read about various species in the animal kingdom that go into mourning, experiencing a deep depression upon losing an offspring or a mate. In *Al Khalouj*, it is unclear whether the mother camel's sorrow signifies her acceptance or her denial of her calf's death, but the poignancy of the story struck a deep chord within my grandfather, and continued to do so until his final days. He never forgave himself for failing to return home to Unayzah to see his mother.

In the days of my grandfather's youth, it's true, poetry had served as a political ploy, a kind of war propaganda, to gain the community's allegiance. By reciting poems, passing them from man to man and repeating them around every campfire, the poet transported his message to the far-flung corners of the Arabian Peninsula and stirred the sentiments of its people, inspiring them personally and politically. *Al Khalouj* had certainly moved my Grandfather as a grown man in ways he never would have suspected as a child. Of course, I wasn't privy to any of this when I visited him in 1978. I would learn this after his death. At the time that I gave my

Semm Yubah

grandfather the recording, I was only aware of his abiding love for the poem.

So what I had thought would be a joyous occasion for my grandfather turned out to be quite the opposite. Some days later I asked my grandmother why he had looked so sad, and she told me that although he appreciated the gift, the poem brought back some difficult days of his youth when he had been separated from his family. She left it at that but did make a point to tell me later that he had listened to the tape when he was alone with her. I discovered afterwards that whenever he heard the recording he wept.

Looking back now on that moment I realize Grandfather Abdulrahman had been in the final years of his life, at a time when one usually calculates regrets and calibrates the cost of one's missteps. He was already an old man in his eighties when I had given him the tape, and I had been only slightly older than he had been when he embarked on the journey that would forever change his life, a journey that would leave him with a yearning for a time and place, and a family long gone.

* * *

My grandfather grew up where he was born, in Unayzah, a city that has been in an important region of the Arabian Peninsula for centuries. The oldest city in the northern Saudi province of Al-Qassim, Unayzah lies northwest of the capital of Riyadh, in the heart of central Arabia, and in the greater Najd "uplands" region. It is the land of farms and orchards, palm groves and ancient wells, blessed with an abundance of good soil and, more importantly, water. Unayzah's climate is typical of most cities in the center of the Arabian Peninsula, extreme heat with low humidity, and cold and semi-rainy winters. Many of the great camel-herding Bedouins spent at least part of the year in the region as they migrated from one place to another.

Adel Alsuhaimi

The Lebanese poet, Ameen Rihani, and friend and advisor of Ibn Saud, had called Unayzah "the Queen of Qassim," and "the Paris of Najd," when he visited the oasis in the early 1920s, and said it was "the fortress of freedom and the stopping place of travelers." He went on to describe it as a small, calm, peaceful place that:

> *"... enchants you with its colors—like a picture painted by Manet illustrating a story from A Thousand and One Nights...a pearl in a plate of gold with a border of lapis lazuli. Unayzah is tranquility personified. It is though this tranquility built for itself a temple among the palm trees and decorated it with golden sand and crowned it with a wreath of tamarisk..."*[14]

Historically, Unayzah was the main stopover for thousands of Muslim pilgrims journeying by caravan from Mesopotamia (present-day Iraq) and Persia (Iran) southwest to the holy city of Makkah. During the time my grandfather was growing up there, Unayzah was a village, populated with merchants, artisans and craft workers, but mostly farmers of dates and figs, wheat and barley, citrus fruit and pomegranates, etc. and whose only water wells were dug by hand.

The Arabian Peninsula is the largest in the world at three times the size of Texas, with Unayzah deep in its interior. Once, Unayzah had been isolated from the outside world, surrounded by vast deserts and a mountainous chain. Trade was crucial for its people, and a mutually beneficial alliance had developed between the nomadic Bedouins and the sedentary population of the town. Locals traded with nomads for such needed items as ghee, wool, and horses and camels, which "led to the development of long distance trade to other urban centers in the Arabian Peninsula, and Syria, Egypt,

---

14 Edited by Hopkins, Nicholas S.; and Ibrahim, Saad Eddin; Arab Society: Class, Gender, Power and Development, Ch. 2, "A Change in Saudi Arabia, A View from 'Paris of Nejd.'" By Altorki, Soraya and Cole, Donald P.; Pg. 29-30.

Semm Yubah

SAUDI ARABIA

Iraq and eventually as far away as Bombay, India."[15] In turn, the nomads bought their agricultural products—dates and grains—along with household utensils, and the tools and implements for herding as well as those goods imported by local merchants—coffee, cardamom, tea, sugar and rice.[16]

Still, violence remained a constant in the region, making local trade and supply routes dangerous but not impossible to navigate. Locals had long grown accustomed to tribal warfare, and had adapted and did whatever was needed to circumvent it. Besides, they had far worse things than tribal warfare to contend with—the threat of famines and the spread of fatal epidemic diseases.

The Unayzah of yesteryear had been controlled by various rulers and judges. The townspeople visited the *Amir* (the ruler) in his *majlis* (Arabic for "a place of sitting"), the reception area of his home, to lodge complaints of civil disputes and various other issues. Most conflicts pertained to minor affairs, but if a person transgressed the limits, he or she would be punished according to *Shariah* law. (An Arabic word meaning "path" or "way," *Shariah* is the personal set of laws and code of ethics derived from the *Qur'an* and from the *Sunnah*, the teachings of Mohammed (PBUH), that practicing Muslims follow.) At his *majlis*, the Amir also consulted prominent merchants and other learned men on local issues, and reached a decision by consensus.[17]

The townspeople had feared a punishment's social implications more than the punishment itself. With such close-knit communities, no one wanted to risk being shunned or even ostracized by family or neighbors, and it prompted shame and honor among the people.

---

15 Altorki, Soraya and Cole, Donald P., Arabian Oasis city: The Transformation of Unayzah; University of Texas Press, Austin, Texas; 1989; Pg. 25.

16 Altorki, Soraya and Cole, Donald P., Arabian Oasis city: The Transformation of Unayzah; University of Texas Press, Austin, Texas; 1989; Pg. 24.

17 Altorki, Soraya and Cole, Donald P., Arabian Oasis city: The Transformation of Unayzah; University of Texas Press, Austin, Texas; 1989; Pg. 27.

Semm Yubah

In addition to maintaining law and order in the community, the *Amir* was also responsible for its safety, and he had at his disposal a group of local men for his militia.

Yet, even the *Amirs* couldn't prevent tribal fighting. Although they formed alliances with many Bedouin tribes, the Amirs were unable to sustain those relationships.

Since 1823 the Alsulaim family had ruled Unayzah (with occasional interruptions by rival forces) after they took control of the city by assassinating the Ottoman-appointed governor of the region, Abdullah Al-Jamei. To this day, Unayzah continues to be ruled by the Alsulaim family as part of a treaty they had made with the Saudi royal family.

History of Early Unayzah

The mentioning of Unayzah dates back to pre-Islamic poetry, although it is unclear whether the ancient poets were referencing the same city known today as Unayzah.[18] Others have written that the region has been inhabited for thousands of years. What is known with more accuracy is how settlements occurred during the Roman influence in the region and before Islam became dominant in the 7th century. Before Islam, no major world power had dominated the Peninsula although both the Romans and Persians had tried.[19]

The inhabitants of the Arabian Peninsula in pre-Islamic times had to contend with the same things that my grandfather did—tribal warfare and a hostile environment: limited arable land, lack of grasslands for livestock, and scarcity of water. It was the same borderless country without boundaries or demarcation of any kind. Rivalry over a water well or better grazing lands could fuel a feud that could last for centuries, and sometimes did. Allegiance to the family was paramount and, out of necessity, extended to the

---

[18] Altorki, Soraya and Cole, Donald P., Arabian Oasis city: The Transformation of Unayzah; University of Texas Press, Austin, Texas; 1989; Pg. 15.

[19] Khaira Ummah 2013, Pew Forum on Religion & Public Life, accessed 18 July 2017, <http://lostislamichistory.com/what-was-special-about-pre-islamic-arabia/>

tribe and became an integral part of the social unit, making tribal allegiance the driving political force of the peninsula.[20] The tribe had provided protection and enabled the people to survive.

After the region was dominated by Muslims and prior to 1686, the location of present-day Unayzah was inhabited by scattered groups of the Subaie tribe of central Arabia: Aloqailiah, Alkhuraizah, Almalihah, and one from the Bani Khalid tribe, the Al Janah. After the Sharif of Makkah, Ahmad Bin Zaid, ransacked their villages during an unprovoked attack, the various tribes united in one castle and built a protective wall around their settlements. In 1686, they appointed Fawwaz Bin Humaidan Alsubaie as their ruler, who remained in power until 1704 when the Al Janah clansmen, a branch of the Bani Khalid tribe, believed they were more qualified to rule the land and assassinated him. These episodes of killings and seizures of power were a constant reoccurrence in Unayzah while the Alsubaie competed for control, until the first Saudi dynasty was established in 1744. The Alsubaie ruled Unayzah unchallenged then until 1823 when the Alsulaim family (who were also from the Alsubaie tribe) killed Abdullah Aljamie Alsubaie and assumed control of Unayzah.

Yet despite the political upheaval, word had spread of the more fertile land of Unayzah, and prompted many tribes to migrate there.

My own family members had migrated to Unayzah from the Ushaiqar region (about 60 miles west of Riyadh) in 1563. I don't have any details other then they left Ushaiqar to avoid escalating family feuds and tribal warfare as most did then.

Nomadic tribes had lived in makeshift homes, lightweight tents of woven goat or camel hair that were easily dismantled and transported in a hurry. When my ancestors had reached Unayzah, they found a surplus of that rare commodity—water, and the land suitable for farming, the town welcoming and safe, blessings for any

---

20 Ibid.

Semm Yubah

desert wanderer. Finally, they were free to abandon the nomadic life and looked to establish more stable dwellings.

Their early homes were simple, made of mud bricks and mortar, with reinforced roofs of tree bark, woven ropes and palm tree fronds. The trunks of *athal*—tamarisk trees—served as beams.[21] A layer of mud and tar coated the top for protection against the elements. Rooftops often provided the coolest place to sleep during summer nights. The construction of the house included a unique and natural ventilation system, utilizing wind and draft currents to circulate fresh air from the upper to the lower level of the house, a design both practical and economical.

The typical Unayzah house had three different entrances, and had been similar to my grandfather's boyhood home. There were separate entries for the men and women, and a third for the delivery of supplies and the family's animals. (Cows, chickens and rabbits were an essential part of any Unayzah home.) The entrance to the men's side of the house led directly to the male reception area, the *majlis* which was a spacious room, its perimeters lined with cushions, the walls with shelves of steel pots and handle-less glass cups (*finjaan*), and there was a fireplace to brew tea and *gahwah* (Arabic coffee) for guests. In contrast, the women's entrance funneled directly to the house's interior, which had a long corridor of a courtyard with access to all the other rooms. Most houses consisted of ten rooms since many people lived together in one dwelling, unlike today, and rooms were added as the family needed.

Houses were grouped close together in a single neighborhood along winding, narrow, dusty streets unlike the grid system of today's modern communities. Up to twenty-five houses were located in the same vicinity, and separated by farms and clusters of palms, with each neighborhood housing its own mosque. People of different economical backgrounds lived together, promoting brotherhood

---

21 Altorki, Soraya and Cole, Donald P., Arabian Oasis city: The Transformation of Unayzah; University of Texas Press, Austin, Texas; 1989; Pg. 20.

between rich and poor, and it wasn't unusual for people from diverse social groups to develop close ties.

For this reason, even the poorest among Unayzah's citizens hadn't felt isolated, but instead had become an incorporated part of its society. However, there was gender segregation. Women socialized in the *hasu* area surrounding the well used for laundry, bathing, and ablutions. Men washed and showered at the mosque.

The old city of Unayzah had become a haven for those fleeing warring factions and arid land, and earned a reputation as a close-knit and extremely hospitable community. The Lebanese poet, Ameen Rihani, had been so impressed with Unayzah society that he wrote in the early 1920s:

> *"Unayzah has old families with ancient lineages and long traditions of virtuous behaviors. Its fathers have toured the distant countries of east and west; and travel has made them kind and charming...so that they elevate hospitality to the level where they open the doors of homes and hearts. Indeed, the stranger forgets in this city, that he is a stranger—whether he is Muslim or infidel, whether he believes in one God or many. Here, he feels he is among people who are accustomed to meeting people like him. And more than that, they are people who are used to being hospitable to a guest no matter who he is... The stranger enjoys himself very much and gratefully welcomes their invitations. "Come in for coffee!" ...the head of the household serves you himself from the minute he welcomes you until the minute he bids you farewell."*[22]

And earlier, in 1918, British Arabist, explorer, and colonial office intelligence officer, Harry St. John Philby, had echoed the sentiments, saying Unayzah was "a gem among Arabian cities" and a "highly civilized and even cultured society," the people offering an "open-

---

22 Edited by Hopkins, Nicholas S.; and Ibrahim, Saad Eddin; *Arab Society: Class, Gender, Power and Development*, Ch. 2, "A Change in Saudi Arabia, A View from 'Paris of Nejd.'" By Altorki, Soraya and Cole, Donald P.; Pg 29-30.

handed hospitality…complete freedom from any kind of religious or sectarian bigotry."[23]

He also noted that:

> "…the stranger within its gates, far from being an object of aversion and suspicion, was regarded as the common guest of the community to be entertained—somewhat mercilessly and regardless of his own feelings—by every household that claimed to count in the local scheme of things."[24]

More than thirty years earlier, Lady Anne Blunt, granddaughter of Lord Byron, and the very first western woman to set foot in central Arabia,[25] had also remarked on the hospitality of those she encountered in the Najd region:

> "Wherever one goes in Arabia, one only has to march into any house one pleases, and one is sure to be welcomed. The Kahwah[26] stands open all day long, and the arrival of a guest is the signal for these two forms of indulgence: coffee and conversation, the only ones known to the Arabs. A fire is instantly lighted and the coffee cups in due course and handed round."[27]

I'm not at all surprised. My grandfather used to tell us stories of how his father, Saleh, learning that visitors had newly arrived in Unayzah, dropped everything and rushed out to greet them. In fact, it was not uncommon for neighbors to race to be the first to welcome a stranger to the community and have the honor of serving them coffee and a meal, as guests in their home.

It was in this kind of neighborhood that my grandfather was born and raised, as was his father, Saleh.

My great-grandfather was born in 1864 and his early life was

---

23 Ibid.

24 Altorki, Soraya and Cole, Donald P., Arabian Oasis city: The Transformation of Unayzah; University of Texas Press, Austin, Texas; 1989; Pg. 21.

25 Peter Harrigan 2004, Special to Review, Arab News, accessed 18 July 2017, <http://www.arabnews.com/node/248066>

26 *Kahwah* (or *Gahwah*) Arabic for Arabian coffee, or the place where it is offered.

27 Blunt, Lady Anne, Blunt, Wilfred Scawen Blunt; *A Pilgrimage to Nejd*: The Cradle of the Arab Race, Vol. I, Pg. 190; London, John Murray, Albermarle St, 1881.

uneventful but certainly not uncomplicated. He and his family had endured the same hardships of his ancestors: feudal wars, famines, droughts, an unforgiving climate, and a scarcity of resources.

As a young boy, Saleh had remained in the shadows for his own safety when he worked alongside his father, Abdulaziz Ibrahim Alsuhaimi, at their farm at the outskirts of Unayzah. Our family history of revenge killings had required it; besides, the political atmosphere had been tense with feuding factions. The second Saudi state (1824-1891) had diminished with the defeat of Imam Faisal Bin Turki Al Saud by their rivals, Al Rasheed clan of Ha'il.

Since the farmer depended on his offspring to help with the work, children were considered an extremely valuable commodity. Many of Saleh's siblings had died either from famine and disease or complications at birth. (That accounted for the fifteen-year age difference between Saleh, born in 1864, and his younger brother, Sulaiman in 1879.) Saleh and Sulaiman were the only surviving children as far as I know, and Saleh's father could not afford to lose another child.

At around seven, Saleh had been sent to a *Madrasa* (religious school) to learn the *Qur'an,* and the basics—writing and arithmetic. A few years later, Saleh assumed responsibility for providing for his family. Politically, it was a volatile time, and his father had left the family to join forces with the rest of Unayzah's male inhabitants who had been engaged in battle to defend their region, and Saleh as eldest had to stand in for him. He rose to the challenge as best he could and worked diligently at various jobs, bartering with nomads and farmers for necessities and digging irrigation water wells by hand.

This continued for a few years, and he became known in the community as an honest, competent and diligent worker. But despite his long hours, he was unable to provide sufficiently for his family. When his father died, Saleh assumed charge of the farm and family. He bore no ill feelings when his younger brother, Sulaiman,

Semm Yubah

pursued his studies in Unayzah and Makkah instead of helping him on the farm. My great-grandfather had accepted his duty as the eldest, and had been proud of his brother's advancement. (Sulaiman later became known in the region as a well-versed and respected scholar of religion and science.) Besides, the differences in life paths for Saleh and his brother had been established when they were still both young. It wasn't merely the 15 years age difference; it had been clear that Saleh was the more pragmatic and physically stronger of the two, possessing the physique and temperament more suitable for farming. Sulaiman, on the other hand, was the academic in the family, interested in research and science. I suppose as the youngest, Sulaiman had the luxury of a choice, but as my elders have pointed out, Saleh had never questioned his role, at least not to them.

As I already stated, Unayzah was unstable then, and a lawlessness prevailed throughout the region where the 'might is right' was standard recourse. This hard-knocks life had inculcated Saleh with the necessary traits for future success—patience, humility, adaptability, and a work ethic born out of need—the same qualities he had instilled in his son, Abdulrahman, which had eventually paved the way for establishing the family legacy. It certainly helped my grandfather build a thriving business, spanning multiple industries, making him a key player in the future economic development of the eastern province of Saudi Arabia. But I'm getting ahead of my story.

My great-grandfather, Saleh, an imposing figure at six foot, with sharp features, had married late according to the traditions of his time, and was most likely due to his lack of financial means as well as the region's political unpredictability. Yet, once he did marry, married life agreed with him, and soon he was blessed with good news—a baby was on the way, a beam of hope. His first son—Abdulrahman, my grandfather—was born in 1899 in Unayzah, and was considered good luck, another pair of hands to work the land and help with trade. A decade later, after a number of stillbirths and infants' deaths, Saleh's second son, Mohammed, was born.

But while Saleh had been rejoicing these treasures of life, his joy, unfortunately, would become short-lived.

Security in the region was, as usual, deplorable with political rivalries between warring clans raging nonstop. Even though it was an accepted way of life, it was also a highly stressful one.

The troubles in the region never subsided. Conditions improved intermittently, the fighting halting for only brief periods, but when it finally resumed, as it always did, it was always worse than before.

Bloody battles and deadly incidents occurred with such regularity that the inhabitants of the peninsula name the year after whatever tragic incident occurred. The year that my grandfather's brother, Mohammed, was born, 1910, was called The Year of Hunger, and 1912, The Year of the Measles, for an epidemic so dire it spread to nearly all of the region, killing thousands, making matters far more problematic for the people. Saleh dutifully shouldered on, but his concerns for providing for his extended family became ever more paramount.

From the onset it is evident that security and survival were the two most important factors determining the course of Saleh's life, and by extension, my grandfather's.

In 1915, my great-grandfather found himself in a precarious position. Farming wasn't providing sufficient income, nor was digging water wells by hand. He was faced with a difficult decision. He was the only means of support for his extended family. The region was rife with tribal conflict, and western countries now instigated the inevitable overthrow of rulers by political rivals. WWI was starting its second year, and the diminished Ottoman Empire (Turkey), who ruled much of the Arab world since the 1500's, had signed a secret pact with Germany back in August 1914 and entered the war against Britain and France. The British, concerned about their own WWI prospects, were already laying the groundwork for the Arab Revolt (held the following year) to help them in their war efforts. 1915 was already known as the "Year of the Jarrab Battle," a proxy WWI fought that January when Abdulaziz Ibn Saud (linked with the British) had been defeated by his rival Al Rasheed, (who was supported by the German-allied Ottomans).

And the largest oil reserves in the world hadn't even been discovered yet.

All of this affected daily life and prompted Saleh's decision. If his family were to survive, he couldn't stay in Unayzah. He had no choice but to migrate north of the Arabian Peninsula if he hoped to find sustainable work.

Yet another more disturbing factor had also influenced my great-grandfather's decision and the reason Saleh had learned to lead an unassuming life as a boy. Revenge killings had been prevalent in the region, and the Alsuhaimi family had not been spared, (which I will detail in the next chapter). Even though it had happened five years before Saleh was born, and decades before the birth of his son, Abdulrahman, it had still remained a viable threat. Historically, spilled blood demanded more blood, and usually that of the first-born, and decades could pass—generations even—before someone might avenge their dead. Saleh had wanted to remove even the remotest possibility of a revenge killing occurring again in the family, and to do that he needed to take his first-born son with him.

I believe this was the underlying factor for my great-grandfather's trip. He wanted to protect Abdulrahman, and keep him safe, preferably in a region where he would be free from revenge killings and tribal clashes. Of course, Saleh wanted to safeguard the future of all his children, but Abdulrahman, as his eldest son, was the primary target.

Still, it wasn't an easy decision. Saleh loved his wife and family, and the neighborhood he considered home. But five years after his youngest son was born, he opted to join the trade migration trekking north, and his oldest son, my grandfather, Abdulrahman, was going with him.

This was the first time my grandfather traveled to a different part of the country, He was 16 in 1915, a teenager, and since teenagers are similar no matter the generation or the ethnicity, I'm sure the prospect of an adventure thrilled him, the chance to see new and exotic lands.

But there may have been another reason for my grandfather's enthusiasm, one less obvious, and an even darker one urging him forward. My grandfather's paternal side of the family descended from Alsubaie tribe nobility. There are no records of Abdulrahman's mother's origins, and my elders claim they never learned anything about her, which I doubt. Maybe they are protecting my grandfather's privacy or his mother's ancestry. I'm not sure. It is interesting to note, however, that no one in the family will admit to knowing my great grandmother's name. Was it because she was from a lesser tribe? Or that she was non-Arabian? It's disappointing to say the least that I'll never learn anything about her. But what I did ascertain from conversations with my relatives is that she was different from the other mothers of the neighborhood, and I think that might have affected my grandfather at 16-years-old. Prejudice is not unique to any country or for that matter to any period in history, being different brings its burdens no matter who you are or where and when you live, and the other boys may have mocked Abdulrahman for being the son of an unconventional woman. There is no doubt in my mind that my grandfather loved his mother but he may have viewed this trip as an opportunity to escape his peers' taunts.

Still, all this makes me question why he chose to marry her, knowing how restricting society was then, and that an unconventional marriage may have caused him and his family unnecessary heartache. Had he fallen so deeply in love with her that he blatantly disregarded the social norms of the day, risking any stigma that marrying an outsider such as his bride might bring? Or did he marry her for a more practical reason, being the practical man he was known to be?

As I mentioned, my family had lived in a tight community, and although its benefits were numerous, any positive can become

Semm Yubah

a negative when living in such close proximity. Everyone in town knew each other's family and their history, both the good and bad. A family's misfortune was never kept secret for long. And my family had their share of tragedy. The Alsuhaimi family had already been the victim of a revenge killing five decades earlier, with the assassination of Saleh's distant cousin, Prince Nasir. I will discuss this in depth in a later chapter but suffice it to say that although the murder of Saleh's cousin had taken place more than fifty years earlier, it was by no means forgotten and certainly no secret. I can't help but think that my great-grandfather may have chosen his bride because no one else in his tribe wanted his or her daughter to become his wife. Revenge killings spanned generations, and I'm sure other families feared for their daughter's safety as well as their family's. It may sound odd but it would indicate the thinking of the day.

What is certain is that the political and economic disruption had swayed Saleh's decision to leave his wife, younger son and extended family and his beloved Unayzah. He and Abdulrahman had lived there all their lives and now were about to set off on a journey to foreign lands. There were no guarantees they'd find sustainable work, and I often wonder if my grandfather understood the challenges he and his father would face, if he comprehended the full scope of such a huge undertaking. I wonder if he ever dreamed that this journey would alter the course of his life.

CHAPTER 2

A Journey of a lifetime

The second year of "The Great War" saw more and more countries being drawn into the global conflict, including the Arabian Peninsula. In January of 1915, Ibn Saud and his men, prompted by the British, had already fought and lost The Battle of Jarrab to his enemies, Al Rasheed, loyalists of the Ottomans who had allied themselves with Germany. Rival countries crisscrossed the Peninsula, promoting their own agenda and competing for Arabian support. Danger and uncertainty stalked the region and commandeered most everyone's attention except my grandfather's. He was about to embark on the journey of a lifetime.

Abdulrahman couldn't wait to commence his adventure, thrilled at the prospect of voyaging to new lands, having never ventured beyond the Najd region, and never even stepping out of Unayzah. I'm sure he must have romanticized the escapades he'd have, travelling north through the desert, speculating about the foreign countries he'd see. Still, I doubt he ever envisioned the hardships he might endure or considered the emotional cost of such a trip, what he might lose in the exchange. He was a teenager, after all, and like most young people, his myopic vision prevented him from long-range sight. Most

Semm Yubah

likely he felt invincible, immune to life's tragedies believing like most his age, that bad things rarely happened to the young.

Was he aware of the dangers of the desert? Had he calculated the strength he and his father would have to summon if they were to endure the hundreds of miles across the immense tracts of endless sand? Or had he assumed any adventure outweighed all the risks? If I had to venture a guess, and knowing something about teenage boys, I would say the latter was closer to the truth. My elders said he did have genuine concerns about leaving his mother and younger brother behind. He was conflicted, often distressed at the notion that they had to remain in the turbulent area, and although they had not been far from their extended family and friends, they still had to fend for themselves. So as enthusiastic as Abdulrahman was about his upcoming trip, perhaps it is safest to say his feelings were mixed, his longing for adventure at odds with his love and allegiance to his family. Nevertheless, his uneasiness soon gave way to joyful expectancy.

It was not common practice for an Arabian boy to accompany his father on such an extensive journey. Although Abdulrahman had not been privy to his father's reasons for taking him, he recognized that this trip as a great privilege and an opportunity to fulfill his childhood dreams.

Ever since he had been a child, he had fantasized about epic voyages across the desert, imagining himself a brave Arabian warrior, galloping under sun and stars across its dunes and oases, greeting strangers, visiting exotic places. As a young boy, he had listened with wide-eyed wonder while elders narrated tales of the region's nomads, and he placed himself in the stories, casting himself in the hero's role.

To Abdulrahman, this dream-come-true would allow him to live among his beloved "desert people," the fierce nomadic Bedouins who frequented Unayzah, and whose hospitality toward strangers was legendary. A Bedouin never turned away someone in need of food and shelter, and was bound to share whatever he owned. The

Camel Caravan travelers hunting antelopes, circa 1910s.

Bedouin code of honor demanded he oblige his guests. It was, and still is, not unusual for a Bedouin to unroll his carpet in the middle of the desert and offer sustenance to a weary traveler. No doubt the prospect of experiencing their way of life had softened those trying moments when Abdulrahman was ambivalent about leaving his mother and brother. Still, I don't believe it ever occurred to him that this trip would also provide some of life's most painful, albeit, valuable lessons.

The day for their departure was fast approaching. Much work needed to be done before the long desert journey, and as soon as the sun rose, Abdulrahman assisted his father in gathering the necessary equipment and supplies: dried and salted meats that would not spoil on the long and hot trip, rice, bread, dried dates, the thick, gritty green-bean coffee, and of course, the great staple of the Bedouins—*eggit* (pronounced eejit), a dried, baked yoghurt processed from camels' and sheep's milk, and rich in protein. He also secured enough woolen blankets for those cool nights and portable tents (easy to strike camp at a moment's notice, and made from nature's best insulators, camel's wool).

Semm Yubah

Their first stop would be at an oasis in the northwest, the remote city of Ha'il, bordered on the north by the Great Al Nefud desert with its great horseshoe of sand and steep banks, and on the west by the massive Shammar mountains, both making the city inaccessible to foreign invaders. It was also still the home of Al Rasheed clan, the historic rivals of Al Saud family. In later years, the region would come under the control of Abdulaziz Ibn Saud, after the Emir of Al Rasheed dynasty, Abdulaziz Ibn Mitab Al Rasheed, was killed. The opposition from Al Rasheed would weaken then and once Abdulaziz Ibn Saud married one of their family's members, the mother of the former King of Arabia, Abdullah, and part of the Shammar[28] clan.

The authority of Ibn Saud eventually had a significant impact upon Saleh, and Abdulrahman, as well as the countless Arab people living there. But during the time that Saleh and Abdulrahman had traveled to Ha'il, Unayzah had still not aligned themselves with neither Al Rasheed nor Ibn Saud, even though Al Rasheed ruled their neighboring city of Buraidah, just north of them. Unayzah was still considered a coveted prize that needed to be won, and the key to controlling the remaining Najd region in the interior. By maintaining a neutral position, Unayzah had hoped to avoid conflict, but it only increased political tensions and made the citizens of Ha'il suspicious of anyone traveling from Unayzah.

Yet Saleh would not even consider passing through the city without spending the night with his relatives there, giving Abdulrahman the chance to meet his uncles for the first time. Besides, Ha'il was a regular stopover for any caravan en route to the northwest and the perfect place to rest and regroup after their approximately 180-mile camel trek from Unayzah.

By today's standards, the distance between the two cities translated to less than a three-hour car ride on a highway but in

---

28 The Al-Shammary tribe originated from this region and named themselves after the massive Jebel Shammar.

1915 the trip took Abdulrahman and his father 5 to 6 days, since they had to traverse desert sands—the dunes and wadis—on the back of a camel. Although capable of traveling up to 90 miles in a day the camels my grandfather and Saleh rode were part of a long caravan of two hundred or more camels, and probably traveled no faster than five miles per hour.

There were no paved roads. Horses and wagons, common in western countries, were still extremely expensive to purchase on the Peninsula—a convenience Saleh could not afford—and not practical for crossing the Arabian Desert.

A camel caravan was their logical (and only) choice for the most efficient mode of transportation through the northern part of the peninsula. Saleh had contracted *Al Ogailat*, well versed in the safety of the route and the navigation of its terrain, and vital to the their caravan's success.

Al Ogailat were a group of scouts whose origins dated back to the 1700s when they were employed by the Ottomans during various campaigns on the peninsula, helping troops navigate the desert and providing them with inside knowledge to the Arab world, skills the Ottoman officers often lacked. Most *Al Ogailat* came from the Qassim region—Unayzah and Buraidah and other smaller towns in Najd and Ha'il. They had the ability to locate a water well in the middle of the open desert or reach their destination by simply tracking the stars. They knew which sandy stretches to avoid where a camel might sink to disaster or where raiding bandits might ambush a caravan. These desert specialists passed their knowledge and skills from one generation to the next and were highly respected and in demand.

With the Ottoman Empire weakened, most of *Al Ogailat* had disbanded, some finding work with other armies crossing the desert, others working as guides for camel caravans. *Al Ogailat* were known for their bravery, honesty, and commitment. When anyone needed a caravan transport across the desert, they contacted *Al Ogailat*.

Semm Yubah

The group typically had a regional *Ogailat* chief who ascertained the type and size of caravan that someone needed, and selected a suitable Caravan Master from a pool of qualified Arab Sheiks, (tribal leaders or their representatives from the nearby cities) who had experience and the trust of many *Al Ogailat*. These tribes generally co-existed peacefully with each other and the Ottomans, but occasionally had raided a neighboring tribe's desert pastures or revolted against the Empire. Therefore, choosing a sheikh who was acceptable to both Ottomans and the tribes had become a sensitive and difficult undertaking.

The Caravan Master selected his own squad of men—the guards, laborers, camel jockeys and caretakers—from various tribes to ensure safe passage since a tribe would not attack a caravan if one of their tribesmen was escorting it.

Each member of the caravan master's team carried his tribe's 'flag' or band and whenever tribal warriors appeared on the horizon, those 'flag' men moved to the front of the caravan to be clearly visible, ready to display the same tribe's flag to the approaching and, possibly unfriendly, group. Once, the tribal warriors identified themselves to the flagman who was a member of their tribe, they were invited to a feast with the caravan master. In the end, the Caravan Master paid fees to the tribal warriors—and sometimes provided an additional gift of coffee or cardamom or other rare spices—to guarantee the caravan's safe passage through that particular stretch of land.

Each caravan always had a religious scholar with them to call for daily prayers and act as arbitrator for any disputes that might arise among the itinerant merchants.

Al Ogailat had kept my grandfather's caravan safe as it made its way through the desert. They provided the four camels Saleh and Abdulrahman had needed for the journey, one for each of them to ride, and two more to transport goods and supplies. But the number of camels involved in my grandfather's caravan was most

A Caravan guard with his valuable prey protecting stock and travelers, circa 1910s.

likely about 200, small by standards of the day when the camels' numbers reached more than 2000.

Abdulrahman had been raised in a desert and farming community and had been familiar with riding a camel although apparently not as skilled as he thought. Riding a camel is different from riding a horse. The camel needs to be in a seated position before a rider can mount it. Camels extend their back legs first and then rise to a standing position, and an inexperienced rider will catapult forward if not properly braced. Still, after a few mishaps, it hadn't taken Abdulrahman long to get the knack of it.

The camels' unique capability to adapt to the grueling desert climate and carry hefty loads had made them ideal candidates for trekking into the peninsula's interior. To Arabs the camel has long been a symbol of community, fortitude, and survival. Who else could endure and thrive in such an exacting environment?

Their bodies were uniquely designed for desert journeys. Arabian dromedaries with their singular hump store more than 80 pounds of fat, and when metabolized, it acts as a source of energy, allowing them to travel up to 100 miles without water.

Their big, padded feet are suitable for traversing the sinking and hot sands. A double set of eyelids with long lashes protects them from wind storms; a third, a nictitating membrane, is drawn across the eyeball and swipes it clean. Their nostrils voluntarily close to prevent entering sand, and their small round ears have hairs that block blowing dust. They can survive in blistering heat for as long as a week without water, longer in colder temperatures. They rarely sweat, and their urine is more concentrated than most animals and thus they lose less water; their kidneys and intestines are efficient at retaining water. All of these qualities have earned camels the title, "ships of the desert."

In his book, *The Last Camel Charge*, Forrest Bryan Johnson elaborates on the camel's capabilities and describes in detail how they became a crucial part of a military experiment conducted in 1836 by the American Corps when they were used for transporting military supplies between the urbanized American east and the developing California. The Army Quartermaster George Hampden Crosman had first proposed the use of camels instead of horses and mules for a trip to the American Southwest, championing their talent to travel without water and carry three times more weight than a mule, perfect for transporting the huge supplies they needed to survey the best route for a railroad track connecting the east with the west.

Of course, Abdulrahman hadn't been aware of any of this, and hadn't come to fully appreciate these desert ships, at least not yet. It was an ordinary occurrence—Arabs riding camels long distances in the desert. Had he developed a fondness for his camel the way people do with their horses or dogs? Most Arabians do, and I suspect my grandfather was no exception. He loved to watch them graze in the desert and listen to their bleats. Sometimes he'd talked them, and I imagine as a teenager he had become quite familiar with his camel's individual quirks, the usual grumblings and grunts, the throaty bellows, the lowering of his head to greet him. I am sure he had a special name for his constant companion for the trip. Perhaps he called his *naqah, Gazlan,* for her gracefulness, or *Jahamah* for her likeness to the predawn sky, or *Ga'ood* for his *jamel's* youthful strength and endurance wading through the deep sand. No doubt at the end of his trip he had a better appreciation for these ships of the desert.

The time had come for Abdulrahman to depart Unayzah with his father, and after morning prayers, the sun rising high in the skies, he made his final goodbyes to his mother and younger brother and left to join the caravan. They were met by the Caravan Master, a wizened looking man from decades roaming the desert, but quite skilled and experienced and well-versed in the unmapped terrain and possessing a cosmic sense of the stars, the expert who would lead them out of Unayzah and north into Ha'il.

I often wonder what those first few nights were like for my grandfather after he and Saleh rode out of town, their caravan cresting the dune, and Unayzah and everything familiar dwindling and disappearing from sight. Perhaps Abdulrahman experienced a welter of emotion, even stole a glance or two back before staring straight forward, his body in synch with the rhythm of his camel, the air palpable, bristling with hope.

Semm Yubah

I don't know how long they rode that first day or if he welcomed the chance to rest when they finally broke for camp that night. The camels had to be secured, the tents raised, their food cooked and consumed, prayers recited. Still, he had to have been too excited for sleep, still intoxicated by the promise of adventure to shut his eyes. Eventually I suppose exhaustion won over, and he surrendered to the Arabian moon.

There is something mysterious about the desert at night, something haunting in its austere beauty, the pitch dark of the sky, the flickering stars. The chance cry of an Arabian Red Fox piercing the stillness can unsettle even the steadiest of nerves the first time you hear it. Still, the desert's nocturnal air is crisp and cleansing and soothing and, by morning it can lull any troubles away, or at least make them seem less ominous. Two years before Abdulrahman made the trip with his father, Gertrude Bell, explorer and British political officer, had written about the wonders of the desert as she had traveled to Ha'il.

> *"Sometimes I have gone to bed with a heart so heavy that I thought I could not carry it through the next day… Then comes the dawn, soft and beneficent, stealing over the wide plain and down the long slopes of the little hollows, and in the end it steals into my heart…."* [29]

My guess is Abdulrahman slept well that first night once he gave himself to it and he had woken reinvigorated. Although most likely Saleh rose first and before the sun and nudged Abdulrahman awake for the *Fajr*, the dawn prayer, supposedly God's favorite.

In a week's time they would arrive in Ha'il and soon at their relatives' home to enjoy the family's hospitality, a generosity as grand as the proverbial Hatim's.

---

[29] Clive Irving 2014, Gertrude of Arabia, the Woman Who Invented Iraq, accessed 12 Oct 2017, <https://www.thedailybeast.com/gertrude-of-arabia-the-woman-who-invented-iraq>

Hatim, legendary chief of the Taiy tribe, one of the largest in Ha'il, was a Christian desert dweller known for generations as a magnanimous man who fed and sheltered anyone who showed up at his camp. It is said he kept a fire burning on the Samra mountaintop near his pastures to welcome travelers through the barren wilderness. His generosity led him to frequent bankruptcy but it never stopped his hospitality to strangers. His reputation spread across the Peninsula as well as to other parts of the Levant and Asia. Some believed Hatim's fame reached as far as Italy and influenced Boccacio's writing of the *Decameron* in the story of "Mitridanes and Natan." There's a strong possibility that as my grandfather's caravan neared the mountain where Hatim is supposedly buried, tales of his good deeds and altruism were told.

When my grandfather's caravan approached the walled city of Ha'il, Abdulrahman had been impressed with its towers, the historic grand Barzan Palace, and the bustle of merchants in the square.

Their group set up camp nearby to rest for the night but Saleh and my grandfather made their way to their relatives' home. Abdulrahman had often heard his father and his Uncle Sulaiman, Saleh's brother, speak with great affection of their relatives in Ha'il. He knew that he was remotely related to royalty, Prince Nasir, a distant Alsuhaimi family relation who had lived in Ha'il, and that Nasir once ruled his hometown of Unayzah, but that was all he knew of his distant cousin. So when he entered the city of Ha'il and visited for the first time the very home of a famous Alsuhaimi political figure, he was enthralled. No doubt there was a celebration given in their honor at the Alsuhaimi Ha'il household, a gathering with neighbors and family for a dinner feast of roasted lamb and rice; the traditional Arabian dish of *Jareesh* made from crushed wheat and milk; *Margoog*, a Najdi dish of vegetables, meat and wheat flour; and *Thareed*, a stew of lamb and vegetables, and many other rich entrees. After dinner, only Saleh, Abdulrahman and their cousins remained at the Alsuhaimi's *majlis* for their coffee

Semm Yubah

Hail Barzan Palace Towers, the name comes from the Turkish word for fort or barrack (Kişla) and the purpose in building it was to host the troops that were protecting the northern part of the Kingdom. After that it was used as a prison until the end of the principality of bin Musa'ad.

with cardamom and a chance to catch up on family news, talking until the early morning hours, discussing which direction Saleh and Abdulrahman should go after they headed north.

Their choice was between two routes, each posing its own set of challenges. If he and Abdulrahman maintained a northern direction, it meant traveling deeper into Ottoman-controlled territories and risked clashing with Hashemite forces (on the verge of a British-sponsored Arab revolt). On the other hand, if they trekked northeast, they would end up in the British-controlled territories of Basra in Mesopotamia (present-day Iraq) or Kuwait. Ultimately, they chose what they considered the safest route—the one heading toward Basra and Kuwait.

When the sun strong, and after prayers had been said, Saleh and Abdulrahman bid farewell to their relatives, and left to rendezvous with their caravan.

As my grandfather's caravan exited the city they traveled through the Province of Ha'il, passing by some spectacular rock art, ancient ruins more than 4000 years old though I doubt anyone explored it. Some extraordinary petroglyphs dot the landscape there, too spectacular not to mention here, unique paintings and carvings, many of which depict camels and Arabian horses, exquisite works of art.

From Ha'il they journeyed northeast with a stop at Zubair in the desert where many Najdi merchants had settled, and continued on in the direction of Iraq and Basra, a big city with a vibrant economy where Saleh hoped they'd find opportunities. But first the caravan had to pass through the magnificent Al-Nefud Desert, a natural barrier with the Arabian Peninsula on one side, and Iraq and Jordan on the other.

I have never had the pleasure of traveling through Al-Nefud but had often visited Dah'naa desert between Dammam and Riyadh. My first trip was in 1973 when I needed a visa to travel to the U.S. after high school. After dawn prayers I departed home for a four-hour trip of 400 kilometers. The scenery was serene—sand dunes stretching as far as the eye could see, all of it a light rust color, its iron oxide giving it that gleam when the sun is low in the sky. But my earliest memory of the desert involved a family trip to the Levant (Jordan and Syria) in 1964 when I was 8 years old. The roads were in poor condition and it took us three days. I remember the crispness to the morning air when we rose to wash

Semm Yubah

and help my mother and grandmother prepare breakfast. There was a clarity and peacefulness to our surroundings with the sounds of distant birds chirping, the fire wood sparking against the sand, the sweet water boiling in the kettles. But my experience had been a far cry from my grandfather's when the desert had been truly an unmapped wilderness without roads or superhighways, before cars and oil fields and urbanization.

The Al-Nefud is an erg, (from the Arabic *arg*, meaning dune field*)*, a broad, flat area the size of Iceland, with large masses of shifting sands, huge crescent shaped dunes carved by brutal winds and sand storms. Abdulrahman must have been intimidated by its sheer size or left speechless by its beauty when he first glimpsed it.

Thirty seven years earlier, Lady Anne Blunt, who had traversed the Arabian desert, gave her own first impressions of it in *A Pilgrimage to Nejd*:[30]

> *"...we saw a red streak on the horizon before us, which rose and gathered as we approached it, stretching out east and west in an unbroken line. It might have first been taken for an effect of mirage, but on coming nearer we found it broken into billows, and but for its red color not unlike a stormy sea seen from the shore, for it rose up, as the sea seems to rise when the waves are high above the level of the land. Somebody called out 'Nafud,' and though for a while we were incredulous, we were soon convinced. What surprised us was its color, that of rhubarb and magnesia, nothing at all like the sand we have hitherto seen, and nothing at all like what we had experienced...."*

She was the first European woman to cross Al-Nefud, in 1878. In her journal, she described this great desert in detail as she made the trip with her husband. Although she dreaded the journey initially and was exhausted at the end, she was taken with its beauty:

---

30 Blunt, Lady Anne, *A Pilgrimage to Nejd: The Cradle of the Arab Race; 1881*, pg. 155-56.

> *"The thing that strikes one first about the Nafud is its color. It is not white like the sand dunes we passed yesterday, nor yellow as the sand is in parts of the Egyptian desert, but a really bright red, almost crimson in the morning when it is wet with dew... It is however a great mistake to suppose it barren. The Nafud, on the contrary, is better wooded and richer in pasture than any part of the desert we have passed in leaving Damascus. It is tufted all over with ghada bushes, and bushes of another kind called yerta..."*[31]

The Blunts had noted a series of huge hollows in the desert, some a quarter of a mile across, but "all precisely alike in shape and direction," and compared them to the track of an unshod horse.

> *"... the toe is sharply cut and perpendicular, while the rim of the hoof tapers gradually to nothing at the heel, the frog even being roughly represented by broken ground in the centre."*

She is referencing what we call in Arabic, *falj*,[32] those deep horseshoe depressions between dunes that are sculpted by the violent winds of the Al-Nefud.

So this was what my grandfather glimpsed when his caravan had entered the immense Al-Nefud, its grains sparkling crimson at the height of the desert sun, star dunes and crescent-shaped ones stretching across the terrain, ghada bushes and acacia, the occasional scrub tree. Here amidst the brilliance and sparseness of the desert Saleh confided in his son. He waited until they broke for camp before telling him. That was when Abdulrahman first learned of the darker side of the Alsuhaimi's past.

History Of The Alsuhaimi Family
Decades-long tribal warfare had engulfed generations of young Arab men, but so had the revenge killings that had victimized countless people. Revenge killings were horrific practices of retaliation older than the Qur'an, the Bible, even the Torah itself, but for my family

---

31 Ibid.
32 Zahra Freeth and Victor Winstone 1980, Aramco World, accessed 18 July 2017, <http://archive.aramcoworld.com/issue/198003/a.journey.to.hail.htm>

Semm Yubah

the cycle of revenge killings had begun several years before my great-grandfather, Saleh, had been born.

The Alsuhaimi family's first encounter with a revenge killing dates back to the early 19th century. Unayzah was under the regime of Al Saud II (the Second Saudi State) between 1824 and 1891 and ruled by Imam Faisal Bin Turki Al Saud after a distant cousin had assassinated his father, Imam Turki Al Saud, and founder of the Second Saudi State. (Faisal had the cousin executed to avenge his father's death.)

The desire for power in the region had prompted some to resort to violence to eliminate their political rivals, and often resulted in the assassination of the opposition, with the effects rippling across the Peninsula. When Imam Faisal Bin Turki Al Saud had appointed my great-grandfather's distant cousin, Prince Nasir Alsuhaimi, the ruler of *all* of the districts of Unayzah he impacted the Alsuhaimi family as well as the region. His decision had incensed the Al Sulaim clan.

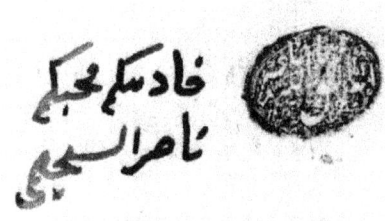

Signature & ring stamp of Prince Nasir Alsuhaimi, Ruler of Unayzah, 1843-49.

Imam Faisal's appointment had contradicted Al Sulaim's original one. In 1847 Al Sulaim had designated Prince Nasir as the man to govern *only* the pilgrims' routes through Unayzah, and nothing else. The appointment was the result of a long-standing conflict between Imam Faisal Bin Turki Al Saud and the Al Sulaim clan who had ruled all of Unayzah since 1823. The Al Sulaim family had overthrown the Ottomans after Prince Yahya Al Sulaim had assassinated the Ottoman-appointed governor, and Prince Yahya Al Sulaim had remained the ruler until his death in the Battle of Bag'a.

Imam Faisal Bin Turki Al Saud's decision to decree Prince Nasir Alsuhaimi as the ruler of all of Unayzah quickly turned into a fierce political feud.

After Nasir's appointment, the usurped Al Sulaim clan set out to eliminate their opposition by planning assassination of Nasir at the Governor's Palace in Unayzah, the headquarters of his uncles.

That day, Nasir left the Palace as he often did in the evening after *Isha* prayers, the fifth of the daily prayers, and was on his way home when two of the Al Sulaim brothers and one of their guards ambushed him, opening fire. Nasir was struck and fell to the ground, and his assailants, assuming he was dead, charged the Palace, ready to force their way inside. Nasir's blind brother Mutlaq, had heard the fired shots and ordered the gates closed and a counter attack. Only one of the Al Sulaim's entourage was killed, the rest escaping into the night. [33]

Nasir had recovered from his injury and tracked down a close relative of the assassins but the relative claimed ignorance of the event and the whereabouts of the group. Still, Nasir had him executed, claiming that as a member of Al Sulaim's clan, he shared responsibility for the attempted assassination, and used that reasoning as justification for the man's death, which reflected the cultural thinking of the time.[34]

Nasir's rule ended in 1849 after the entire Al Qassim region suffered a major defeat at the hands of none other than Imam Faisal Bin Turki al Saud himself who had originally appointed Nasir as Unayzah's ruler. After losing power, Nasir regrouped, and headed south with his brother, Mutlaq, and their families to seek asylum in the Al Hilaliyah town, approximately 75 miles west of Riyadh and not far from Ushaiger, his ancestors' birthplace, where they would

---

[33] HRH Khalid bin Sultan 2020, Muqatel, accessed 16 October 2018. Qasim turmoil and Prince Nasir political events that led to his assassination (in Arabic), <http://www.moqatel.com/openshare/Behoth/Atrikia51/Saudia2/sec03.doc_cvt.htm>

[34] Ibid.

Semm Yubah

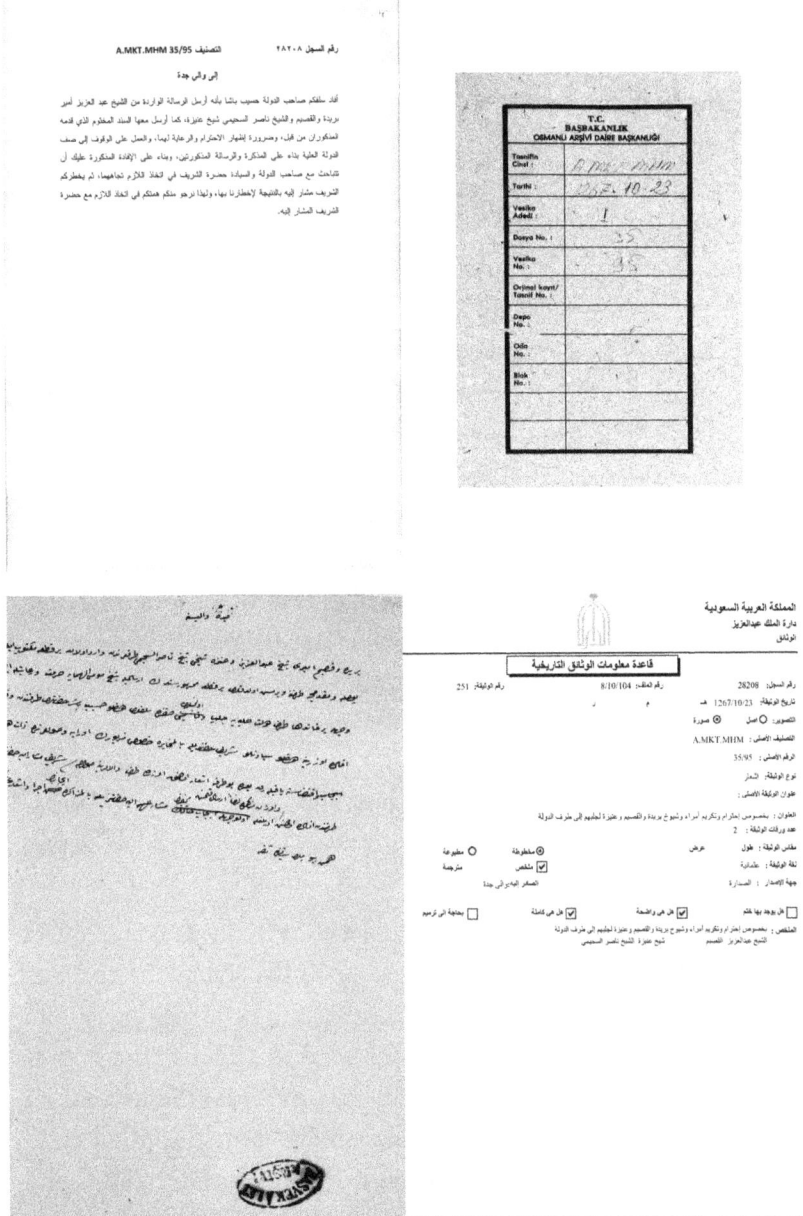

Exchange of telegrams between Jeddah Ottoman commander and his superiors requesting favorable considerations for Unaizah ruler Shiekh Nasir Alsuhaimi & other rulers of Qassim who showed respect to Ottomans, August 21, 1851.

be under the protection of his uncles and cousins. However, the Al Sulaim family wanted blood-revenge for the killing of one of their men, and they were determined to ensure that any opposition contending for the rule of Unayzah was permanently eliminated, no matter how long it took.

Nearly a decade after the former Unayzah ruler had lived in asylum in the Al Hilaliyah town with his cousins, Nasir had been attacked once again in 1859. The Al Sulaim clan had ten years to prepare and it gave them the edge they needed.

His assailants had staked out Nasir's quarters, discovering the best time to attack was after noon prayers when he retired and help was not accessible. The workday began at sunrise, and during the noon hour most people rested. Al Sulaim's scouts had observed Nasir for a few years and knew noon was his most vulnerable time.

Two of Al Sulaim's sons traveled clandestinely for days until they reached Nasir's estates in Al Hilaliyah. They came prepared to battle Nasir's guards, and brought along backup, a large group of slaves and mercenaries. They split themselves into smaller teams, each team entering town through a different gate to avoid detection, and dispersed among the townspeople and merchants, infiltrating the market and the outskirts of town. They were aware of Prince Nasir's routine of napping after noon prayers at his horses' stables at the Bhujaih Palace.

Two of Al Sulaim's sons remained with the main assassins' squad, and once they found Prince Nasir asleep in the stable, they gagged his mouth, bound his limbs and killed him, this time making certain he was dead. Al Sulaim's men did not stop the killings there; they tracked down the rest of Nasir's family and murdered them to ensure that none of his progeny would ever challenge their authority in future years. Any surviving members of Nasir's family escaped and fled and changed their names from Alsuhaimi to Althuwaini[35] to

---

35 Dr. Mufid Alzaidi 2004, Encyclopedia of Saudi Arabia's History. Prince Nasir Alsuhaimi rule & assassination events (in Arabic), <http://www.sobee3.com/showthread.php?t=10829>

Semm Yubah

avoid further persecution and a possible revenge execution. Mutlaq, Nasir's half brother, and his family escaped too, but changed their name to Alhinaki. (Both Althuwaini and Alhinaki families belong to the same Subaie tribe as Alsuhaimis.)[36]

After witnessing the horror of the blood feud and the extent of the killing spree, the remaining Alsuhaimi families fled Unayzah and went into exile, settling west of Riyadh, in the region of Ushaiqar.

That proved ironic. As early as 1562, the Alsuhaimi family had made the crucial decision to immigrate to the far better destination of the Qassim Oasis, near Unayzah, seeking a safe haven, away from the local conflicts of where they had lived—Ushaiqar.

Meanwhile, the Second Saudi State had been locked in severe clashes between the sons of Imam Faisal Bin Turki and the Ottoman-backed Al Rasheed dynasty of Ha'il. Then the great Battle of Mulayda (1891) took place, resulting in the final defeat and fall of the Al Saud II dynasty.

The peaceful life of the Alsuhaimi family was disrupted once again, and they were forced to seek asylum elsewhere. Realizing that their sanctuary in Al Hilaliyah wasn't as secure as they had thought, some Alsuhaimi families decided that it was safe to return to Unayzah; that was in 1864, the year my great-grandfather, Saleh, was born.

Saleh had purposely kept this information from his son. Now, he felt he was old enough to learn the truth.

Abdulrahman had spent his childhood in Unayzah, no different than other children there, attending school, studying the Qur'an along with reading, writing and arithmetic. Children there were like children everywhere, and sooner or later someone would get into a competition over who was the strongest or fastest. Abdulrahman was tall and well built, giving him an edge in any

---

[36] Details of this account can be found in the 2013 edition of the US Saudi Arabia Diplomatic and Political Cooperation Handbook, USA International Business Publications.

skirmishes that broke out with his schoolmates, and sometimes a simple scuffle could lead to a full-blown dispute. Adults often were drawn into their offspring's fights, and when tempers flared, there was a greater potential for escalation and a power struggle between the families and local clans. Saleh had worried that this dangerous behavior might lead to revenge, and the tragic past would repeat itself, once again.

He waited until their caravan had left the city of Ha'il and headed for the north and they were safely under the desert moon before he revealed to his son the story of Prince Nasir. Maybe it was being surrounded by all that open space or the soothing light of the desert stars but Saleh felt secure enough to share the tragic side of our family history. My elders have told me that Saleh wanted his son aware of the challenges he might face, and understand why it had been crucial that Abdulrahman not engage in conflict while in Unayzah, and that it was imperative he continued to circumvent it and learn the art of diplomacy if he were to live his life in harmony. Of course, Saleh had wanted his son smart in the ways of their world but more than that, he wanted to keep his son safe, he wanted his son to enjoy a long and healthy life. He did not wish history to repeat itself. He would not let that happen to his family again.

CHAPTER 3

The Great War

When I think of the unpredictability of the Arabian Peninsula then, the reverberations of the Great War extending deep into its interior, both the Ottomans and Europeans viewing the region as a means to an end—a way to protect their interests and expand their influence—coupled with ongoing tribal warfare across the land, I'm amazed at Saleh's courage and tenacity. He had been determined; the future of his family had depended on his success. Still, it had to have been difficult knowing he couldn't guarantee his son's safety, but my great-grandfather had been stalwart in his duty as head of his household and devout in his love for family, as was my grandfather.

To get a broader understanding of the challenges they faced, it is important to put their trip in historical context and explore the backstory of central Arabia and those events leading up to the Great War as well as the those incidents and circumstances that affected the Middle East during that time.

The turn of the 20th century saw a shift in the balance of power across the world. Empires of old were falling away, giving rise to new factions and alliances, and resulting in the emergence of a new world order.

OTTOMAN EMPIRE 1914

Semm Yubah

This change in world politics saw the clash of three distinct ideologies: Capitalism, Communism, and Islam. Communism was emerging as a powerful set of concepts of labor rights and economic injustices in Soviet Russia under the leadership of Vladimir Lenin. Capitalism, on the other hand, was masquerading in the form of real estate investments and corporate takeovers in regions, such as India, the Ottoman controlled territories, and Africa.

Islam had been steadily losing its political hold on Europe and elsewhere as frictions increased within the Ottoman Empire, prompting many of its enemies to exploit the Empire's instability, an opportunity to occupy its lands. Nationalism was on the rise, distorting the Islamic ideas of unity and brotherhood. Consequently, many Muslims identified themselves as Turks or Arabs, fueling their desires for separate control and political patronage of their individual lands.

Ottoman influence in 'Muslim lands' had weakened, and their hold on the Arabian Peninsula had been fragmented, nominal at best. Their decrease in power had created a political and economic vacuum, perfect for political rivals (including local tribal rulers and outlaws) for takeover of the region.

The Ottoman Empire and the Arabian Peninsula

Since the sixteenth century the Ottoman Empire had ruled the Arabian Peninsula. The seeds of the modern Saudi state in central Arabia were not sown until 1744 when the local ruler, Muhammad Ibn Saud (1689–1765), joined forces with another native of the Najd region, the Islamic reformer and purist (and founder of the Wahhabi conservative religious movement), Muhammad Ibn 'Abd al-Wahhab (1703–1792) to create a new political entity which helped establish the House of Saud. (The alliance allowed Muhammad Ibn Saud control over military, political, and economic matters and gave Muhammad Ibn Abd al-Wahhab responsibility for religious concerns.[37] Muhammad Ibn Saud ruled the First Saudi State until his death, and afterward was succeeded by his heirs.) Through the nineteenth century, the Saud family had spread their influence over the Arabian Peninsula but the extent of their territory fluctuated along with their fortunes, as they also had to contend with Egypt, the Ottoman Empire, and other rival Arabian families—primarily Al Rasheed—for control over the peninsula.

The House of Saud competed fiercely with their archrivals, Al Rasheed, for the interior of the peninsula, but in 1890, Al Rasheed succeeded in occupying Riyadh. Abdulaziz Ibn Saud, a direct descendent of Muhammad Ibn Saud and the House of Saud, was 15 then and already passionate about restoring his family's authority, but he waited a year before attempting to regain the region. But Al Rasheed had proved too powerful, emerging victorious in battle and forcing Abdulaziz Ibn Saud, his family and followers from their homeland and into exile for more than a decade.

The Al Saud family found refuge first with the Bedouin tribe of Al Murrah in the southern Arabian desert, later relocating to Qatar for two months and then on to Bahrain before settling in the British protected emirate of Kuwait where they remained until 1901. Abdulaziz Ibn Saud was twenty-six then with plans to take back the family's lands, and rode from Kuwait with seventy of his clansmen for a desert raid on the Najd region and was so successful that the following year they struck again. On January 21, 1902, they recaptured the ancient capital, Riyadh, and reclaimed the family's ancestral home. Al Rasheed had requested aid from the Ottomans but the young Abdulaziz Ibn Saud had the support of the Ikhwan, a tribal nomadic army of dedicated followers. In the end Ibn Saud's charisma and reputation as a warrior had earned him the region's high praise and more than enough supporters to help him defeat

---

37 John L. Esposito, Ed., in The Oxford Dictionary of Islam 2007. Oxford Islamic Studies Online, accessed 18 November 201, <http://www.oxfordislamicstudies.com/article/opr/t125/e916>

Al Rasheed. By 1906 he had successfully ousted Al Rasheed clan along with any of their allies from Najd, prompting Al Rasheed to retreat to the city of Ha'il in the northwest.

In 1913, Ibn Saud reached yet another major milestone when he took the Al-Hasa region from the Ottomans, giving him control of the entire Al Hasa coast in eastern Arabia (where oil reserves were eventually discovered). He aimed to extend his expansion to the entire Najd region (central Arabia) and establish his base in Riyadh but it would take him many more years (not until 1932) before he consolidated his dominions into the kingdom of Saudi Arabia and declared himself its king.

In the years leading up to WWI, Britain had fostered relationships with two powerful rulers of the Arabian Peninsula: Sharif Hussein of Makkah, the Hashemite Arab leader who controlled the Hejaz region of western Arabia including the holy cities of Makkah and Madinah; and Abdulaziz Ibn Saud who was still vying with Al Rasheed for dominance of central Arabia.

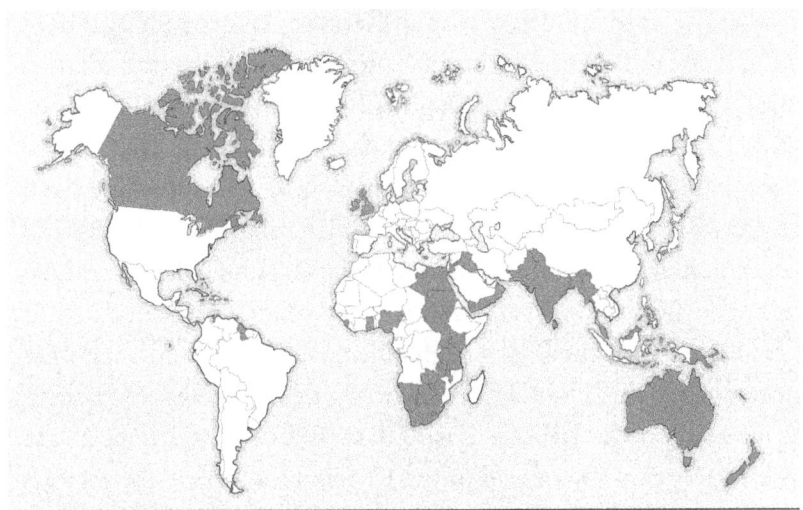

RISE AND FALL OF BRITISH EMPIRE

Adel Alsuhaimi

Young King Abdulaziz Bin Saud visiting Kuwait with
British Military Commander, circa early 1920s.

Britain's relationship with Ibn Saud had been an on/off affair depending on what was occurring in the Al Hasa Gulf, and did not grow serious until the Ottomans and Germans sought a stronger hold of the Arabian Peninsula with plans to extend a European railroad from Turkey to the cities of Baghdad and Basra in Mesopotamia (Iraq), and southward, possibly as far as Al Hasa. That would strengthen Germany's and the Ottoman's military supply lines, and threaten British dominance in the Al Hasa and Oman Gulfs and their colonies in India, Indonesia, Malaysia, Hong Kong, and so forth. The British were not keen to see a united Arabia emerge if it conflicted with their own imperialistic concerns, and they were encouraged by the United States who wanted to protect its nascent oil interests in the Middle East. (It should be noted that, at the time, the British were ahead of the U. S. in recognizing the region's "oil revolution," having beaten everyone else to Persia—present day Iran—and in the southwestern part of Iraq where they had found encouraging signs of oil deposits sites, and formed the Anglo

Persian Oil Company in 1908. Although the U.S. oil industry had marketed abroad extensively before the war, it owned few foreign properties.)

Throughout this time, Ibn Saud had relentlessly pursued his campaign of territorial expansion despite opposition on the various fronts.

Captain William Shakespear

In 1910, while in Kuwait, Ibn Saud developed an influential relationship when he met the young Captain William Shakespear, British diplomat and political agent, amateur photographer, botanist and explorer. It may have been Shakespear's fluency in Arabic that enabled the two men to develop a strong friendship. In Shakespear's account of that first meeting he described Ibn Saud as "a fair, handsome man, considerably above average Arab height with a particularly frank and open face, and after initial reserve... of genial and very courteous manner."[38] In turn, Shakespear had

Young King Abdulaziz Bin Saud visiting Iraq, circa early 1920s.

---

38 Harrigan, Peter, The Captain and the King 2002, Saudi Aramco World, 2002, accessed 18 July 2018, <http://archive.aramcoworld.com/issue/200205/the.captain.and.the.king.htm>

impressed Ibn Saud with his knowledge of the desert and his grasp of Najdi Arabic. Shakespear said of their encounter, "He offered me a welcome should I ever contemplate a tour so far afield as Riyadh."[39]

Near the end of his five-year post as political agent in Kuwait, Shakespear took him up on the offer, traveling in 1914 to Riyadh in the central Arabian Nejd desert region, where Ibn Saud had greeted him warmly. "Tea, coffee and sweets and talk until the evening prayer," Shakespear recorded in his diary, "and then again afterwards until nearly 9:30 when I came back, escorted as before to camp and dinner."[40]

Shakespear remained in Riyadh for five months, from February to June.[41] Soon afterwards he wrote to London seeking Britain's help for Ibn Saud whom he considered "the rising, dominant element in the region, the only one with the widespread support and capacity to drive out Turkish influence." But to Shakespear's disappointment, the British did not offer any support.[42]

With the outbreak of WWI, the British had a change of heart, realizing they needed help shoring up their regional interests. In late 1914, as part of a plan to take the southern city of Basra (in Mesopotamia, now Iraq) from the Ottomans, Britain dispatched the thirty-six-year-old Shakespear back to Arabia to gain Ibn Saud's help in allying Arabian tribes with Britain against the Ottomans. In the early days of January, 1915, Shakespear sent his commanders the first draft of a formal treaty between Ibn Saud and the British.[43]

Shakespear never lived to see the treaty signed; on January 24th he was shot and killed at the famous Battle of Jarrab, where WWI

---

39 Ibid.
40 Harrigan, Peter, The Captain and the King 2002, Saudi Aramco World, 2002, accessed 18 July 2018, <http://archive.aramcoworld.com/issue/200205/the.captain.and.the.king.htm>
41 Terry Boardman 2015, New View magazine No.75, accessed 18 July 2018, <http://threeman.org/?p=2179>
42 Harrigan, Peter, The Captain and the King 2002, Saudi Aramco World, 2002, accessed 18 July 2018, <http://archive.aramcoworld.com/issue/200205/the.captain.and.the.king.htm>
43 Matthew Priest 2015, Esquire, accessed 20 June 2017, <http://www.esquireme.com/culture/features/shakespear-saudi-king>

had been fought by proxy, Ibn Saud's army battling his rival, Ibn Rasheed who had pledged allegiance to the Ottomans. (Details about Shakespear's death are unclear. Ibn Saud had insisted he stay behind that day, but the Captain wanted to observe the battle. He went dressed in western attire—against Ibn Saud's advice—and had been an easy target, clearly identifiable as an Englishman. His death deeply affected Ibn Saud, and when asked later to name the greatest European he had ever met, it is said he replied without hesitation, Captain Shakespear.)[44]

Ibn Saud's control weakened in the Najd region after he lost the Battle of Jarrab, and again when he suffered another defeat, this time by the Ajman tribes at the Battle of Kanzan where his younger brother was killed. The Ajman tribes attacked Najd, eventually capturing the entire Al-Hasa region, except Hofuf and Qatif, creating major predicaments for the Najd's inhabitants and adding to the chaos in the region.

The Shakespear's treaty was eventually signed in December of that same year by Ibn Saud and Major Percy Cox for Britain on the Gulf Island of Darin.

The Treaty of Darin

The Treaty of Darin designated the land ruled by Ibn Saud a British protectorate and attempted to define its boundaries. It also supplied him with guns, ammunition and a monthly subsidy. The treaty guaranteed Britain's sovereignty of Kuwait, Qatar and the Trucial States and, more importantly, cemented their relationship with Ibn Saud who finally agreed to enter WWI as their ally against the Ottoman Empire, and promised to safeguard British territories and refrain from any acts of aggression toward them.

It should be pointed out, however, that before WWI had even begun, Ibn Saud had aligned himself, albeit by default, with the

---

44 A Brief Biography of Captain William Henry Shakespear 1997-2020, The Shakespear Family History Site, accessed 20 June 2017, <http://freepages.genealogy.rootsweb.ancestry.com/~shakespeare/military/capt_wm_hy/biog.htm>

Young King Abdulaziz Bin Saud visiting Shiekh Khazal of Ahvaz, South of Iraq, circa early 1920s.

Turks, hoping to avoid their interference in the Najd region. Later, when war broke out in 1914 he had remained neutral, determined to keep his options open, but he had certainly been savvy enough to know the Ottomans would take full advantage of the situation and attempt to rekindle tribal and religious feelings against the British, at least, that's what he told them, according to a British report.[45] However, only when his relationship with Britain was firm did he finally agree to be their ally in WWI, demonstrating in the process, his dexterity in politics. It's conceivable that Gertrude Bell saw this in Ibn Saud when she wrote:

> *"He combines with his qualities as a soldier that grasp of statecraft which is yet more highly prized by the tribesmen. To be 'a statesman' is perhaps the final word of commendation."*

Britain's objective had always been to use Ibn Saud to weaken the Ottoman influence by defeating Al Rasheed, and help dismantle Ottoman hegemony. Ibn Saud had agreed not to attack British

---

45 Report on Najd Mission 1917-1918; British Library, India Office Records and Private Papers, Pg. 427; IOR/R/15/1/747, Qatar Digital Library. East India Company 1917-1918, 'Report on Najd Mission,' accessed 9 June 2017, <https://www.qdl.qa/en/archive/81055/vdc_100022698600.0x00000f>

protectorates, but his 1915 agreement did not include his other rival—Sharif Hussein of Makkah, the Hashemite Arab leader who controlled the western part of the peninsula, which also included the holy cities of Makkah and Madinah. (Ibn Saud had been unaware, at the time, of Britain's concurrent talks with Sharif Hussein—McMahon Hussein Correspondence—which I discuss later in this chapter.) He had strategically avoided any form of alliance with Hussein, telling the British he was "a trivial and unstable character and could never be depended on."[46]

But it was more likely their intense rivalry over political aspirations and disputes over the boundaries of their respective jurisdiction that prompted lack of cooperation between Ibn Saud and Hussein. Associating with Hussein would have diminished Ibn Saud's hard earned military reputation and placed him in direct confrontation with the group who had destroyed the first Al Saud dynasty—the Ottomans. Also, Ibn Saud relied on the support of the Ikhwan, the Fundamentalist tribal fighters who disliked Hussein for allowing the Ottomans to introduce non-Islamic practices to their religion. The Fundamentalist Ikhwan considered Hussein a non-believer and, subsequently, not worthy of being the leader of the Islamic world. Still, despite the Ikhwan's dislike of Hussein, Ibn Saud thought it best not to engage in direct conflict with him.

The Treaty of Darin had one other stipulation—Ibn Saud was to ask the clerics to issue a religious pronouncement (*fatwa*) to bar Arabs from joining the Ottoman Army. They represented a large percentage of the Levant and Iraq, and a *fatwa* was pivotal in reducing the numbers of Arabs in the Ottoman army. In return, Britain would offer substantial military support with weapons and funding to help Ibn Saud unify the Arab Peninsula.

---

46 East India Company 1917-1918, 'Report on Najd Mission,' accessed 9 June 2017, <http://www.qdl.qa/en/archive/81055/vdc_100022698600.0x00000f>

Adel Alsuhaimi

The "Sick Man of Europe"
Even before WWI broke out in 1914, the Ottoman Empire had already been in serious decline, known since the mid-nineteenth century as "The Sick Man of Europe." The Sultan, Abdul Hamid II, had been reduced to a figurehead, his authority having been weakened two years prior, after losing much of the Empire's European territory in the First Balkan War.

The Sultan had limited influence within the CUP-led government (the Committee of Union and Progress) since all decisions were controlled by a powerful triumvirate: Mehmed Talaat Pasha, the Grand Vizier Minister of the Interior; Ismail Enver Pasha, the Minister of War; and Ahmed Djemal Pasha, the Minister of the Navy. Known as "The Three Pashas," they were largely responsible for the Empire's joining the war and sided with Germany against the Allies in an attempt to prevent further foreign encroachment. On Nov. 14th, 1914, in the Empire's capital of Constantinople, the religious leader Sheikh-ul-Islam proclaimed a holy war or *jihad*, urging Muslims around the world to defend the Empire against their common enemies.[47]

Yet, the move to join forces with Germany and become a member of the Central Powers (along with Austria-Hungary and Bulgaria) had made more enemies for the Ottomans, and they were unable to manage all of the external threats.

Blockade of seaports in the Eastern Arabian region
The decline of the Ottoman Caliphate and the efforts of Britain and others to gain political ascendency contributed somewhat, to the incidents in the Hejaz region in the west of the Arabian Peninsula. Political frictions in the region continued to increase, and for desert dwellers this meant greater hardships.

Britain's and France's exertion of economic pressure on the

---

47 History.com Editors 2009, History, accessed 14 June 2017, <http://www.history.com/this-day-in-history/ottoman-empire-declares-a-holy-war>

Germans and Ottomans at the inception of the war had a disastrous effect on Arabs. When they issued a blockade against eastern Arabian seaports to restrict supplies from India reaching the German and Ottoman armies, they also prevented food from reaching Central Arabia; the Al Hasa Gulf had been affected the most. It led to famine, resulting in the death of thousands—and was a major catastrophe for the Arabian population.

The McMahon-Hussein Correspondence and the Arab Revolt
By 1915 although the Ottoman Empire was weak it still maintained some control over much of the Arabian Peninsula. The British continued to exert their own influence since Arabia was centrally located between Europe and its prized colony, India. The Ottoman Sultan's call for a *jihad* the year before had concerned the British who now feared that it might provoke an attack on their protectorate of Egypt, in particular, the strategically critical Suez Canal. At 101 miles long, it connected the Mediterranean with the Red Sea and gave the British a much shorter route to their possessions in India, Asia and Africa, as opposed to the longer southern route round the Cape of Good Hope. The British didn't want to risk compromising their position in Egypt, and the Ottoman army allied with Germany posed a serious threat. To keep the Ottomans from marching toward the Suez Canal, Britain needed a diversion. If they harnessed growing Arab nationalism to their advantage, they would have one.

Many Arabs, having been ruled by the Ottomans for over 400 years, were more than ready for independence and would welcome the chance to liberate their lands from Turkish control. And the British needed someone to divert their Ottoman enemy and mitigate the *jihad* called by the Ottoman Sultan in 1914. An Arab uprising against the Ottomans would achieve that. Secret correspondence began in 1915 when a series of letters were exchanged between the British governor of Egypt, the High Commissioner Sir Henry

McMahon, and Sharif Hussein bin Ali, Amir and ruler of Hejaz in western Arabia and guardian of the two holiest cities of Makkah and Madinah.

McMahon wrote to Hussein requesting his help with mounting a rebellion in the region against the Ottomans. In exchange, Britain would provide the guns and cash the Arabs needed for a revolt, *and* at the end of WWI return the land previously ruled by the Turks to the Arabs who lived there. Hussein saw it as a chance to liberate Arab lands from Ottoman oppression; the English saw it as way to keep the Germans and Ottomans at bay. In the end, the English reneged on their promise, disputing Hussein's claims when the correspondence became public. However, Britain's promise to Hussein was contained in a letter dated Oct. 24, 1915, and later became known as the McMahon-Hussein Correspondence. Although the exchange culminated with the Arab Revolt in 1916, the correspondence had never been formalized into an official treaty; its terms, couched in vague language, had been left open to interpretation. Confusion over the correspondence continued to complicate Middle Eastern history for decades.

The French learned of the secretive McMahon-Hussein Agreement, which included giving the Arabs the land that they had desired, and were not at all pleased. The British had made a separate deal with them in 1916, the Sykes-Picot Agreement that contradicted the deal the British had made with the Arabs, promising the French the same land they had designated for the Arabs.

The Sykes-Picot Agreement
The agreement that Britain had made with France served as the blueprint for the creation of a new Arab region, and one that would have fateful repercussions for decades to come. Both the French and British had imperial designs on the Middle East, and between 1915 and 1916, they conducted private talks about how to carve up the area, post WWI, if the Allies won. Each wanted some jurisdiction

Semm Yubah

over it and thought their country better suited to assume leadership over the Ottoman territory. During the same time that Britain and France entered into a secret agreement, the British were in secret negotiations with Sharif Hussein and his sons about starting an Arab revolution to establish an independent Arab kingdom in the region. But the secret agreement that Britain made with France was the one that would have immense political impact on the Arab world for generations.

Two young diplomats were charged with the task. The first was a thirty-six-year-old from Britain, Sir Mark Sykes, whose understanding of Arabs and their politics was limited, as British historian James Barr states in his outstanding book, *A Line in the Sand*:

> *"Sykes's reputation on an authority of the Middle East rested on a series of books he had written on the region, the latest being a two-inch tome that he published earlier that year. The Caliph's Last Heritage was part history of the rise of Islam as a political force, part dyspeptic diary of his prewar travels through the Ottoman Empire. Spiced with Arabic phrases and comical dialogue, the book implied a deeper understanding than the author truly had."* [48]

It is striking that the British had considered Sykes such an expert, since his misunderstanding of Arabs, and Bedouins in particular, is so apparent. As early as 1905, in his book, Dar-ul-Islam: A Record of A Journey Through Ten of the Asiatic Provinces of Turkey,[49] Sykes had written:

> *I would as soon trust a London pickpocket as a desert Arab, for their greed of gold shows that the sons of Ishmael still have some of the characteristics as the sons of Isaac, and it is a blot upon their nature. On the other hand, their treachery and*

---

48 Barr, James; *A Line in the Sand: The Anglo-French Struggle for the Middle East, 1914-1948;* W.W. Norton & Company, New York; 2011; Pg. 4.

49 Mark Sykes 1904, Dar-ul-Islam: a record of a journey through ten of the Asiatic provinces of Turkey, accessed 14 June 2017, <https://archive.org/stream/darulislamrecord00sykeuoft/darulislamrecord00sykeuoft_djvu.txt; chapter 2>

avarice only show when dealing with strangers or enemies at war. Their lives are clean and moral, they know nothing of the evils of civilization and luxury, and rare deeds of violence, owing to their fiery tempers, are the only social crimes known among them.

And earlier in the same chapter,

Now the Bedawin intertribal wars have been going on for some six thousand years at least, probably without ten years of perfect peace. It is obvious that war was necessary for the purpose of infusing manliness into the race and relieving the boredom of the desert....the Bedawin wars appear at first sight so absurd to an European soldier; but I think anyone who considered the Bedawin as wanting in courage would be committing a grave error. My own idea is that they would give way to a foreign aggressor until some vital interest, such as a grazing or camping ground really essential to them, was threatened, when they would astound their adversaries by a sturdiness and bravery of which their previous conduct had given no hint."

It's quite clear to me that the British government's choice of Sykes was intentional; they didn't want a person with a deep knowledge of Arabs to do the surgical dissecting. Dismembering the Muslim world needed ruthlessness; the British feared that an expert would be sympathetic to the Arab people and their desire for independence after nearly eight centuries of Ottoman rule and neglect.

The other person involved with redesigning the Middle East was forty-three-year-old François Georges-Picot from France, who, as historian James Barr tells us, was well aware of the Arabs' desire for autonomy.

"While serving as France's consul in the booming port of Beirut immediately before the First World War, he had received letters from educated and ambitious young Arab army officers, lawyers and journalists who wanted France to help them achieve their

Semm Yubah

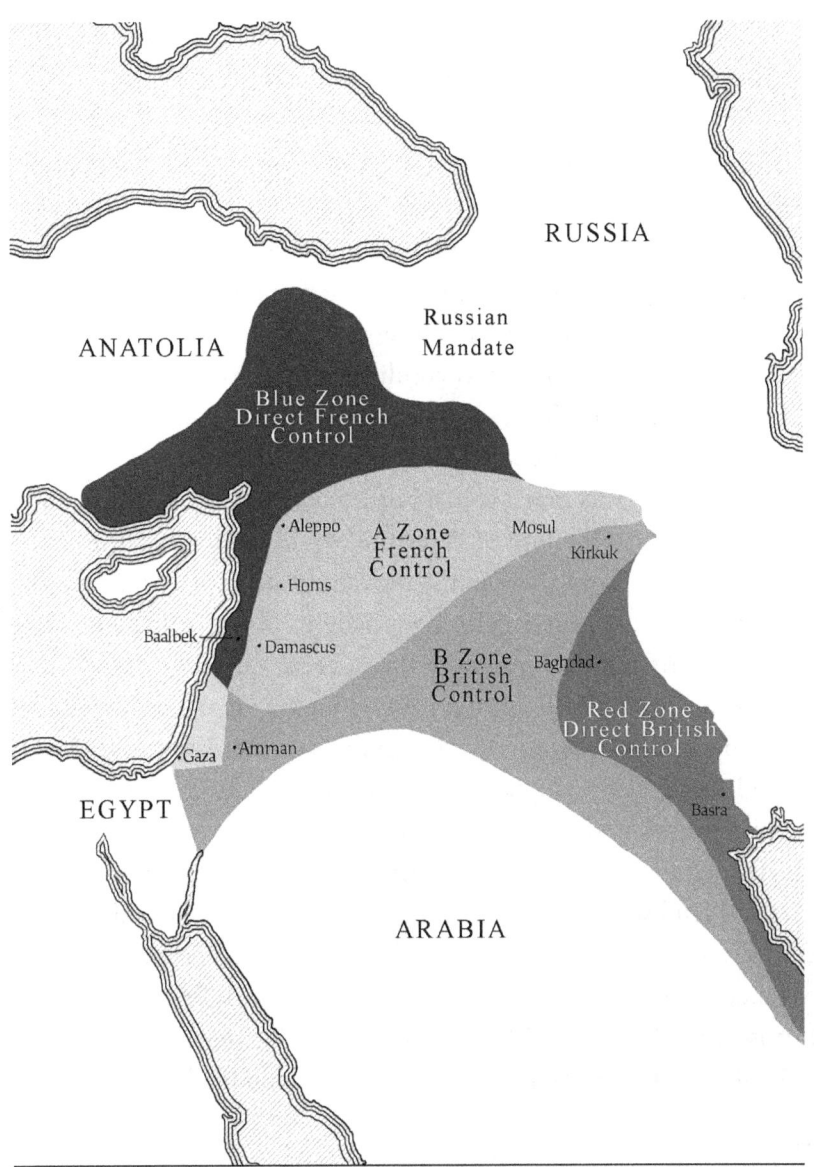

SYKES-PICOT, 1916

goal of autonomy within the Ottoman Empire. The Arabs even held a congress to discuss this aim in Paris in 1913, but the French government was unwilling to help them, because of its financial stake in the Ottoman endurance, and Georges Picot could only file the hopeful approaches carefully away."[50]

Sykes and Picot divided up Arab lands into French and British spheres of influence without any regard to ethnic or religious communities, the actual people who lived there. The agreement was later known as the 'Sykes-Picot' agreement and signed on May 19, 1916, (a few weeks before the official start of the Arab Revolt) and set the terms and conditions for carving the Arabian Peninsula into multiple Arab states. The agreement granted Britain control of what is currently Iraq, Kuwait, and Jordan; France, on the other hand, was given control of Lebanon, modern Syria, and southern Turkey. The fate of Palestine would be determined later, due to pressure from the Zionist movement to settle on the land, while the promises the British had made to Hussein and his sons were now proving nothing more than deception.

Still, in 1916 Sharif Hussein was unaware of the Sykes-Picot Agreement, and believed a revolt would give the Arabs a separate unified state, one independent of Ottoman rule. It is not clear whether he wanted an Arab independence due to his rejection of the nationalist agendas of the Ottoman's Three Pashas, or due to his personal feud with the Ottoman regime. Or because he had simply desired a kingdom for himself and his sons. Nevertheless, on the 5th of June, 1916, the Arab Revolt was carried out with British support. It was initiated by Sharif Hussein but led by his older sons with an estimated 30,000 Bedouins and other tribesmen by their sides.[51]

---

50 Barr, James; *A Line in the Sand: The Anglo-French Struggle for the Middle East, 1914-1948;* W.W. Norton & Company, New York; 2011; Pg. 16.

51 O'Brien Browne 2020, History Net, accessed 23 June 2018, <http://www.historynet.com/creating-chaos-lawrence-of-arabia-and-the-1916-arab-revolt.htm>

Help from Lawrence of Arabia

A year later Sharif Hussein and his sons received additional British support from the popular and charismatic military officer and intelligence expert, T.E. Lawrence. Thomas Edward Lawrence who earned fame in later years as "Lawrence of Arabia," and even more notoriety decades after that in the epic film of the same name, was at 5'5" not as tall as his Hollywood counterpart, Peter O'Toole. Lawrence first found his affinity for the Middle East and the Arab people when he traveled there as an archeology student, learning their language and customs. With the outbreak of WWI, he joined the British military as an intelligence officer in Cairo, working at a desk job for two years before being sent to Arabia in 1916. He fought the Ottomans under Faisal's command, one of Sharif Hussein's sons, and provided the military strategic support to the Hashemite forces. He had a strong rapport with Faisal and ensured him that his Arab northern army would become the main beneficiary of British aid. The turning point for Lawrence came when he had to convince the Arab leaders to co-ordinate their attacks and decisions in line with British interests.

In the introduction of his book, *The Seven Pillars of Wisdom* (1926) he says:

> *The Cabinet raised the Arabs to fight for us by definite promises of self-government afterwards. Arabs believe in persons, not in institutions. They saw in me a free agent of the British Government, and demanded from me an endorsement of its written promises. So I had to join the conspiracy, and, for what my word was worth, assured the men of their reward. In our two years' partnership under fire they grew accustomed to believing me and to think my Government, like myself, sincere. In this hope, they performed some fine things, but, of course, instead of being proud of what we did together, I was bitterly ashamed.*
>
> *It was evident from the beginning that if we won the war these promises would be dead paper, and had I been an honest adviser of the Arabs I would have advised them to go home*

and not risk their lives fighting for such stuff: but I salved myself with the hope that, by leading these Arabs madly in the final victory I would establish them, with arms in their hands, in a position so assured (if not dominant) that expediency would counsel to the Great Powers a fair settlement of their claims. In other words, I presumed (seeing no other leader with the will and power) that I would survive the campaigns, and be able to defeat not merely the Turks on the battlefield, but my own country and its allies in the council-chamber. It was an immodest presumption: it is not yet clear if I succeeded, but it is clear that I had no shadow of leave to engage the Arabs, unknowing, in such hazard. I risked the fraud, on my conviction that Arab help was necessary to our cheap and speedy victory in the East, and that better we win and break our word than lose."

Lawrence had dissuaded the Arabs from making a heavy assault on the Ottoman stronghold of the Arab holy city of Madinah, and instead, orchestrated their efforts to coordinate with British war strategy and attack the Hejaz Railway[52], which had supplied the garrison of the Turkish army. When the railway was attacked, the Turkish army had been forced to repair and protect it while fighting the Hashemite forces. This gave Hussein and his sons a major opportunity to destabilize the Ottoman army.

Perhaps T. E. Lawrence wanted the Arabs to continuously engage the Turkish army rather than try to regain Madinah and Makkah. If Hussein had recaptured those two holiest Islamic cities it might have given him an opportunity to tap into Muslims everywhere—from Morocco to Indonesia and central Asia to Somalia. That

---

52 Construction of the Hejaz Railway had been commissioned by the Ottoman Sultan Abdul Hamid, and the project ran from 1901 to 1909. The original intent behind the construction of the railway was to establish a direct travel route from Istanbul to Makkah, and reduce the travel time from forty days to five. But the start of WWI disrupted all construction effort, and the railway tracks, as a result, only reached as far as Madinah (approximately 282 miles north of Makkah), and the railway soon became a military target. The Turks used the railway to transport troops and supplies, and during the Arab Revolt, parts of the railway were destroyed under the guidance of British military officer, T.E. Lawrence and his Arab allies—Sharif Hussein with his sons.

would have created the possibility of a resurrection of the Muslim Caliphate, and in my opinion, would have terrified Britain and the other European/Western democracies.

The aftermath of the WWI left Britain occupying vast territories of the Ottoman Empire that later became Syria, Lebanon, Palestine, Iraq, and Trans-Jordan. Russia was left crippled with civil wars and foreign intervention, while France had a minor military influence in the Middle East. Britain emerged as the true victor of the war, remaining unchallenged and gaining considerable influence over the Middle East region.

With the Ottoman Empire now paralyzed, Britain had the legitimacy in crafting the terms for a new, albeit fragmented, modern Muslim Arab world.

However, in November, 1917 the Russian Bolshevik government exposed the terms of the Sykes-Picot agreement. After the Russian Tsar was overthrown in 1917, the Bolshevik communists, led by Lenin, discovered a copy of the Sykes-Picot agreement in the government's archive records. Lenin's colleague Leon Trotsky published a copy of the agreement in *Izvestia* newspaper on November 24, 1917, wanting to disclose what Lenin called "the agreement of the colonial thieves."[53]

It prompted a political scandal for Britain and France, but wouldn't be the only source of friction between the Arabs and Britain.

The Balfour Declaration

In 1917, one year after signing the Sykes-Picot Agreement, the British once again promised Arab lands with another possible ally which contradicted both the McMahon-Hussein Agreement and

---

[53] Contributors: Aljazeera.Net & Aljazeera Center for Studies 2016, accessed 5 June 2017, <http://interactive.aljazeera.com/aje/2016/sykes-picot-100-years-middle-east-map>

the Sykes Picot Agreement. Britain initiated talks that became the Balfour Declaration, promising the Zionist movement a political authority in Palestine, a region where the modern creation of a Jewish state would later take place.

It wasn't altruistic on Britain's part. "…Lloyd George had come to see British dominance in Palestine—a land bridge between the crucial territories of India and Egypt—as an essential post-war goal." [54]

In addition, the British hoped a formal declaration in favor of Zionism would curry Jewish support for the Allies in neutral countries like the U.S. who had not yet entered the war. The British government also came under lobbying pressure from the Zionist movement, calling for the rights of Jews to live in Palestine. Sympathetic Parliament members responded, and one was the Foreign Secretary of Britain, Arthur Balfour. On November 2, 1917, he drafted a letter to a leader of the Zionist movement, Baron Rothschild declaring full official support of Britain for the creation of a Jewish home in Palestine, which later resulted in the conflict of three different agreements—the first with Sharif Hussein and his sons, the second with the French in dividing Arab lands, and now the third promising Palestine as a homeland for the Jewish people.

Foreign Office
November 2nd, 1917
Dear Lord Rothschild,

I have much pleasure in conveying to you, on behalf of His Majesty's Government, the following declaration of sympathy with Jewish Zionist aspirations which has been submitted to, and approved by, the Cabinet.

His Majesty's Government view with favour the establishment in Palestine of a national home for the Jewish people, and will use their best endeavours to facilitate the achievement of this object, it being clearly understood that

---

54 History.com Editors 2009, A&E Television Networks, accessed 19 March 2017, <http://www.history.com/this-day-in-history/the-balfour-declaration>

nothing shall be done which may prejudice the civil and religious rights of existing non-Jewish communities in Palestine, or the rights and political status enjoyed by Jews in any other country.

I should be grateful if you would bring this declaration to the knowledge of the Zionist Federation.

Yours sincerely,

Arthur James Balfour[55]

The Hungarian-born Jewish author and journalist, Arthur Koestler, had astutely said of the agreement, "…one nation solemnly promised to a second nation the country of a third."[56]

Britain needed a third party to resolve the conflicts in a legitimate manner, but one that would ensure hegemony of Britain. A League of Nations was established that drew mandates for different Muslim Arab states.

Both Britain and France received these mandates, based on the terms laid out in the original Sykes-Picot agreement. The extra condition proposed by the League of Nations was that the authority of these regions rested with Britain and France until the states were able to function independently.

The League of Nations drew up maps around the Middle Eastern countries, as we know it today, paying no regard to the ethnic, religious, and geographic boundaries. This resulted in the modern creation of several independent Arab nation-states, each of which would have a new colonized identity based upon nationalism and regional boundaries. Therefore, the differences between Iraqis, Jordanians, Egyptians, and Syrians were now based upon the mandates drawn by the League of Nations.

---

55 Jennifer Rosenberg 2018, Thought Co, accessed 23 September 2018, <https://www.thoughtco.com/balfour-declaration-1778163>

56 Ian Black 2017, The Guardian News & Media Ltd., accessed 14 September 2018, <https://www.theguardian.com/news/2017/oct/17/centenary-britains-calamitous-promise-balfour-declaration-israel-palestine>

As a result, both Britain and France gained influence over the Middle East, and Sharif Hussein and his sons were granted their kingdoms under British protection. Prince Faisal, son of Sharif Hussein, was made king of the land that later became known as Syria and Iraq, while his brother, Prince Abdullah, was crowned King of Jordan. However, in reality, the British and French maintained the real authority.

Britain's Role in the Creation of Saudi Arabia
All of this leads me to question the role of Britain in the creation of Saudi Arabia. How long had Britain backed Ibn Saud to eliminate the influence of Al Rasheed in the region? After all, Al Rasheed remained loyal to the Ottoman Empire, and Britain would only benefit from the downfall of the Ottomans in the run-up to WWI. Also, as I mentioned earlier, Ibn Saud was aware of the Ottomans' attempts to stir tribal and religious sentiment against the British. So, why hadn't Britain become a supporter of Ibn Saud sooner? One possibility was that the British weren't that confident in their fight against the Ottomans, since in the first four months of the war, both Britain and France had suffered nearly a million casualties,[57] to be followed by a humiliating defeat on the Dardanelle Straits and at the Battle of Gallipoli in 1915, when they grossly underestimated the enemy and lost 200,000 of their men. None other than Winston Churchill, 40-years-old and First Lord of the Admiralty, had promoted the maneuver. "A good army of 50,000 men and sea power," he said, "that is the end of the Turkish menace." (Although it should be pointed out that Britain refused to send him the necessary troops. Still, he advanced with the number of men he had.)[58]

---

[57] Klein, Christopher, Winston Churchill's World War Disasters. Christopher Klein 2014, History Net, accessed 20 June 2017, <http://www.history.com/news/winston-churchills-world-war-disaster>

[58] Ibid.

The following year they suffered defeat again, this time in Basra, Iraq, losing nearly 60,000 soldiers.[59]

Also, it's interesting to note that Ibn Saud did not confront Sharif Hussein who controlled western Arabia until Britain no longer supported him. After WWI, Hussein's reputation as a genuine Arab leader had diminished, and Ibn Saud took full advantage of public opinion. With British aid (they had withdrawn their support from Hussein once he had become problematic), the forces loyal to Ibn Saud would easily outmatch those of Sharif Hussein. Ibn Saud's allies, the Ikhwan, had now clearance to invade Hejaz, enabling Ibn Saud to take the city from Hussein. (Later the Ikhwan were ousted from the alliance with Ibn Saud after they attempted to occupy the British protectorates of Iraq, Kuwait, and Trans-Jordan.) Hussein, in his seventies, fled from Makkah to Madinah in 1924 and later went into exile, escaping to Cyprus.

There has been some criticism of Ibn Saud pertaining to his relationship with Britain and using their help to achieve his military goals in the Najd and Hejaz. The Saudi government and others believe that Ibn Saud was fighting the injustices of the Ottoman-controlled areas, particularly in Najd, and an Islamic revivalist movement was required to restore the lost dignity of Islam to the region.

However, what is clear is that Ibn Saud had purposely sought Britain's support to help increase his legitimacy in the region, diminish the influence of the Ottoman Empire and continue his territorial expansion.

Ibn Saud may have learned this political tactic during his exile in Kuwait, which had been protected and supported by a British political officer in the region. He had witnessed first-hand the reign of Kuwait's Amir, Sheikh Mubarak Al Sabah, who, without the control of the British Empire, could never have remained in power. And in 1901 still exiled there, Ibn Saud saw evidence of British

---

59 Wright, Dean, British Military Defeats; Dean Wright 2009, FriedGold.co.uk, accessed 21 June 2017, <http://www.friedgold.co.uk/battles.html>

might when their warship, HMS Perseus, successfully blocked the invasion of Kuwait by Al Rasheed family who were on the verge of capturing the entire region.

It is safe to say that Ibn Saud's forces did not have the capacity to fight Al Rasheed or Hussein on their own, and needed the sponsorship of the British. If they had lost, it would have meant a resurgence of the Ottoman Empire in the region, thwarting Britain's as well as Ibn Saud's goals.

It wouldn't be until 1927 that the Treaty of Jeddah was signed in the central Hejaz of western Arabia, superseding the Treaty of Darin, and recognizing the independence of Ibn Saud and his sovereignty over the Hejaz (the western) and Najd (central) provinces. The growing relationship between Britain and Ibn Saud would culminate in 1932 with the unification of Hejaz and Najd into the Kingdom of Saudi Arabia with Ibn Saud declaring himself its king. The warrior had proven true what Gertrude Bell had said about him, "His star is in the ascendant..."[60]

Needless to say, when my grandfather journeyed with his father on the peninsula, there was certainly more than enough chaos—famine, epidemics, tribal wars, neighboring sheikdoms under siege, local skirmishes as numerous and contentious as ever, and conditions so bleak that often left the inhabitants of the Najd region in despair. Did the Najdi then have any inkling of what was to come, that the various clashing clans and tribes who battled over the looting of sheep or stolen grazing lands, would stand united in one kingdom and under the rule of one man? It must have been unthinkable to most, that even Ibn Saud would have the tenacity and skill and diplomacy to achieve such a feat.

As a father myself I can only imagine the angst Saleh must have felt embarking on their journey. Each direction, a potential

---

[60] Howell, Georgina, Editor, *Gertrude Bell, A Woman in Arabia: The Writings of the Queen of the Desert*, Pg. 123.

Semm Yubah

landmine. It is one thing to put oneself in danger, but to risk your child's safety is something entirely different. But urgency and desperation are powerful motivators and certainly propelled him forward, despite the risks. Still I wonder, what were Saleh's thoughts traveling alongside his son through the desert, when the wind turned deadly, and the sand rushed their ears and blinded their eyes?

CHAPTER 4

The Majestic Deserts of Arabia

It was more than a century ago when my grandfather and great-grandfather had sojourned through the majestic Al Nefud desert. It was such a different place then, a wilderness of austere beauty, untouched by time. What was the affect of crossing that sea of sandy red? Had it left its mark? Had the desert etched itself into their souls, something unnamable, unimaginable, claiming them in a way they could have never foretold?

"No man can live this life and emerge unchanged," wrote the explorer and travel writer Wilfred Thesiger in his book, *Desert Sands*, about living among the Bedouins in the Empty Quarter of the Arabian Peninsula in the 1950s. "He will carry, however faint, the imprint of the desert, the brand which marks the nomad; and he will have within him the yearning to return, weak or insistent according to his nature. For this cruel land can cast a spell which no temperate clime can match."

It's true the desert can be a desolate place, devastating when the weather turns hostile, more than unforgiving. But it can also be restorative, a sanctuary, soothing in its silence, even mystical in its isolation, healing with its blooms of desert rose, silver hamat

Semm Yubah

and pitch-green arder, inspiring with its bursts of nasi and sobot,[61] pale as straw.

Some say they feel transformed after spending time in the desert, inexplicably changed by its shape-shifting winds and stark scenes; others feel blessed long after they have departed, as if still held by its allure. Perhaps it is true what Lady Anne Blunt said, "The Nafud accounts for everything." Still, I wonder. Had my grandfather at sixteen experienced any of this? Had Saleh? Had they emerged transfixed, instilled with a benevolent sense of peace? Perhaps I'm imposing my modern perspective on my grandfather's tale, drawing conclusions from the vantage point of a much more comfortable life, and romanticizing what it was like then. I'm sure Saleh's concerns were far more basic and pragmatic, fraught with anxiety over the well being of the wife and young son he left behind and the immediacy of his current situation—how would he and his son survive the journey? Would their food and water supply last until their next stop? Would they get caught in a lethal *shamal* or the crossfires of local tribal clashes, collide with marching Ottomans and Brits, or the warring Al Sauds or Al Rasheeds or Hashemites? And once they arrived at their destination, would they find sufficient work? Saleh certainly had much to contemplate, although traveling through the Great Al Nefud would have been the right place for that, and may have strengthened his resolve.

It seems that they had encountered their share of mishaps, one with lasting effect. My grandfather rarely spoke about the incident but my elders have told me about the day when Abdulrahman's and Saleh's caravan had been caught in a severe sandstorm. They can be fierce, winds sometimes stronger than 50 miles per hour, making visibility

---

61 Watts, David; Al-Nafie, Abdulata H. Vegetation and Biogeography of the Sand Seas of Saudi Arabia, Routledge, 2003. Watts 2003, Vegetation & Biogeography of The Sand Seas Of Arabia 1st edition, accessed 14 June 2017, <https://books.google.com/books?id=RaOsAgAAQBAJ&pg=PA3&lpg=PA3&dq=Nafud+desert+description+1915&source=bl&ots=4KDUc9lrdt&sig=wowRiRc5-U56gVYmFhiAapqqWuA&hl=en&sa=X&ved=0ahUKEwjAq9KZlJXSAhULi1QKHY2kBscQ6AEIPDAF#v=onepage&q=Nafud%20desert%20description%201915&f=false>

poor, horizons disappearing, the sand rising, swirling, forcing its way into your eyes, ears and nose, mouth and throat and lungs. Legend has it that once a caravan had disappeared during a brutal storm, buried by a tsunami of sand. A sandstorm can quickly turn deadly.

My grandfather's caravan had resumed their progress after spending a night under the stars, making a slow trek across the sand when the sky had suddenly turned ominous, the sun disappearing. The Master Caravan directed everyone to close ranks and get in ring formation. Abdulrahman and Saleh had taken cover, huddled in the shelter of their tent and covered their faces, the wind howling, the air dense with sand, infiltrating and permeating every available crack and crevice with grit. It was hard to hear anything other than the roar of the wind, their eyes shut tight against the sand. They prayed it would end, and the storm had only lasted a day but it seemed longer the way the sand had invaded their tent and clothes, burrowed deep into their eyes and ears and nose. The next morning they regrouped and continued onward but Abdulrahman's eyes had become inflamed, and later infected after a cloud of sandflies descended, one landing into his left eye and exacerbating the irritation. A Bedouin had applied some kind of homemade poultice to my grandfather's eye, but the infection grew worse, and by day's end he had difficulty seeing out of his left eye, and it lasted throughout the trip. His eyesight had greatly diminished as a result, and years later he lost complete vision in it. I'm sure at sixteen he was frightened at the prospect of losing his vision in that eye but he had learned from his father to take hardship in stride.

When Saleh and Abdulrahman and the caravan finally left Al Nefud, they continued northeast, entering another Ottoman-controlled region the Arabs called *Al Iraq*. (Iraq as we know it today did not exist.) Translated, *Al Iraq* means "to be deeply rooted."[62]

---

62 Christopher Hitchens 2007, The Atlantic, accessed 3 November 2017, < https://www.theatlantic.com/magazine/archive/2007/06/the-woman-who-made-iraq/305893/\/>

Semm Yubah

It occurs to me that the meaning might have held some greater significance for Saleh, resonating with him on some subconscious level. Perhaps it resuscitated hope, reassuring him that his ambitions were not merely dreams. Did he see Iraq as some kind of sign? Maybe he believed that if this land could provide the sustenance needed for its people to stay rooted, it would also deliver, *In sha Allah*, for his own family. I can only guess at what my great-grandfather and grandfather felt as they approached the region.

Once, the region had been the economic and educational center of the Islamic Golden Age, but the Iraq of the early 20th century was a victim of a power struggle between the German supported Ottomans, and the British and French. For centuries, the Ottomans controlled Iraq, but during WWI in 1917 Britain had captured the once-prosperous city of Baghdad and took 45,000 prisoners. Two years after the War, in 1920, Iraq came under British control per the Sykes-Picot agreement between Britain and France, and in 1921 it became a Hashemite monarchy under the protection of the British with the appointment of Amir Faisal Ibn Hussein as King of Iraq and Syria. Independence was not granted Iraq until 1932.

Three weeks after they exited the desert, the caravan neared their next destination in Iraq, the Al Zubair oasis. Even before they glimpsed it, they caught its distinct pungent aroma in the air, heard the echo of bellows and bleats. Al Zubair served as hub for traveling caravans, and hundreds upon hundreds of herds of camels were corralled at its outskirts. Caravans parked their camels here before they continued to the town's center. It was also the place where camels were sold and rented. Al Zubair proved a convenient stopover for caravans, and afforded desert travelers a basic luxury, a place to clean themselves up after such an arduous journey, and a chance to change into more formal clothes before advancing into the city for business.

I'm not sure why but at Al Zubair, Saleh and Abdulrahman decided to leave the caravan and travel the rest of their journey alone.

It must have seemed like home to my grandfather and Saleh seeing so many native Najdis. Many had relocated to Al Zubair to set up shop, selling their supplies to the commercial caravans at the open market. Trade had produced a thriving business for them and motivated other emigrating groups to make the trip there.[63]

It was no surprise that Saleh had befriended transplanted Najdis who had been more than happy to share their secrets of the local trade and open markets.

In 1916, a year after my grandfather first set foot in Al Zubair, Gertrude Bell gave her own impressions of the town when she wrote to her stepmother.

> "...a funny little desert place, something like Hail, 9 miles from Basrah... The road was all under water and mud – Euphrates floods – till we reached the high edge of the real desert about a mile from the town.... I was put up at the post office in room with a mud floor furnished with my own camp bed and chair and bath and a table lent by Captain Marrs, but the shaikh of the town insisted on entertaining me, and we went in to him for all our meals and unlimited gossip about the desert with which he is always in the closest touch since the caravans come in to Zubair. He lent us some horses in the afternoon and we rode out to Shaibah [Shu'aiba (Ash Shuaybah] where we have a small cavalry post. The officers took us round the battlefield, or part of it, and we galloped back to Zubair at sunset."[64]

Saleh and Abdulrahman remained in Al Zubair for several months, and rented a small place to live and store their supplies

---

63 Firas Sami Abdulaziz Alqatrani 2015, The Old City of Al Zubair; The Emergence and Physical Reality (1571-1882 Iraq), accessed 21 July 2017, <https://www.degruyter.com/downloadpdf/j/bog.2015.27.issue-27/bog-2015-0002/bog-2015-0002.pdf>

64 Letters, Gertrude Bell to her father, Sir Hugh Bell 1916, University Library, Newcastle University, accessed 28 September 2017, <http://www.gerty.ncl.ac.uk/letter_details.php?letter_id=164 >

Semm Yubah

Gondolas in the Basra Shatt Al Arab waterway shuttling people and goods, 1915.

and equipment. Al Zubair served as their base, and soon after their arrival they traveled southeast to Basra, a seaport very close to Al Zubair, but a much more modernized metropolis. They shuttled daily between the two places, buying supplies, some for their own consumption, most for resale. They purchased a wagon along with several additional camels to transport their goods, each camel capable of holding between 520 and 540 pounds of merchandise and equipment.

The historic Iraqi city of Basra was once known as the "Venice of the east," and one can understand why when perusing the historic photographs and seeing its many canals and lagoons and gondola-like flyboats, its golden domes and arched windows and colored glass. Some called it the city of *Shanasheel* for its unique architectural element prevalent since the Middle Ages—oriel windows enclosed with intricately carved wooden latticework. The *Shanasheel,* or *Mashrabiya,* was located on the street side and upper floors of a building. The word *mashrabiya* is derived from an Arabic root meaning the "place of drinking," and was adapted to accommodate the first function of the screen, "the place to cool the drinking water."[65]

The lattice wooden screen supplied the needed shade and air currents to cool the clay vases of water wrapped in damp rags kept there, and it helped refresh the house and its inhabitants, no small feat when the temperature climbed to 105.[66]

Basra means the over watcher and might have referenced the city's origin as an Arab military base against the Sassanids.[67] Strategically located between Iran and Kuwait, Basra sits on the western bank of Shatt Al-Arab, the waterway formed by the confluence of the two great rivers, the Euphrates and Tigris. In 1914 when the British decided to protect its interest in the Near East, especially the Suez Canal and the oil fields surrounding Basra, it sent British and Indian troops into the city, and in November of that year, Basra became the first Ottoman city to fall to Britain and India occupation. (In early spring of 1915, the year that Saleh and Abdulrahman were traveling, the Turkish army staged a counterattack in Basra, but was defeated.) After the British seized control, they modernized its port, and subsequently trade and industry flourished, and the city developed a prosperous economy, although the foundation for its success was laid centuries before that. In the 7th century, Basra became, as historian and Arabist Paul Lund writes,

> *"the largest and most ebullient city in the Islamic world, its population exploding from zero to 200,000 in three decades. The streets were thronged with Arabs, East Africans, Persians, Indians and Malay-speakers from "Zabaj" (Indonesia). A clearinghouse for information, it was here that practical knowledge of Southeast Asia and China began to reach the*

---

65 John Feeney 1974, Aramco world, accessed 21 September 2017, <http://archive.aramcoworld.com/issue/197404/the.magic.of.the.mashrabiyas.htm>

66 Mashrabiya 2020, Wikipedia, accessed 10 December 2017, <https://en.wikipedia.org/wiki/Mashrabiya>

67 Basra 2004, Wikipedia, accessed 10 December 2017, <https://en.wikipedia.org/wiki/Basra>

Semm Yubah

Arabic-speaking peoples and gradually find its way into both sober works of geography and entertaining wonder books... 'Our sea is worth all the others put together,' Basra's most famous writer, the ninth-century polymath al-Jahiz, wrote, 'for there is no other into which God has poured so many blessings. It flows into the Indian Ocean, which extends for an unknown distance.'[68]

The city served as a gateway to shipping and trade to India and the far east, with ample opportunity to make a very good living, a fact that would have appealed to Saleh, along with other merchants. Ships arriving in Basra offered rare goods and agriculture produce, and much of the merchandise from the north or east changed hands here before making its way to Kuwait and into the heart of Arabia.

In the days of Babylonia's prosperity the Euphrates was hailed as the soul of the land, and the Tigris, the bestower of blessings,[69] and the river banks yielded rich, fertile lands allowing locals to grow everything from grains to vegetables and fruits. Many boats and ships arriving from Asia and India carried exotic spices and silks, rubber and ropes and bamboo. Basra's merchants bought and sold rare goods earning themselves a hefty profit, and Saleh soon learned that most everything sent inland could be sold for ten or fifteen times more than what a merchant originally paid for it. Coming from a town struggling for survival, Saleh must have been overwhelmed by the potential. He certainly must have seen Basra and later Kuwait, as the gold-ring opportunity to improve the family's quality of life.

My elders have told me many stories of Basra, and one in particular stands out in my mind. When Abdulrahman and Saleh

---

68 Paul Lunde 2005, Aramco World, print edition. pages 20-29. accessed 3 July 2018, <http://archive.aramcoworld.com/issue/200504/the.seas.of.sindbad.htm>

69 Donald A. Mackenzi 1915, The World's Wisdom in the Palms of Your hands, Myths of Babylonia and Assyria, accessed 3 July 2018, <http://www.sacred-texts.com/ane/mba/mba08.htm; Mackenzie, Donald A. *The World's Wisdom in the Palms of Your hands, Myths of Babylonia and Assyria*, 1915>

had first approached the historic city by sea, they could not believe what they saw—mountains rising up from its port, as if by some conjuring. Surely it must have been a figment of their imagination since Basra's land is actually flat, but I soon learned what it was they saw. As they sailed closer they realized those mysterious mountains were made of grain transported from ships and piled four to five stories high.

Gertrude Bell had also resided in Basra for most of 1916, and described it in a letter to her father:

> *"Even Basrah has a burst of glory in April. The palm gardens are deep in luxuriant grass and corn, the pomegranates are flowering, the mulberries almost ripe and in the garden of the house where I am staying the roses are more wonderful than I can describe…" The following month she spoke of "an uninterrupted North wind, and the temperature never above 105… not at all oppressive, the nights quite cool on the roof. Sometimes one even needs a blanket…so far there's nothing to complain of…"*

Though she found the number of mosquitoes trying, and the city's muddy banks.[70]

For Abdulrahman, living in Basra had been a feast of delectable firsts. It was the first time he ever glimpsed the luminous blue-green sea and inhaled its briny air, the first time he heard a steam ship clanking across water, the first time he tasted both sweet water and gulf fish, the first time he beheld a car. He must have experienced sensory overload from the city's myriad smells, sounds, and sights—the hiss and slap of paddle steamers, the bobbing of slender flyboats, the clamor of the railroad with its stacks of smoke, the mule carts and telephone wires, the palm groves and apricot trees and walled gardens, the open market with its striking wares and spices. I would have loved to have seen his expression the first

---

70 Gertrude Bell to her father, Sir Hugh Bell 1916, University Library, Newcastle University, accessed 9 July 2017, <http://www.gerty.ncl.ac.uk/letter_details.php?letter_id=164>

time he witnessed a parade of British and Indian troops, the Red Cross nurses, the officers' wives in western attire, their pale arms and faces exposed, his fellow Arabs dressed in jacket and trousers, some with a Tarboosh or Fez on their heads.

Here in Basra, Saleh schooled Abdulrahman in the ways of the world. Although Saleh considered it a city with immense prospects he also recognized the unforeseen threats a big city posed. In the early twentieth century Basra was, in some ways, not unlike the towns of the wild west, and his son was young, gullible, with a teenager's healthy dose of inquisitiveness and passion to experience life. But Saleh didn't want Abdulrahman unduly influenced by misguided peers or exploited by fast-talking merchants. For Saleh, more important than the business of earning a living, was the upbringing of his son. Raising a boy to become a man required guidance as well as love. Before Saleh even began to establish connections and set up a shop, he taught his son how to read faces and negotiate with strangers, how to navigate the streets and canals, which were the best and safest routes to travel, and the ones to avoid.

As soon as they rented their stall in the open market Abdulrahman assisted his father with transporting the purchased wares from the dock back to their stall. Sometimes he went alone. I'm sure as a sixteen-year-old boy traveling through a new city, crossing bustling bridges and canals, he was curious to explore. Had he wished for an hour to sneak off and wander alone? Was there some winding street beckoning, some old shop crammed with exotic objects calling him? Of course, Abdulrahman and his father had traveled all this way for one purpose—to earn money to provide for his mother and younger brother and other family in Unayzah. So any thoughts of fancy probably weren't entertained long, and if they were, he certainly would have kept them to himself.

Three months after they arrived in Basra, they had accumulated the inventory needed to set up a shop at the next city. In the early morning hours, Saleh and Abdulrahman, kneeling, bowed toward the west and Makkah, saying the *Istekhara* Prayers to God for guidance and blessings, asking Him to keep them safe on the next part of their journey. With their wagon and camels packed to capacity, they started on the road again but this time traveling alone, and heading for Kuwait.

The distance between Zubair and Kuwait was not very far, approximately eighty-six miles of hard compacted mud as a makeshift road, with small settlements dotting the landscape. Even though they were no longer part of the caravan, it still took them several days, and they were careful to pace themselves to maintain their strength and endurance, what with the scorching heat and blinding desert sun.

Since there was no *Al Ogailat* to navigate for them, they had to depend on their own skills for survival. They had no modern instruments to determine their direction, nothing like today's GPS, no compasses or maps. Instead, they used the same methods the Bedouins had employed for hundreds of years, and that some still use today: during the day they relied on the rising sun and a cane. (The cane was stuck into the sand, and the shadow the rising sun made determined points west; other directions were located by the shadow's advancing position). At night, they depended on the position of the moon, and a reading of the stars—Polaris the North Star and others—to help them advance from one point to the next. They also interpreted the terrain, using its various elements as navigational tools, noting the shape and swell and position of certain dunes, the prevailing direction of the wind and sand flow, the specific trees, rock formations and watering holes, all known landmarks to any desert dweller.

Their hard work and ingenuity were rewarded with Kuwait's appearance on the horizon. My grandfather had been unaware at the time that his favorite poet had once resided here. He'd learned later Al Ouny had traveled to Kuwait to escape the famines and epidemics of the Najd region.

Semm Yubah

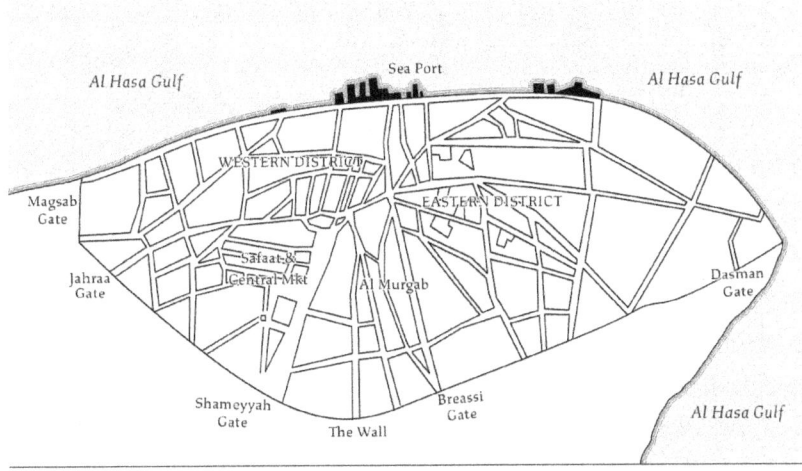

KUWAIT CITY AND SHORELINE

A British Protectorate, Kuwait was small (the size of Hawaii), arid and flat with low hills and shallow depressions, predominantly a sandy desert except for the few oases and the shore, a natural harbor which gave rise to the flourishing fishing, pearling and shipbuilding industries. Located in the northwest corner of the Gulf, Kuwait is flanked by Iraq to the north and west, the Arabian Peninsula to the south and southwest, and the Gulf to the east. The historic city was a small town built in the early 18th century and looked out on the aquamarine water. Originally called *Grane* or *Qurain*, Kuwait was bounded by a mud wall with gates leading out to the desert.[71] That could be the reason, by the mid-eighteen century, it was renamed Kuwait, the diminutive for the Arabic word, *kut*, which means fortified town.

It had remained a small desert community until the Al-Sabah family took control and built the first fortified settlement in the mid-1700s when Arab tribes from the central Arabia migrated to the more hospitable shore of the Al Hasa Gulf. "The journey of migration itself," Professor Jill Crystal tells us in her book, *Oil and*

---

71 Dawlat Ahmed Sadek 2019, Encyclopedia Britannica, Inc., accessed 2 September 2019, <https://www.britannica.com/place/Kuwait/People>

Politics in the Gulf: Rulers and Merchants in Kuwait and Qatar, "was a key formative event in establishing the sense of community by creating a new social bond among the migrant families." By the time the migrants reached Kuwait, "they considered themselves not merely members of the Arabian tribes they had left, but members of a new tribe, the Bani Utub. Indeed, the name Bani Utub may have its origin in the act of migration." Professor Crystal credits the Arab historian, Ahmad Mustafa Abu Hakima, for its meaning. "…the name Utub comes from the arabic root *ataba,* to travel from place to place (*Bani,* people of.*)* [72]

In an effort to move away from Ottoman rule, the small Gulf Country became a British protectorate in 1899. Kuwait had a rich maritime heritage and a long history of pearl trading to its name, and before the appearance of oil, was celebrated for its pearling industry. When Saleh and Abdulrahman arrived, the demand for pearls was on the decline and would get worse with the Great Depression and with Japan's cultured pearls flooding the market, and a few years later in 1921 only 329 of Kuwait's 700 pearling boats would set sail for the banks. [73]

In the 19th and the first decade of the 20th century, and before the discovery of its oil, Kuwait remained prosperous and the center of boat building in the Gulf region, and well established in pearling and long distance commerce. Kuwait-made ships carried the bulk of international trade between the ports of India, East Africa, and the Red Sea. And Kuwait was on the trading caravan road between Arabia and Iraq.

When Abdulrahman first entered Kuwait he was staggered by the show of dhows, those Arabian sailing vessels with teak planks and graceful triangular sails, and the Jalboot pearling boats, crowded with *Jazwa* or pearl divers who risked their lives every time they

---

[72] Jill Crystal 2016, Kuwait: the Transformation of an Oil State, accessed 17 June 2017, <http://bit.ly/2KsOT3G>

[73] The pearl fishers of Arabia 2014, BBC News, accessed 11 January 2017, <http://bbc.in/2LvAu78>

sunk deep beneath the sea, the *Nakhodhas* or boat captains at the helm, and other fishermen at the piers, swapping stories.

The pearl divers and harvesters were well known to my family. When my father, Abdulaziz (1929-2013) was a boy living in the seaport of Jubail, (just south of Kuwait) he listened to the divers sing before they set out to sea and was enthralled by their music and rhythmic clapping, and I assume my Grandfather's experience in Kuwait was similar. The divers' escalating chants and mesmerizing drumming and dancing attracted viewers from afar; women and children peeked over their house walls in the dark of night to witness the event.

The life of a pearl diver was difficult. Every time they sailed out to sea, they placed themselves in peril with 30 to 40 dives a day, their bodies oil-coated, their ears plugged, their nostrils clipped shut, a rope basket dangling from their necks for oysters. While clutching a heavy stone tethered to another rope, the divers sank deep, up to 60 feet, with a knife to scrape the oysters off. Aboard ship another man stood ready to yank up the rope tied to the rock, waiting for the diver's tug signaling he wanted to be hauled to the surface.[74]

Some claim pearl divers were no more than indentured servants, always in debt to their captain, who, in turn, owed money to the merchants. Others say they were slaves. Diving had enabled some men to work off their debts, but if their loans weren't repaid at the time of the pearl divers' deaths, then their sons or brothers inherited their debt.[75]

At the end of the divers' long seafaring journey, sailors beat their drums and tambourines in celebration. As soon as the ship's sails were spotted from shore, families and friends rushed out to greet them, the women beating the beaches with palms, singing their

---

74 The pearl fishers of Arabia 2014, BBC News, accessed 11 January 2017, <http://www.bbc.com/news/blogs-magazine-monitor-30042226>

75 Kareem Fahim 2010, The New York Times, accessed 15 January 2017, <http://www.nytimes.com/2010/08/13/world/middleeast/13kuwait.html>

One of Kuwait castle wall gates, 1900s

hopes—may their loved ones be among the lucky men returning home.

At first, Saleh and Abdulrahman stayed at the home of a family friend in Kuwait. There were no hotels in town, and even if there were a small eatery with a few rooms for rent, Saleh preferred to reside with friends until he and his son found their own place and a stall in the open market. Saleh knew Kuwait was the major port for exports to Najd and for imports arriving from as close as Basra and as faraway as India and southeast Asia.

I've been told by my uncles that after they settled in Kuwait, Saleh relied more and more on Abdulrahman and after he felt confident, he sent his son on his first solo trading voyage through the Shat Al Arab water way between Kuwait and Basra in early 1917.

In Basra, Abdulrahman purchased the merchandise they needed: grain, vegetables, coffee, sugar, rice, and fabric, woods and other products—and then he hauled his supplies back to Kuwait. Saleh resold the goods at the open market and contacted the camel caravan and Bedouins who took those hard-to-find products back to the inner peninsula and Unayzah for resale. Kuwait gave merchants access to the interior of the Arabian Peninsula and the Najd region.

For weeks, Saleh and Abdulrahman spent their days in the open market and commuted between Basra and Kuwait. Saleh observed how self-assured and amiable his son was with the merchants and customers. Abdulrahman had grown in the year and a half they had been away from Unayzah. No longer was Abdulrahman a gangly, tall boy. The time had come for Saleh to help him find other work and he spoke to a friend, one of the Kuwaiti merchants, about

Semm Yubah

Abdulrahman working at his stall in the open market. As luck would have it, the merchant needed the extra help. Abdulrahman was now working two jobs: one with the merchant, selling foodstuff and household items, fabrics and garments, and building materials, and doing the accounting, processing the paperwork at customs and dealing with government officials, and at the same time still helping his father with the family business. As weeks grew into months, and the seasons gave way to another year, father and son fell into the routine of daily life, and the city didn't feel as strange at dusk.

With Abdulrahman earning extra income, he had what his father had always wanted for him—independence. Saleh had felt equal measures of relief and pride. His son, now had the means to support himself, and it comforted Saleh in ways Abdulrahman hadn't completely understood. But a great burden had been lifted from Saleh's shoulders. He no longer was the sole provider of the Alsuhaimi family.

Three years later, Abdulrahman was well on his way towards establishing a career as a merchant. He now was allowed to have his own shop. Most merchants imported and exported goods from the same traders of India, Indonesia, China, and some European countries as well as offering goods to local customers. Saleh was now shuttling the 550-mile distance between Kuwait and Unayzah (a month's camel journey) on a fairly regular basis. Abdulrahman was just two years shy from becoming a fully mature adult. Despite his missing his mother and younger brother, he had adjusted to his new Kuwaiti home, and was familiar with the customs and traditions of the British-controlled Arab society and understood the locals' culture, which only helped him in his business.

Each morning Abdulrahman rose before the sun for *Fajr* (predawn) prayers and afterwards prepared *Iftar*, his breakfast of dates and camel milk. At sunrise, he walked to the bustling marketplace, the Safat Central Market, where he traded successfully with nomad merchants for their array of merchandise, everything from rugs of woven sheep and camel wool to dairy items, ghee, grains, dates and other foodstuff.

For so many years Saleh had been struggling under difficult conditions in Unayzah, and despite his hard work, had been unable to provide sufficiently for his family. But with his eldest son now earning his own income, and contributing to the family fund, the idea of a stable and secure life was no longer a dream, and the only thing remaining for Saleh was to bring back his wife and son and his younger brother's family to Kuwait and live peacefully with his entire family.

For the first time in a long while, he felt a lightness to his step and a steadier breath. It was still the early months of 1918 when a man from the caravan brought him a letter from home that would change all that.

CHAPTER 5

A Family Loss

The sun was in a slow descent, its rays reflected across the Gulf when Abdulrahman stepped into their house. His father awaited, letter in hand. Saleh's voice wavered when he spoke. Abdulrahman stood in shock, not sure he heard his father correctly. His beloved mother was gone? How could that be? Saleh consoled him as best he knew how.

I'm not certain how long it took for Saleh to learn of his wife's death. It was 1918 after all, communications nonexistent on the peninsula—no telephones or telegraphs. The letter carrier from Unayzah had to trek by camel across the desert and the 550 miles stretch to Kuwait, and the delay only intensified the family's despair. Neither Saleh nor Abdulrahman had been at his mother's side for her last days.

I never learned the exact cause of her death or when she grew ill or if Saleh had any inkling. I do know she died the same year the worldwide influenza epidemic had struck the peninsula, when at its height, the death rate had risen to 100 a day in Riyadh, just southeast of Unayzah.[76]

---

76 Michael Darlow & Barbara Bray 2012, Ibn Saud: The Desert Warrior who Created the Kingdom of Saudi Arabia, accessed 2 February 2018, <http://bit.ly/3nyTgIQ>

Saleh had commuted between Kuwait and Unayzah during this time and must have surmised she had been exposed to it as well as to smallpox, another epidemic ravaging the region, but then everyone had been at risk, and he may have believed her strong constitution (and good luck) would prevail. He had felt guilty about leaving her in Unayzah, a place not equipped to provide her with proper medical care. If illness had repeatedly plagued her, it would have eventually taken its toll. The fact that Saleh had deliberately chosen to leave his wife behind added to his remorse.

Equally troubling was the fate of his eight-year-old son, Mohammad, who was now without a parent at home. Saleh's only brother had already departed Unayzah with his family for his new position as a religious teacher in Hejaz, newly appended to the Najd kingdom by Ibn Saud, and in need of judges and religious clerics for teaching the proper form of Islam, one not corrupted by the Turks. Frantic about his younger son's well being, Saleh departed immediately for Unayzah, leaving Abdulrahman alone in Kuwait to keep the family business afloat.

It had been three years since they first left Unayzah, the last two spent in Kuwait. By now, Abdulrahman, had adjusted to the city, and had assimilated into their everyday life. He felt confident running the family business at the *souq* or open market, and had no reservations about his father departing, comprehending the gravity of the situation. All would be well, he reassured his father. Still, Abdulrahman felt a void. He had difficulty reconciling himself with his new reality. Like many teenagers, he had assumed his mother would always be there. Her love had nourished him for all these years, and now she was gone. He wasn't prepared. That emptiness would stay with him for the rest of his life.

Until now, Abdulrahman lived under the supervision of his father. With Saleh in Unayzah, Abdulrahman had to rely on his own wits when making decisions that affected the family and business. For the first time in his life, Abdulrahman, at 19 years of age, was on his own.

Semm Yubah

The atmosphere in Kuwait at this time was highly charged. With the end of WWI nearing, rumors swirled of an escalating dispute between Ibn Saud and Kuwait's current ruler, Salim Al-Sabah. In 1917 Salim had begun his new rule as Sheik on shaky ground for having given sanctuary to Ibn Saud's enemies. Although this had occurred during Salim's father's rule, Sheik Mubarak Al-Sabah (from 1896 to 1915), Ibn Saud hadn't forgotten that Salim had been head of the Kuwaiti forces.[77]

The spring of 1920 also brought territory clashes between Kuwait and Ibn Saud's Ikhwan forces in the desert outside of town. Tensions increased throughout the year, and culminated in October when the Ikhwan attacked Salim's forces at the Battle of Al Jahra, west of Kuwait.[78] The Kuwaitis drove back the Ikhwan with Britain's aid. Still, Kuwait's political climate was strained at best, and provided the backdrop for the series of events that would play out in Abdulrahman's life over the next few years.

A gregarious young man, he made friends easily and possessed a knack for dealing with difficult personalities, which served him well in business, and he was regarded in the mercantile community as a fair and prudent negotiator. He worked hard at his job and, hoping to start a family of his own, married a young woman, Fatima Al Issa. She gave birth to two daughters but neither survived infancy, and their deaths deeply affected my grandfather whose dream of a cohesive family seemed elusive. But the family business continued to prosper over the next few years, and his acumen and affability in the marketplace did not go unnoticed.

The elite merchants of Kuwait were an extremely successful and wealthy group whose economic power wielded strong political influence, and the city's ruling family had generally conferred with

---

77 Jill Crystal 2016, Kuwait: the Transformation of an Oil State, accessed 12 March 2017, <http://bit.ly/383p0zC>
78 Ibid.

them on major issues. The majority of them had grown concerned about rising political unrest in the seaport, and as a precautionary measure decided it best to transfer most of their merchandise 250 miles south of Kuwait to the Gulf coast city of Jubail in the eastern province of Arabia. Some of those elite merchants were Al Humaidhi, Al Ghanim, Al Issa, and Al Mudayan, and they needed a candidate to spearhead their project, someone reliable, industrious, congenial, but above all, trustworthy. When they approached Abdulrahman for the job, he was honored and certainly surprised.

The sea city of Jubail represented a stable place for the merchants to conduct their trade, and one that offered new and safer business opportunities. Their decision to relocate, however, was also predicated on the reopening of the ancient Uqair seaport.

The Uqair Seaport

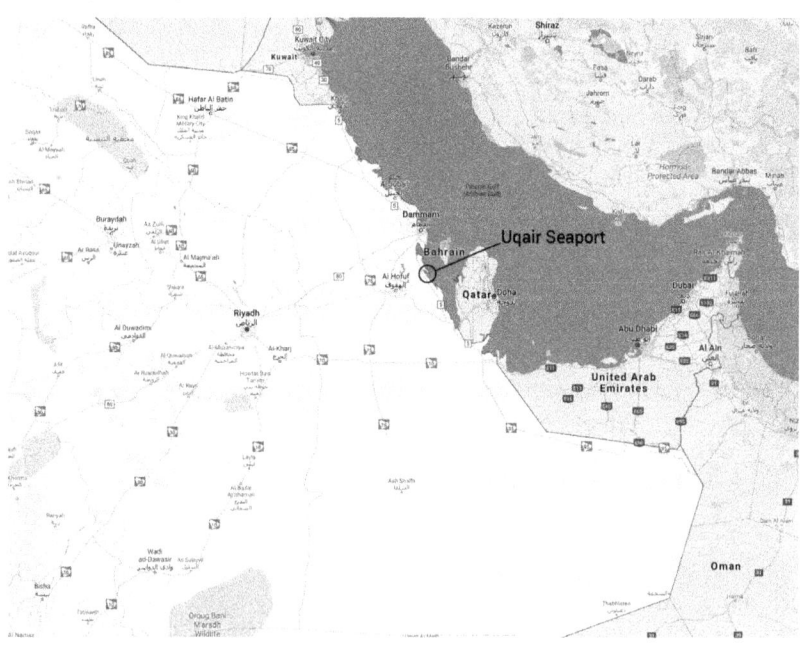

Al Uqair Seaport location in the Alhasa Gulf relative to Bahrain, Jubail, & Kuwait Seaports. Map data ©2021 Google, Mapa GISrael, Saudi Arabia.

Semm Yubah

The old seaport of Uqair lay 400 miles southeast of Kuwait, but only150 miles south of Jubail, and was of Islamic origin. When Ibn Saud had reopened it in the early 1920's it became a source of income for many Arabian Peninsula traders.

Since 1910 Ibn Saud had been involved in the unification of the various tribes and regions as part of his vision of resurrecting the Saudi State for the third time. But he needed a major logistical advantage that would keep his army well supplied, and at the same time, prevent provisions from reaching the Egyptians and Ottomans.

He chose the Uqair seaport for its location and reopened it, hoping to redirect most desert trade there. Besides, the seaport was in close proximity to his stronghold in the Al-Hasa region.

Throughout history, the Uqair seaport has been a subject of much discussion, and many have linked it to the ancient city of Gerrha, which had once belonged to the Dilmun civilization, more than four thousand years ago.

According to contemporary explorer George Potter, part of the team responsible for the Nephi project, the Uqair seaport in Hofuf

Al Uqair Seaport main building of 1920 protected for restoration.

dates back to antiquity. Some historians believe the combined regions of Hofuf and Uqair were part of the wealthy city-state of the ancient Gerrha civilization. Others claim Uqair "was the first city to arise in this rich Mesopotamia delta, and possibly in the entire world."[79]

Potter believes Uqair was the ancient harbor of Hofuf, which is considered the largest natural oasis of the world. Other historical accounts indicate that Hofuf had shown signs of habitation since prehistoric times, possibly as a result of its considerable area of fertile land and large date palm plantations.

When Potter and his team headed into Arabia on an expedition of the Jaredite trail from Uqair, they discovered the remains of the ancient caravanserai halfway between the harbor and the oasis, where food and shelter and, more importantly, water would have been available for caravan travelers. Travelers in 4000 BC would

Al Uqair Seaport central storage areas of 1920 protected for restoration.

---

[79] Arabic and Islamic Cultures 1963, Aramco World, accessed 15 Feb 2018, <http://archive.aramcoworld.com/issue/196302/a.visit.to.some.early.cities.htm/ *Saudi Aramco World*, Feb.1963, print edition; pg. 8-10>

Semm Yubah

have found Uqair an impressive city with its productive land, irrigation system and surplus food, unlike anything they had seen before, "...a street lined with strange houses. The walls low and made of mud-daubed reeds or baked mud bricks, topped with flat roofs. Doors of reeds or wood, and pivot on hollow stones...inside, five or six individual rooms."[80]

British explorer and Intelligence officer Jack Philby had a different perspective, albeit a more limited one, and described the Uqair seaport in his 1922 book, *The Heart of Arabia, A Record of Travel and Exploration Arabia, November 1917-1918*[81]

Henry St. John Bridger Philby, Arabian explorer.

Uqair, situated on a narrow and barren strip of foreshore between the sand-hills and the sea, has in all probability never been more than it is today, a caravansarai of growing commercial and decreasing strategic importance, whose floating population of troops and merchants eke out a weary existence at the call of business or duty until relieved. Its name and excellent harbour tempt one sorely to speculate whether this may be the site of Ptolemy's Gerra, an identity for which, I am aware, there are other candidates, but speculation is idle in the absence of material remains, and it is unlikely that any permanent settlement could have existed in a location where today there is but a single well. The old seaport of Gerra, whence before the beginning of the Christian era and for a few centuries

---

80 Ibid.
81 Philby, H. St. J. B. 1922, The heart of Arabia, a record of travel and exploration, accessed 23 March 2017, <https://archive.org/stream/heartofarabiarec01philuoft/heartofarabiarec01philuoft_djvu.tx>

of it flourishing caravan routes radiated to the uttermost ends of Arabia—to 'Uman, to the Hadhramaut, to the Yaman and to Petra—is doubtless to be identified with an extensive ruin-field said to have been discovered long since at the southern angle of the Gulf of Bahrain. It lost its importance probably when the southern caravan routes ceased to be practicable and was supplanted by Qatif at the northern extremity of the Gulf opposite Bahrain, while 'Uqair cannot be of any great antiquity, though its name—'Uqair, 'Ugair or 'Ujair—seems almost certainly to preserve the name of the original settlement and port.

Be that as it may, the only buildings of 'Uqair are a square turreted fort and a large warehouse, forming together a continuous oblong block of clay, some 150 yards in length and 70 in breadth, facing the jetty, which projects southwards into the arbour from a blunt promontory of low-lying land jutting out from the mainland to within 100 yards of the long thin spit of Al Hadd. The harbour is enclosed by the mainland, the 'Uqair promontory and Al Hadd, between whose southern extremity and the coast opposite lies the entrance, itself protected on the south by the island of Zakhnuniyya several miles distant. A narrow channel, lying between the 'Uqair promontory and Al Hadd, connects the harbour with a lagoon extending about a mile northwards to the point at which the spit of Al Hadd projects from the mainland. Eastward of the warehouse lies a flat stretch of sahne land, which serves as a camping ground, while westward, between the fort and the sand-hills, runs a broad line of reeds and bushes, on the farther edge of which is the well already mentioned, guarded by the circular watch-tower of Abu Zahmul. A small and dilapidated cemetery completes the scene, commemorating the forgotten sojourn of a Turkish garrison.

The Motive for the Kuwaiti Merchants' Decision
Prior to Ibn Saud's reopening of the Uqair seaport, Kuwait monopolized trade to Arabia's interior. The reopening of the Uqair

Semm Yubah

seaport provided stiff competition after Ibn Saud took full control of all trade activities to and from the region. A few years later, in 1923, he forbade Bedouin caravans from trading with Kuwait and placed an embargo on Kuwait that would last until 1937.

The reopening of the Uqair seaport had undercut the Kuwaiti merchants' profits, creating a major crisis. They had no other option but to look for alternatives for their trade and opted to migrate south of Kuwait to Jubail. If they remained in Kuwait their businesses and families would suffer. Up until this point Abdulrahman had been earning an exceptionally high income, but the seaport had affected him as well, and when the elite merchants presented him with the opportunity, he realized it was in his family's best interest to accept their offer. On the verge of turning 21, he was ambitious and passionate and his decision would prove to be one of the hallmarks of his life.

The merchants had one stipulation—Abdulrahman's move to Jubail had to be permanent, at least for the next few years. Fatima's parents were very old, and as their only child, she felt it her responsibility to remain with them in Kuwait. The young couple reached an understanding and amicably divorced. Decades later my grandfather, having a sense that something was wrong with his first wife, would send my grandmother to track her down. We don't know why or how he came to this conclusion but my grandmother dutifully went to Kuwait with her daughter to search for Fatima. Unfortunately, Fatima had died a few years prior. Family has survived her but my grandmother had been unable to track down any of Fatima's relatives. It didn't surprise me when I learned my grandfather had been concerned about his first wife's welfare, even after so much time. That was the kind of man he was.

Abdulrahman had never traveled south of Kuwait, but the last five years had prepared him for his latest venture. Living in Kuwait had given him a major advantage over other merchants, since he had expertise at pricing and handling merchandise, knowledge

Letter from Al Hasa merchant Al Ajaji to Bahrain merchant Fakhro informing him of an imminent King Abdulaziz economic blockade of Kuwait with Nejd territories, May 1921.

of the best supply routes and transportation methods, and the flexibility to handle the challenges posed by each. His mercantile experience would serve him well in the unfamiliar region of Jubail, nearly 400 kilometers to the south. Still, he had no idea what to

Semm Yubah

expect when he got there. Would the town be similar to Kuwait, populated with other Najdis, Iraqis, Pakistanis and Indians? Would he find the people hospitable or aloof? The trip would take him past scattered settlements and stretches of desert with sand dunes, the shore snaking south, the gulf sneaking in and out of view so he would have had plenty of time to consider what Jubail would be like. But to him, challenges and the uncertainty that came with risk only added to an adventure. Besides, he was young, strong, and resilient, and had been known for never refusing challenging work, all qualities that had appealed to the elite merchants.

Interesting enough, Abdulrahman wasn't their first choice. One of the prominent merchants lobbied for his son to lead the caravan to Jubail but too many of them had claimed the merchant's son would show preferential treatment toward his father, promoting his merchandise over theirs. Finally, after much deliberation and debate, they unanimously agreed that Abdulrahman was the better candidate and an unbiased one.

It was a risky undertaking. The Kuwaiti Traders were planning to send most of their merchandise to Jubail, and it necessitated quarterly relays of more than 100 camels for however long it took Abdulrahman to transport and sell through the 570 tons of their goods. Any disruption along the route would result in a delay, and the traders would risk losing a substantial amount of money. It was Abdulrahman's responsibility to ensure the merchandise arrived safely at the Jubail seaport, 400 kilometer southeast of Kuwait and in a reasonable amount of time. He would have to plot his route to avoid surprise raids by desert bandits and heavy custom duties (that would eat into the merchants' profits) and he'd have to stay under the radar of Ibn Saud's forces, hard to do when each caravan consists of more than 100 camels. One misstep could result in disaster. If he crossed into Ibn Saud's territory he risked a confrontation with his Ikhwan forces. And if the caravan was mistaken for smugglers, they chanced imprisonment.

Despite the risks and uncertainty and knowing he would have only a few armed guards to accompany the caravan, Abdulrahman accepted the job. It was a major test for a young man on the verge of turning twenty-one. But he was ever more focused, mindful that the elite merchants' trade prospects as well as his own depended on his success.

To evade Ibn Saud's forces and increase the success rate of the caravan, Abdulrahman decided to alternate his methods of shipping the merchandise between the land and sea. A camel caravan would take approximately 8 to 10 days to reach Jubail whereas a boat traveled the distance in a mere two and half days, although shipping the goods generally resulted in paying higher custom fees. To avoid detection and steep fees, he employed both methods. He calculated the cost efficiency of each and weighed his options, deciding how much merchandise he should ship by land and by sea, the sea being faster but more expensive.

Since the volume of the elite merchants' goods was enormous, and storage space in Jubail was limited, Abdulrahman planned to test the new market first, seeing how well the early shipments went, while gathering information about the town and its Bedouin trading caravans. The Bedouin population was sparse in the south in Arabia, and Jubail was still unknown to many, having only been established in 1911 with a very small population with little infrastructure. It would take time before it gained a reputation among traveling tribes as a viable source of food and supplies, and a worthwhile alternative to the more popular Kuwait. Besides Abdulrahman wanted to avoid flooding the market with goods which would only result in pushing his prices down. He had learned from working with his father about the dynamics of supply and demand.

Now he was ready to put all his experience to the test. He alone was responsible for the safe delivery of the caravan of merchandise, as well as his crew of men and herd of over 100 camels. This must have been a heady proposition for him, and may have unleashed

Semm Yubah

some arrogance in another young man, possibly resulting in a show of bravado, rash decisions and costly mistakes. But my grandfather was pragmatic and grounded, if anything, and fully aware of his limitations as well as his capabilities as a leader, and never underestimated either one.

I'm not sure about the exact route that they took traveling via land between Kuwait and Jubail or if they varied it each time but I believe Abdulrahman and his crew hugged the coast whenever possible to avoid warring tribes and desert thieves. The British Navy was still a formidable force in the Arabian Peninsula with a reputation for its firepower and ruthless treatment of anyone compromising their shoreline interests, and inadvertently, the British had provided protection for Abdulrahman's caravan whenever they neared the coast.

The caravan ambled slowly along in their long marches with few stops—providing the weather held—breaking only for sleep and water, attempting to stay close to the coast in their journey south. Abdulrahman kept vigilant, making certain the train of camels was intact. His strategy was simple: the less time spent in the open desert, the better chance of avoiding raiding tribes or Ibn Saud's forces or other marauders. If they traveled during summer they would have rested before mid-day, resuming after sunset, and continuing throughout the coolness of night. In winter, they did the opposite, rousing the camels at sunrise, traveling through sunset and camping at night. Each evening, the packs had to be unloaded for the camels to graze, and afterwards, they were herded into a circle around camp with all the merchandise and their water skins and saddlebags in the center, the guards keeping watch for raiders or wild animals.

When it was time to leave their encampment whether it was under the glare of the harsh sun or a constellation of bright stars, Abdulrahman made certain the herd was packed, the merchandise re-loaded, the crew alert and ready to move forward. Sometimes they rode their camels, more often they walked alongside them not to add to the animal's burden.

Miraculously his train of 100 camels arrived at the small fishing village, the sun rippling across the sea and surrounding dunes and sandy hills, the thatched roofs of the small mud brick houses. The caravan with the first shipment of merchandise intact had reached the town without incurring heavy custom taxes or confronting Ibn Saud's forces or any other belligerent tribes. Abdulrahman allowed himself to breathe a sigh of relief, then quickly set up shop.

Jubail of 1920 was quite a small town in comparison to the more dynamic Kuwait. Still, he hadn't traveled all this way only to have his inventory stolen, and he found a well-guarded storage area near a residence for himself and close to the open market. Within days he began selling, and soon sold through a substantial amount of the merchandise he had brought from Kuwait. The first 100 camels' worth of goods lasted for a period of two months when another shipment arrived by sea, but his makeshift warehouse and shop were stocked to capacity, and he had to work overtime to sell through the merchandise. Four months later, he finally developed a rhythm for selling and restocking goods and everything fell in synch except when the delivery of goods was delayed by political hostilities or inclement weather.

After a few months of experimentation, he adjusted his consignments to the demands and needs of Jubail's market. Eventually, he hired extra help in Jubail and more guards from Kuwait, which allowed him time to run the Jubail shop and the storage unit, as well as travel back to Kuwait (typically, a 2-day sea voyage) via the now empty boats he had used to import goods south to Jubail. He'd return to Jubail with the next caravan, which was about a 10 day camel journey, a trip he had arranged on a quarterly basis.

In a very short time his reputation increased as an affable and honest tradesman, and he became well known in the city as a trader who kept his word and delivered the goods when others failed. The

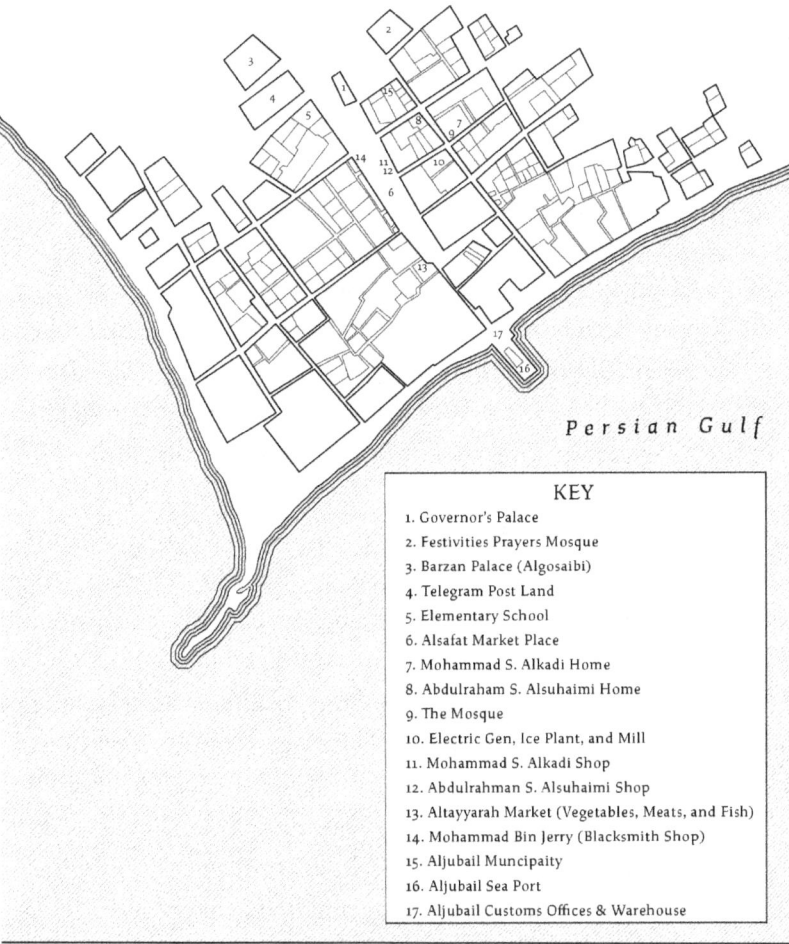

KEY
1. Governor's Palace
2. Festivities Prayers Mosque
3. Barzan Palace (Algosaibi)
4. Telegram Post Land
5. Elementary School
6. Alsafat Market Place
7. Mohammad S. Alkadi Home
8. Abdulraham S. Alsuhaimi Home
9. The Mosque
10. Electric Gen, Ice Plant, and Mill
11. Mohammad S. Alkadi Shop
12. Abdulrahman S. Alsuhaimi Shop
13. Altayyarah Market (Vegetables, Meats, and Fish)
14. Mohammad Bin Jerry (Blacksmith Shop)
15. Aljubail Muncipaity
16. Aljubail Sea Port
17. Aljubail Customs Offices & Warehouse

AL JUBAIL

young town of Jubail, impressed with his skills, was eager to gain a foothold in the peninsula's growing economy, and a mutually beneficial relationship developed.

During this time, Abdulrahman had earned significant revenues from the trade and converted all the profits into gold coins, the available currency at the time. After he sold through the merchandise, it was time for him to return to Kuwait, the city that had become his second home.

It was 1922, and it had taken Abdulrahman two years to fulfill his task. In Kuwait, he delivered the gains in gold to his employers. Delighted by their immense profits, they wanted Abdulrahman to keep any amount he believed was fair compensation as well as giving himself a bonus for his excellent hard work and service.

Abdulrahman, humbled by the generous offer, declined. He said his original fee was a fair share of the profits, and his hard work hadn't warranted a larger amount than his employers originally offered. Most of the Kuwaiti merchants had been very helpful when he and Saleh first had arrived, now seven years ago. They had offered guidance, training, and the chance to make a very good living. My grandfather was eternally grateful for that, and would never forget their help.

The last two years' worth of hard work in Jubail had given him more than just wealth. He told the merchants he now had a vast understanding of the business and an in-depth knowledge of the workings of the Jubail market, invaluable experience which would benefit him in the future.

He requested his employers respectfully relieve him of his duties, and they reluctantly agreed. He finally had earned sufficient money to marry again, and he wanted to settle down in Jubail, where he had developed a strong network of business associates. Besides, Kuwait was still embroiled in political tensions, and it would have interfered with his trading business, and most likely leaved him without a shop and unemployed.

Abdulrahman's prognosis for Kuwait proved true. The political tensions between Ibn Saud and Al-Sabah led to the siege of Kuwait city by Ibn Saud's forces, and as a result, a blockade of all the city's supply routes to the areas outside of Kuwait. The economic siege started in 1923 and lasted for a number of years with many of the traders and merchants suffering great financial losses.

The blockade of Kuwait only ended after Ibn Saud had established the kingdom of Saudi Arabia (1932) and united the surrounding regions under his authority in 1937. During the mid-1930s, Ibn

Semm Yubah

Saud's relationship with Britain weakened as British influence swayed. The United States had gained noticeable power through its capitalist business ventures, and Ibn Saud made a strategic alliance with them by signing various oil exploration agreements, resulting in tremendous geopolitical implications for Saudi Arabia, as well as Abdulrahman's business prospects.

Abdulrahman's analysis of Kuwait's situation reflected a maturity and wisdom beyond his years, and his ability to calibrate the consequences of external factors was indicative of his future success as a tradesman.

But when Abdulrahman requested leave of his job, the merchants only were aware of the excellent job he had done for them, and although reluctant to lose such a conscientious employee, they wished him the best for his future endeavors in Jubail.

After two years working hard at his trade, he was now equipped with the skill and experience for building his own business. It was now up to him to put to work everything he had learned in Jubail.

To this day, I remain in awe of my grandfather, a young man in his early twenties, and his determination to keep marching forward, straight into the unknown, and face adversity, whatever the cost. His adventures only confirm his stature in my mind, and his unique character. I often think back to the first time I learned about this period in his life. I was only a year or two older than he was then, and I don't know if I would have possessed the same self-assuredness, the same strength and depth of character, the courage. I often wonder if he ever felt frightened, sleeping under the desert stars, surrounded by a caravan of 100 camels, in the wilderness en route to Jubail, exposed to warring factions. I suppose he had no choice but to harness his fear, his duty to the merchants and his team taking precedent over nerves, but still, it amazes me, his courage and tenacity, especially during the times.

Adel Alsuhaimi

Jubail: The Birthplace of Alsuhaimi Business
Although his decision to move to Jubail was wise—Abdulrahman had adjusted to their way of life, gained a deep understanding of market dynamics and grown a network of business acquaintances—the region was not free from security risks. Threats of tribal unrests and raids were common here, too, which meant traders could always expect losses.

Jubail maintained a patrol of standing guards, positioned towards the town's outskirts. Some residents, including Abdulrahman, were drafted as part of the security teams, and armed with a dagger, sword, and a shotgun. Abdulrahman, along with others stood watch in the tower, guarding against raiders.

The city's residents lived with uncertainty, never knowing if they were going to be attacked. Many merchants who had migrated to Jubail for the purpose of setting up a business and settling down

Well-designed doorway. Jubail, 1974.

with their families, had to stall their plans since the area was proving too risky for supporting a family or for growing a business.

The History of Jubail

Jubail, situated in the northeast region of Saudi Arabia, had its roots in the ancient civilization of Dilmun, more than 7,000 years ago. Between the 18th and 19th centuries, Al Buanain, a clan of the Bani Tamim Tribe, settled in the area and found Al-Jubail, after they escaped persecution from the competing clans in neighboring Bahrain and Qatar, as did other families such as the Al Khaters.

Abdulrahman had chosen to settle in Jubail, which was controlled by the Al Khater clan. The small town had undergone many changes over the years, its unassuming seaport becoming a key attraction for residents once Ibn Saud expanded it after receiving pleas from the Jubaili merchants who had remained loyal to him. Many of Jubail's settlers had originated from the central Najd region, like Abdulrahman, and the signs of a growing economy were slowly starting to show.

The inflow of migrants had given tradesmen a chance to recover their loss in profits in the aftermath of Ibn Saud's reopening of the Uqair seaport (south of Jubail). However, the security of the

Camels resting in the village square. Jubail, January, 1938.

region had still not stabilized, and any word of thriving trade meant attracting the attention of raiders and thieves.

Still, Abdulrahman had been fortunate up until this point, and he only hoped that his luck would hold out.

Typical house with outer walls in Jubail, 1973.

CHAPTER 6

Life in Jubail and a Unique Friendship

By 1922 life in Jubail had improved for Abdulrahman, although it was not without challenges. His trade business flourished but his personal life fell short of his dreams. He felt incomplete without a close companion at his side, having been divorced from Fatima before relocating, and the absence of his family still weighed heavily.

Although he appeared happy to outsiders, he struggled with his loneliness, and it shadowed him wherever he went. It took the friendship of a young man from his hometown of Unayzah to change that. He discovered a kindred spirit in Mohammad Al Kadi, someone who not only shared his experiences but also nurtured the same hopes and dreams, and understood the meaning of family.

Like Abdulrahman, Mohammad Al Kadi had left home at an early age but instead of heading to the Gulf, he had journeyed west with relatives to the holy city of Makkah where he had remained until his twenties in the employ of a Najdi merchant, a friend of his father's. Later he returned to Unayzah to visit his family and met and married a young woman named Muneera. In 1919 he departed again—only this time he traveled southeast toward the Gulf port town of Jubail in search of better business opportunities. His new bride stayed in Unayzah with his parents until he had deemed it

Abdulrahman Alsuhaimi (left) & Mohammad Alkadi (right). Jubail, 1938.

safe for her to travel to Jubail, and after he secured sufficient work and a house for them to raise a family.

I'm not sure how long Mohammad lived in Jubail before his path crossed with Abdulrahman's. Some family members believe it was sometime in 1920. Although the men never knew each other in Unayzah, once they did meet, they forged a lasting friendship, grown out of a common bond and rooted in their native land and the people they loved and left behind.

The connection between Abdulrahman and Mohammad Al Kadi was not unlike that of close siblings. Abdulrahman hadn't seen his actual brother in more than five years, and Mohammad easily fell into the role of surrogate. Both were without any family in Jubail. Ironically, he bore the same name as Abdulrahman's brother.

Mohammad Al Kadi was good-natured, hardworking and ambitious, with a deep and abiding devotion to family, just like my grandfather. I suppose Abdulrahman saw his own needs and yearnings mirrored in Mohammad, and there had to have been a relief in that, an ease of the tension that isolation from family often brings. The camaraderie had certainly bestowed Abdulrahman with a sense of contentment

Mohammad Alkadi. Jubail, 1945.

Semm Yubah

and peace that had eluded him since he first left Unayzah with his father.

The two young men became inseparable, supporting each other in both their personal and business endeavors, and the locals soon referred to them as brothers. They purchased homes next to each other and set up adjacent shops. Life was still at times desperately hard but it no longer seemed insurmountable.

During this period Abdulrahman had been introduced to a local girl from Jubail, Lulwah al Amer, and he married again but they had no children. The marriage ended for all intent purposes after a year (1922), when they divorced, and remained family friends. Most enter a marriage expecting the best, and perhaps they found they were incompatible, their expectations unrealistic. It's hard to say. I do know he would have to return to Kuwait a few years later if he was to meet the woman who would become his soul mate— Nora Alwazzan, my grandmother.

It was an arranged marriage in accordance with tradition as many still are in Saudi Arabia today, the young couple brought together by family, or a third party who vouches for the groom's character and standing in the community. Both the bride and groom have the chance to decline if the prospective marriage partner doesn't prove suitable.

In my grandfather's day, men and women were not permitted to socialize with each other—so the only way for Abdulrahman to have met Norah in 1924 was if it had been pre-arranged through an outside party. Most likely a woman whose opinion Norah's family trusted and valued made the introduction and arranged for the couple to meet, but it was quite typical then for the family to employ the help of the local *Al-khatabah*, (Arabic for matchmaker or marriage broker).[82]

It was considered serious work, finding the right partner for a

---

[82] Mia Ponzo 2002, The Desert Boutique, accessed 11 July 2018, <http://sites.quickbizsites.com/desertboutique/let_s_get_married___kuwaiti_style___part_two>

family's offspring, and the future happiness of their adult children (and sometimes the families themselves) depended on an appropriate match. The community held a reputable *Al-khatabah* in high regard, and society of yesteryear did not look kindly on a bride who didn't trust the matchmaker's selection. It was considered scandalous for a bride to ignore *Al-khatabah's* recommendations. And, in worst-case scenarios, if a prospective bride broke off an arranged engagement, she risked being ostracized by the town.

It was customary for the bride's father to handle the pre-nuptial negotiations with the *Al-khatabhah* and/or the prospective groom, but in the absence of the father, the eldest living male relative of the bride stepped in. Since Norah's parents had died when she was very young, it fell to her uncle to deal with the matchmaker. Uncle Abdullah was also a merchant by trade and had raised Norah along with her two younger siblings since their parents' death, and his consent had been required before any introduction and meeting were to take place. Afterwards, he presented Abdulrahman with a list of prerequisites—details that had to be ironed out and agreed upon before the marriage. In keeping with tradition, Abdulrahman signed a formal statement specifying what his bride would receive (a gift of money or possessions) before and after the wedding.

The mandatory nuptial gift is known as a *mahr* or *meher*. Usually, the groom presents his gift to his bride at the time the marital contract is signed, and this type of *mahr* is called a *muqaddam*[83] or prompt payment. However, an exception can be made if the couple agree on a *mu'akhar*, [84] a deferred payment. (The word *mahr* is derived from the "Hebrew *mohar*, and the Syriac *mahrā*, 'bridal gift', originally 'purchase-money', and synonymous with *Sadāk*, which

---

83 Encyclopedia of Islam 2012, Brill, accessed 12 April 2017, <http://www.academia.edu/26772149/_Mahr_-Encyclopedia_of_Islam_and_the_Muslim_World_2nd_Edition>

84 Ibid.

properly means friendship, then present…")[85] The terms of the *mahr* varies, and part of it may be due before the marriage ceremony to be used as the bride chooses, and the rest given to the bride throughout her lifetime. [86] In more traditional societies, if a bride's family considers the prospective groom's social standing to be less than theirs, the man has the opportunity "to raise his chances of acceptance through increasing the worth of the nuptial gift."[87]

I don't know if it was the case with my grandparents, but sometimes these negotiations were conducted in complete secrecy, the bride consulted only at the end of the process. Still, Norah would have had her window of opportunity, however slight, to decline the marriage proposal. But it should be said that she would have never been made to marry him against her will. An arranged marriage is not a forced one. It is forbidden in Islam for parents (or others) to coerce or trick anyone into marriage.[88]

That wasn't a concern for my grandfather. I am told he was captivated as soon as my grandmother stepped into the room, cloaked in her floor-length *abaya*, although he didn't see her face since she was veiled. Luckily, her choice of veil (*niqab*) had been lace and afforded him that rare glimpse. In central Najd, Abdulrahman's birthplace, there had been a much stricter adherence to social convention, and such a meeting would have been prohibited, even a stolen glance not allowed. In Unayzah, there had been no such thing as a *showfa*, a "viewing," of a prospective bride; she was strictly and unequivocally off limits to a male, even a prospective groom. If Abdulrahman had been still living in Unayzah, he would have had to rely solely on his matchmaker's or a female relative's advice

---

85   Encyclopedia of Islam 2012, Brill, accessed 12 April 2017, <http://referenceworks.brillonline.com/entries/encyclopaedia-of-islam-2/*-SIM_4806>

86   Robin Beth Schaer 1997, The Knot, accessed 5 February 2017, <https://www.theknot.com/content/muslim-wedding-ceremony-rituals>

87   Encyclopedia of Islam 2012, Brill, accessed 12 April 2017, <http://www.academia.edu/26772149/_Mahr_-Encyclopedia_of_Islam_and_the_Muslim_World_2nd_Edition>

88   Ruqaiyyah Waris Maqsood 2009, Weddings at BBC News Media, accessed 24 June 2017,<http://www.bbc.co.uk/religion/religions/islam/ritesrituals/weddings_1.shtml>

to choose the right mate—and proceed with the marriage without ever meeting her.

But Abdulrahman was in Kuwait, *not* Unayzah, and did get at least a glimpse of his potential bride, despite the veil and was immediately smitten. His first impression left him curious and interested; she was shy but he detected an understated strength in her demeanor and heard a quiet confidence in her voice, qualities he always found attractive, his first wife having possessed similar traits. Each time she spoke, she reaffirmed his belief that she would make a good life partner.

Norah, on the other hand, entertained no such thoughts, and was terrified at the sight of this tall Najdi. Who was this man? Was he kind? Smart? Honest? Hardworking? Would he treat her with the same respect and honor that her uncle had? She loved her uncle and realized he had her best interest at heart. Still. It was as if Abdulrahman was a foreign country. And he looked far too old. (In fact, Abdulrahman was about twenty-five.) She was horrified at the thought of having to marry a stranger, spending the rest of her life with someone she just met.

I supposed mixed in with that fear was some notion of excitement—she was not unlike most young girls of the time, and the idea of becoming a bride had been somewhat appealing, but she had thought it would occur some day in the distant future, and certainly not requiring her to move to some strange small town called Jubail, far away from her beloved siblings. Since her parents' death, she felt a deep responsibility toward her younger brother, Ahmad, and sister, Hessa, and leaving them behind in Kuwait was unthinkable. Uncle Abdullah had to reassure her numerous times, and she was comforted only after he promised to accompany her to Jubail after the wedding and remain there until she felt settled in her new home. So in 1924, based on these conditions, Norah Alwazzan, at sixteen years old, had agreed to marry Abdulrahman.

Semm Yubah

Once the marriage was announced, they had decided that the ceremony should take place in Kuwait, home to the bride, and where Abdulrahman still had many friends. Besides, Kuwait was closer to Unayzah than Jubail, and it wouldn't have been complete without his father and mentor by his side. And like most parents, Saleh did what was needed to insure his presence. None of my elders know if Saleh had attended Abdulrahman's first two weddings (the first to Fatima al Isa in Kuwait when he worked for the elite merchants, and the second, of course, to Lulwah in Jubail) but if I were to venture a guess I'd say Saleh was, indeed, present for only those that occurred in Kuwait. The political climate being what it was, it was still unsafe to travel. And Saleh had never been fond of the Eastern province nor the tribes who had settled near the Gulf, especially in the once Ottoman-run Qatif, 40 miles south of Jubail, which he considered a dangerous place with its transient population, and had been unappealing to most Najdis.

On the day of the wedding the male members of the groom's party had gathered first in the groom's *majlis* after *Isha* prayers. Here, they danced the folkloric *Arda*, a line dance in which two rows of men face each other, wielding their ritual swords to the *Samry* rhythms of drums and song, enticing guests to accompany them to the feast.[89]

Abdulrahman and his father and friends had worn their best *thobe*, and over that, their finest *Bisht*, the traditional black, brown or white flowing cloak reserved for such affairs. A white *gutra* on their head, was secured by the *Ighal*. Some men held

Mubkarah incense burner.

---

89 Unkevich, Lisa 2014, Music and Traditions of the Arabian Peninsula: Saudi Arabia, Kuwait, Bahrain and Qatar, accessed 17 June 2017, <http://bit.ly/2KnOwr0>

oil lamps, similar to lanterns, its flames flickering as they walked. Others carried decorative incense burners, called *mubkarah*, with the *Bukhoor* burning—wooden brick chips steeped in aromatic oils—and anointed the air with its fragrant scents.

Flanked by his father, Saleh, and his dear friend, Mohammad, Abdulrahman led the groom's *Zaffe*, the male wedding procession with some men drumming and singing, others clapping in rhythm as they made their way toward the bride's family *majlis* or wedding hall.

At the entrance to the house, the men of the bride's family had greeted Abdulrahman and his father and led them to their place of honor at the center of the hall, scenting them with incense and perfume as they walked. By now, every room had been fragranced with *Bukhoor*, and while the groom's guests entered the hall, the misting with perfume continued as a gesture of hospitality.

Perfume dispenser.

Since men and women were never permitted in mixed company, even at a marriage ceremony, the female wedding celebration was kept separate from the men, but the same ritual had been done for Norah and her female wedding guests.

The actual wedding ceremony, known as *nikah*, had been held in the men's reception hall. The women did not attend. The groom and the bride's representative had been present, but not the bride. Uncle Abdullah had represented Norah at the signing of the marriage contract, and Saleh stood at his son's side, with the two witnesses and the male guests the only others in attendance.

A religious cleric had presided, and began the ceremony by reminding Abdulrahman that the Prophet Mohammad (PBUH) urged men to treat their wives with the utmost kindness and respect. After the sermon, the cleric recited the first verses of the Qur'an, and then proceeded with the rest of the ceremony. Later that night the groom would be united with his bride on the rooftop room, reserved for the newlyweds.

Traditionally before the bride and groom are united, the women perform *Jalwa* (pronounced *yalwa* in Kuwait),[90] a ceremony to bestow blessings upon the bride.

During *jalwa* the bride was seated on a carpet or a throne-like chair, her head and shoulders draped in a large and decorative emerald-colored cloth *(a khidrah).*[91] Four female relatives lifted *a khidrah* and held it stretched over her head, "each woman grasping a corner like a makeshift roof, symbolic of the bride's new home. The cloth is gently lifted and lowered repeatedly as a religious woman chants prayers and verses from the Qur'an…"[92] After more traditional singing and dancing, two women ferried the bride in her chair or on a mat to the bridal chamber.[93] The woman who initially introduced the groom to the family usually remained with the bride after her other female companions leave, and together the two of them waited for the groom.

The individual festivities of Norah and Abdulrahman had lasted late into the night. And at the proper time, Norah's female relatives escorted her to the wedding chamber on the rooftop where the married couple spent their first night.

My grandfather must have been awed by his petite bride, radiant in the ritual green dress of Kuwaiti brides, embellished with embroidery and cross-stitches, emerald and gold threads woven through the veil crowning her head and sweeping down her back,

---

90 Unkevich, Lisa 2014, Music and Traditions of the Arabian Peninsula: Saudi Arabia, Kuwait, Bahrain and Qatar, accessed 17 June 2017, <https://books.google.com/books?id=gy-cBQAAQBAJ&pg=PA11&source=gbs_toc_r&cad=3#v=onepage&q&f=false>

91 Ibid.
92 Ibid.
93 Ibid.

her delicate hands hennaed in intricate designs, symbols of good luck, health and fertility.

The next day, the bride and groom departed for Jubail, and were accompanied by Uncle Abdullah. Each of them rode separate camels, but Nora traveled in a *Hawdaj*, (which means bed carried by a camel in Arabic), an enclosed cabin placed on top of the camel to make the arduous journey more tolerable. It was basically a canopied cushioned seat mounted to a wooden turret-like plank and a leather saddle, a much more comfortable ride compared to the normal, bumpier and back-aching one that the men endured.

You can imagine Norah's shock when she discovered as they entered the desert that her uncle was nowhere to be found. I remember when my grandmother first told us the story. We had gathered at my grandparents' home, and they were talking about the olden days and someone asked how they met, and slowly the tale unfolded, her indignation rising with her voice as she explained how Uncle Abdullah had stolen away after the caravan was only a few miles from Kuwait's fortified walls. She had been furious and hurt when she realized his trickery, heartbroken at his betrayal and lies, and refused to eat or drink or speak, and broke into tears. Abdulrahman consoled her as best he knew how, serving her hot tea and water, and later hoping to calm her, a meal of cooked lamb and rice with cardamom-flavored coffee. She returned everything untouched. She said not a word, her sobs the only sounds echoing over the dunes and *Kous* winds. Three days passed before things settled down, and only then did she summon the courage to forgive her uncle and accept Abdulrahman as her husband and assume her role as wife.

Did my grandfather have any doubts? Did he wonder what he had gotten himself into at the first sight of her tears? Given my grandfather's sensitive nature, it is more likely that he had empathized with her, understanding the agony of being separated from family. Still, perhaps he prayed that the blue green sea lapping

Semm Yubah

at the shores of their small port town would heal her or the singing sands south of Jubail, or the way twilight descended on her new home. I'm not sure. My grandfather never talked to us about it but it was evident from how he treated my grandmother throughout their life together that he loved her deeply. He praised her to us, and no one ever heard him utter an unkind word. He was a true gentleman, a fact Norah acknowledged repeatedly to her grandchildren. His demeanor and decisiveness had certainly made an impression on her, but it was his kindness and tenderness toward her during those first tumultuous days, she told us, that ultimately won her heart.

In those early weeks my grandfather had been reassured by just how resolute and resilient his sixteen-year-old bride was. He had recognized the value of those qualities when he first glimpsed her, and how they might benefit them both in the future. She definitely had grown into a confident wife, opinionated at times, yes, but always compassionate, dependable, quite capable despite her small size. I believe he was happier for having married such a determined, strong-willed, and self-sufficient woman. It allowed him the time to concentrate solely on his business, knowing their home was in her reliable hands. We, grandchildren, certainly came to experience firsthand her role as empress and understood she ruled the household. We witnessed her assertion of authority to everyone who entered her domain, and saw her yield only to Abdulrahman. Still, her love for us was evident, and whenever we got into trouble she came to our defense and became our hero, saving her grandchildren from any punishment she deemed unjust.

It is clear to me that my grandfather had discovered the love of his life when he met Nora. They lived in Jubail until 1954 when the entire family would relocate to Dammam where they remained until her death at 106 years old in 2012. But I'm getting ahead of my story.

After Abdulrahman had brought Nora back to Jubail, Mohammad Al Kadi thought it was time for his wife to join him, and he left for Unayzah and returned with Muneera.

Abdulrahman and Norah had seven children, and raised their family next door to Mohammad Al Kadi's. Their children grew up together, and much later, a few of them were married to each other. Abdulrahman's first born (1929), Abdulaziz (and my father), married one of Mohammad's and Muneera's daughters—Madawi (my mother)–bringing the two families even closer, binding them in marriage as well as brotherhood.

It had appeared that their lives were finally on the upswing. Their wives and families were at their sides. Business, although demanding, was steady, and their profits strong.

Over the next couple of years (1925-27) Abdulrahman received another blessing when he learned his biological brother, Muhammad was moving to Jubail. A year or two after Abdulrahman had married, Saleh had remarried (a cousin of Norah's, Haya Alwazzan, and he would take another wife, Lulwah, a few years after that), and Muhammad was free to join his brother. They had lived apart all these years, his brother only a small boy the last time he saw him, and now Muhammad was a teenager. Had Abdulrahman recognized him when he arrived? The reunion had to have been overwhelming for both.

Abdulrahman had taken great pride and care to ensure his brother's wellbeing and safety, and helped him acclimate to life in Jubail and trading at the market. They worked well together, and Abdulrahman saw how facile his brother was with merchants and customers alike. Muhammad became a great asset to the family business so it was only a matter of time before Abdulrahman asked Muhammad to join him as his partner.

Soon Abdulrahman and Muhammad discussed expanding the business by going 15 miles east across the Gulf waters to the archipelago of thirty-three islands. Located on the southwestern Gulf coast, Bahrain, which means "two seas" in Arabic (*al-bahrayn*) for its sweet and salty waters, had become a hub for all transported goods from British-controlled India. At the time, Bahrain was also

Semm Yubah

Architectural design of an old doorway. Jubail, 1974.

under British rule, although many of its people wanted independence and demanded a limit to British influence. In 1922 its borders had been established when the British High Commissioner Percy Cox of Baghdad imposed the Uqair Protocol which defined the boundaries between Iraq and Nejd; and between Kuwait and Nejd,[94] with Kuwait losing substantial territory to Ibn Saud. A year later, Britain introduced a number of administrative reforms and made changes to the ruling establishment by replacing Bahrain's Sheikh Issa with his son as the Emir. The political situation of Bahrain may not have been stable, but it wasn't plagued by the same chaos and unrest of the Najd region or the other parts of the peninsula.

Also, it's important to note that in 1923 and 1924 British and American oil companies had secured oil concessions in Bahrain,

---

94 Sheikhdom of Kuwait 2011, Wikipedia, accessed April 2017, <http://cosmos.ucc.ie/cs1064/jabowen/IPSC/php/event.php?eid=156>

Kuwait and the Arabian Peninsula in hopes of finding black gold. In those early days no one really knew if they would strike oil but the race for it in the Middle East had already begun. In 1908, oil had been discovered in Persia (now Iran) prompting further exploration in the region. But as far as discovering oil in commercial quantities in Bahrain, Kuwait and the Arabian Peninsula were concerned, that was still years away.

My grandfather had kept himself well-informed of the myriad changes occurring in the region and had enough experience to consider how any of these might affect his business. Still, Abdulrahman had a more practical reason for expanding their trade operations.

Bahrain was a hub, all of the new merchandise from India arrived there first on ships that were capable of traveling the deep seas. Once the merchandise reached Bahrain it had to be unloaded and reloaded onto smaller boats and then travel west to Jubail and again farther north to Kuwait. Abdulrahm had learned from his experience in Kuwait that merchants had to first order their supplies from traders in Bahrain who in turned ordered from those in India. Abdulrahman wanted to go straight to the source to purchase goods and eliminate the middleman. If he had someone stationed in Bahrain he would save the company money, cutting costs not only on staff needed to move the merchandise before it was shipped out to Jubail and Kuwait, but he would also get first pick on all goods newly arriving from India.

Abdulrahman and Muhammad agreed that conducting trade directly with Bahrain merchants would save them the cost of commissions, decrease their overhead and increase profits. And so the brothers agreed: Muhammad would relocate to the British ruled region of Bahrain, and set up shop and expand their trade operations from there.

They traveled by dhow—the traditional Sanbuq wooden ship with its triangular sails—to Bahrain, Abdulrahman spending a

Semm Yubah

few days there to help his brother find a residence and a stall for Muhammad to conduct trade and storage space for merchandise before he sailed home to Jubail.

It would be another seven years before Muhammad traveled home to Unayzah to marry (around 1935), and he and his bride returned to Bahrain where they raised their family. My father, Abdulaziz, had lived with his uncle in Bahrain for a short time in 1939. My father was ten when Abdulrahman had sent him to attend school there. He became homesick and never acclimated to his new environment, and returned home to Jubail after only one year of school to work with Abdulrahman in his shop. I often wonder how my father's life would have changed if he had remained in school there.

Mohammad Saleh Alsuhaimi (1910-1967); Grandfather's brother. Bahrain, 1930.

Abdulrahman and his brother Muhammad had worked hard to make the expansion of their business succeed, and their efforts were rewarded over the following years until the winds shifted and the political climate changed once again.

CHAPTER 7

Security and Political Uncertainty in Jubail; the need to explore trade sources farther out

A rash of violent forays broke out, tribal raids with an upsurge of looting and killings, the hostilities extending throughout the region. Like many other towns and villages, Jubail depended on its own people to safeguard their residents and businesses.

Both Abdulrahman and Mohammad Al Kadi had answered their town's call to service, taking their turns as guards at the Al Tuwayyah Tower in Jubail's western end. Armed with shotguns, daggers, and the famous Arabian scimitar, *muhaddab*, they were prepared to defend their town *and* safeguard its prized water well. For years Jubail's residents had retrieved their fresh water just north of the town from a well beneath the sea, "...called *Ain Ghumisah*. To fetch water from it, divers had to swim down to the head of the well and hold their leather bags over the bubbling spring to fill them. To provide a more readily available water source to the town's citizens, Al Saud had ordered construction of Al-Tuwayyah Tower over the well with the same name,"[95] and it was completed by 1930.

The instability in Jubail had lasted several years with debilitating

---

95 Al Tuwayyah Tower, Jubail 2020, Wikipedia, accessed September 2017, (in Arabic only, <https://www.marafiq.com.sa/en/operations/opr_desal.aspx>

Semm Yubah

Altuwyyah-Tower Fort. Jubail, 1972.

consequences for local mercantile commerce. Unnerved by the constant conflicts and political disarray, Jubaili merchants now looked for alternatives locations for their businesses. It was common practice for a merchant to commission another merchant to act as their proxy, someone seasoned, reliable, and trustworthy who would travel even as far as India to conduct trade.

The risks of such an undertaking were great, and demanded a highly qualified and skilled individual. The merchants required someone not only facile in trade and familiar with the rigorous conditions that long distance trade imposed—grueling days sailing across the Arabian Sea—but, more importantly, someone fluent in English and with expertise in the customs and mercantile industry of India.

Jubail's population was predominantly young, recent immigrants constituting the majority of its people. Most, including Abdulrahman, knew little, if anything, about India trade. And they hadn't yet had enough experience to gain proficiency in English.

Still, the merchants needed someone with a working knowledge of India and fluent in English. They were hard-pressed to find a qualified candidate and had selected the best of the applicants but someone who, as it would turn out, was a neophyte.

The merchants had provided explicit instructions for the young man, equipped him with a crew and supplies and entrusted him with their merchandise and funds before sending him off on his trip to India with God's blessing. I'm not sure what prompted the merchants' choice but the young man must have had some outstanding quality that elicited their trust. Perhaps he spoke a sufficient amount of English to convince them, or rattled off enough details of Indian life to assuage their doubts. More likely the young man, desperate for work, embellished the truth and did an excellent job of overselling himself. Whatever the reason, he was hired and with the merchants' money and wares in his charge, set sail on a dhow for the city of Bombay, modern day Mumbai.

Named for the local goddess Mumbadevi, protector of all fishermen, Mumbai had been re-named *Bom Bahia*, good bay, when

Taj Mahal Hotel & Gateway of India from Bombay (Mumbai) seaport, circa 1930s.

the Portuguese captured the islands and had established a trading post there in 1534.[96] The English later Anglicized it to Bombay, and its name wasn't officially changed back to Mumbai until 1995.

But, it was still known as Bombay then, and the voyage from Jubail took the young man two weeks and when the port finally came into view, he was enthralled by the 85-foot structure overlooking the Harbor. The "Gateway of India" with its volcanic stone of yellow basalt, stood in all its magnificence against the sky. Near it, loomed the majestic Taj Palace Hotel with its huge domes and turrets, ornate balconies and arched windows, the *mashrabiya*-like casements of Arab homes.

The young man had never seen anything like it, and the bustle and clamor of the crowd had overwhelmed him as soon as he set foot on land.

Bombay was India's second largest city then, with a mixed population of over one million and included the wealthy and destitute, Parsi merchants, Arab traders and Sheiks, the Chinese

Port Mumbai; Maharashtra India, circa 1930s.

---

96 Panorama of Fort, Bombay 2009, British Library, accessed July 2017, <http://www.bl.uk/learning/histcitizen/trading/bombay/history.html>

and Japanese and Malaysians, Afghans, Americans, Portuguese, and British. The city's architecture was just as diverse—an amalgam of modern and ancient constructions, glamorous and dilapidated hotels, commercial modern buildings and tenements, and the blend of old and new cramming the streets with oxen-drawn bullock carts next to automobiles, merchants towing wagons of wares, some shouldering their goods, some balancing it on their backs, others bundling it high on their heads.

It was time for him to navigate the city and deal with the traders at the open market but he was filled with unease. He told my grandfather later he simply lacked the experience and skill to negotiate prudently with the merchants, and his naiveté and lack of street smarts had cost him dearly. A singular mistake in judgment—trusting the wrong person—had led to his demise when he disclosed the quantity of cash and quality of goods in his possession. Some unscrupulous characters had swindled him out of the merchants' funds and goods, leaving him without any belongings or supplies, penniless in Bombay—all within two days.

With no money, food or shelter, he wandered the streets desperate, unable to communicate with the locals, unsure where or to whom he should turn for help. He burned with humiliation, allowing himself to be tricked, cheated and robbed of the merchants' money and goods. At some point the Bombay police found him and took him into custody, and after piecing together his story, informed a resident Arab Sheikh about the young man's predicament.

The Sheik took pity on the young man, advocating on his behalf, and once he persuaded the police to release him, he arranged for his safe passage back to Jubail. The young man, exceedingly grateful and relieved, wasted no time setting sail for home, but as one week turned into two, and his dhow drew closer to his village of Jubail, his apprehension intensified. How would he explain his dilemma to the merchants?

Semm Yubah

His reception by the Jubaili merchants had been as he feared. No one believed his story of being conned by Bombay crooks. They called him a liar and a cheat, a ruthless squanderer of their money, and held him accountable for their losses.

Jubail was small, and it wasn't long before the entire town heard what had happened and treated him as a pariah. When he asked the merchants for an opportunity to rectify the situation, they refused. Their animosity toward him fostered a town boycott, the locals not permitting him in their shops and homes, and forced him into complete isolation.

I suspect it was the young man's forced alienation that was reminiscent of Abdulrahman's earlier years without any family that prompted him to advocate on the young man's behalf.

Abdulrahman had not personally known the young man but when he had learned of his predicament, took it upon himself to talk directly to the merchants.

The young man's only crime, after all, had been inexperience and certainly did not warrant social exile. He used his best diplomatic skills, empathizing with the merchants, acknowledging their great loss but he told them, everyone deserved another chance. The merchants did not agree.

Weeks passed and nothing changed. One day, while Abdulrahman was working, the young man passed by his shop. When my grandfather asked him how he was, he looked despondent, saying his predicament had worsened now that word had spread across the desert to his parents in Unayzah. His actions had disgraced his family, and now he could never return home. Abdulrahman's words of support provided little comfort. The young man was heartbroken but adamant. He wouldn't subject his family to further humiliation by visiting.

The call to prayer interrupted their conversation, and as Abdulrahman rose to go to the mosque, he handed him the keys to his shop and safe. "Take however much money you need,"

Shops along a street in Jubail, 1973.

Abdulrahman said, "for your second chance." He instructed him to record the amount in the ledger, then lock the safe and shop after he was done.

The young man stood speechless. Abdulrahman told him, *Allah*[97] *Yusallmak*, May God be with you, and left for the mosque. The young man hurried into the shop and removed 2000 Indian Rupees from the safe, entered the amount in the ledger, locked up, and headed toward the mosque. After prayers, he met Abdulrahman outside, and thanked him for his generosity and trust in him, and walked away.

It was no surprise to me that my grandfather had demonstrated such compassion and blind faith to someone he hardly knew. Abdulrahman had suffered his share of isolation and desperation,

---

97 The Arabic name for God is *Allah*, and used by Christians and Muslims alike.

separated from his father and brother, losing his mother, experiences that only heightened his capacity to empathize with those struggling.

Besides, he had always been a humble and pious man, a follower of the teachings and ethics dictated by the Holy Qur'an and those of the Prophet Muhammad (PBUH), and his faith had encouraged him to act compassionate toward the needy, whether they were Muslim or not, friend or stranger, rich or poor.

The young man now had received his second chance and wasn't going to waste it. He immediately set sail for Bombay. Upon arriving, he solicited that same Arab Sheikh's help. With his guidance along with a few other local merchants, he set up shop and became quite a successful trader. In a short time he was earning a substantial income, and when he had saved enough to repay his debts, he returned to Jubail but not before thanking the Arab Sheik and reimbursing him for the cost of his previous trip back home.

Ibrahim Saleh Alsuhaimi (1930-2011); half-brother of Grandfather Abdulrahman after relocating from Unayzah to Jubail, 1946.

In Jubail, he couldn't wait to restore his reputation and family's, and regain the trust of his peers and fellow traders, and paid all of his outstanding debts with the merchants and Abdulrahman. He told my grandfather he would never forget what he had done for him, and hoped one day to return the favor.

The young man eventually moved back to Bombay and made it his permanent home. He resumed his trade business, which became a very lucrative operation, making the young man extremely wealthy. Later he became one of the most affluent Arab merchants in the city with his business expanding throughout Saudi Arabia and Kuwait.

The young man had stayed in touch with Abdulrahman, and sometime after 1934 my grandfather became his choice for his business agent. The young man had been true to his word and had never forgotten what my grandfather had done, and rewarded him by making him manager of all of his assets within Dammam and Jubail. Little did Abdulrahman know that a gesture of compassion would, indeed, lead him to becoming the business agent for one of the wealthiest Arab merchants in the region.

At one point, my grandfather would travel to India himself, shuttling between Jubail and Bombay. His first trip there, during the late 30's, was at the invitation of this same young man, now an established and prosperous businessman.

Abdulrahman's singular act of kindness had earned him a true friend for life. The invitation came at a crucial time, since my grandfather needed to learn more about the Indian market. He had heard a great deal about the country, its trade opportunities and bustling marketplaces, and this trip would help him expand his business and give him a chance to spend time with his old friend.

Before leaving India he sent his friend a long list of goods he wished to purchase and import to Bahrain and Jubail. He also made certain he carried a sufficient amount of gold coins for his use during the trip but mainly to help him purchase those goods.

Everything seemed to go according to plan, until he heard the British were levying high taxes and imposing a quota on the amount of gold that could be transported across its various territories. To complicate matters, his vision in his left eye had deteriorated and was giving him problems, made reading the necessary paperwork difficult. This trip wasn't going to be as easy as he thought.

Abdulrahman, who never shied away from risks, decided to proceed with his journey to India. He would carry the same amount of gold coins and hide as much as he could and pray that his demeanor gave him the air of a trustworthy and reliable person.

Semm Yubah

Abdulrahman traveled to Bahrain first, and, hoping for the best, set sail for India from there, a two-week trip across the sea to Bombay. At the Indian port, Abdulrahman and the other passengers unloaded their belongings and waited beside it in a queue at the customs counter. He looked up to the Gateway to India overlooking the harbor, and glimpsed the rooftop of the majestic Taj Palace Hotel and understood how his friend now a seasoned businessman had been overwhelmed as a young man when he first arrived in this city from Jubail.

A British customs officer was inspecting all of the travelers, checking their baggage before issuing a visa entry stamp for the immigration officer.

Any traveler caught carrying gold coins had to undergo a long and costly process by British customs officials who withheld a hefty portion as a tax. Passengers were considered fortunate if they made it through customs with just half of their gold intact.

This was problematic for Abdulrahman, who needed his gold for his trading activities in Bombay. If he was caught carrying gold coins, he risked losing at least half to the officials. Many merchants had fallen prey to aggressive custom checks and high taxes, forced to relinquish a good portion of their money.

As a precaution Abdulrahman secreted his gold coins and pocket watch in his thick vest pocket instead of in his valises. He watched as the British customs officer checked all the baggage of the travelers ahead of him. He told himself he was fine, breathing a sigh of relief, knowing his luggage held nothing of value. But when the customs officer got closer to Abdulrahman, he switched tactics, searching the person of each traveler thoroughly, checking their garments, rummaging through every pocket.

My grandfather's heart raced when the officer came up to him and stared. Abdulrahman hoped it was only because he was much taller than the other passengers, and forced himself to maintain an impassive expression and hold the man's gaze. The officer smiled, grabbed the front edge of Abdulrahman's vest pocket and shook it. No one in the room missed the sound of his pocket watch rattling against his collection of gold coins but Abdulrahman stood confident, looking straight into the British officer's eyes.

My grandfather was never sure why but the officer turned away from him and asked the group if anyone else had any gold to declare before proceeding to the immigration office. The ship's captain at front of the line assured him no one had anything and urged him not to waste any more of their time. In the end, Abdulrahman had to declare very few of his coins and avoided losing the bulk of his money to customs, and was met at the dock by his old friend. The streets were a cacophony of sounds and people, cars and carts and animals, and he was grateful that he had the benefit of his friend's experience and contacts to help him navigate the city. He stayed in Bombay for a number of weeks with his old friend and through his help, successfully set up trade deals with various Indian suppliers, returning to Jubail with a variety of goods—food stuff, building materials, garments and cloth.

Between 1925 and 1940's, Jubail became the main trading post for the people of Najd region as a result of Ibn Saud's embargo on Kuwait until 1937, businesses had flourished, and Jubail's population had increased at a rapid rate with the large influx of immigrants. Ibn Saud continued his territorial expansion, striving to reunite different regions under one kingdom, and many migrated to Jubail looking for a safer haven and a work. The townspeople welcomed the new arrivals. A surge in the number of residents in Jubail only meant more able bodies to help protect the city against attack.

The threat of raids still haunted the town but the round-the-clock tower guards did much to mitigate their fears along with the extra men due to the increase in population. Trade was stabilized, and Abdulrahman's business expanded without much difficulty.

Semm Yubah

Bedouin with his camel loaded with wood, Jubail, 1935.

Even though most regions had to deal with intertribal warfare and raids on caravans, and Ibn Saud's continuing expansion in his quest for one kingdom, Jubail proved a lot safer than most. Kuwait, for one, had suffered more than a decade of siege, along with the devastating effects of Ibn Saud's blockade, and most merchants saw their profits diminish, along with their lifestyle. The townspeople of Jubail, on the other hand, lived a fairly normal life.

Jubail by default, became known for its better prospects and trade, and a safe harbor, a place to raise a family without the insecurity prevalent everywhere else. Most had migrated to Jubail to escape severe hardships due to intense fighting among tribes, epidemics, droughts, and famines.

With so many families now settling in town, children now flooded the streets. The men conducted trade from their shops from early morning until dusk while women worked at home or on the outskirts of the western part of town to help on farms. Jubail had developed a strong sense of community and became known for their hospitality.

Adel Alsuhaimi

Abdulrahman M. Alkadi (left) standing in front of Alshallali (right), Jubail, 1953.

The children were sent to school every day until noon to learn the Qur'an along with writing and Arithmetic. Afterwards, they returned home for lunch and a nap until the scorching heat of Jubail became tolerable for the children to go out and play. Sometimes young boys with a penchant for pranks got into trouble with their elders.

One such incident involved a blind neighbor entertaining dinner guests at his house. While his family prepared their meal, he and his guests attended the mosque to perform Salat ul Asr (afternoon prayers). When they were gone, a group of twelve-year-old boys decided to spend their free time sealing the man's front door with mud from the front yard.

After prayers, the blind neighbor, using his cane, led his guests home

Khalid Abdulrahman Alsuhaimi at Jubail elementary school; stage acting, circa 1946.

Semm Yubah

but when he reached his house he could not locate the front door. He wandered to the left and right, searching, his guests trailing, until he heard some children laughing. He soon discovered the culprits and what they had done. I'm sure when their parents reprimanded the boys and sent them to the old man apologize, and made to help him in his yard.

What struck me most about this story was not the childish and unkind prank, but that the children of Jubail had the time to get into trouble. I had certainly heard enough stories of the early days in Unayzah when small children worked before sunrise to after sunset along side their parents. They had no leisure time to get into mischief. But my elders explained that most children in Jubail had led very different lives from their parents, and knew little of the desperate situations outside of town. These children had never experienced the famines and droughts that gripped other regions, had never gone hungry like other children in the region or even the way their parents had. The children of Jubail lived in a secure and fairly stable environment and spent their childhood playing games and getting into mischief, and had the chance to be

Abdulaziz A. R. Alsuhaimi (my father) standing third from left; Jubail Elementary School Soccer Team, 1942.

children, a luxury that still evaded the children in other regions. Childhood for the young of the other regions had been cut short, as it were for Abdulrahman and with many of his peers, the precarious circumstances in Unayzah demanding it.

The Wise Arbiter of Jubail
By now, Abdulrahman had grown quite popular with the other tradesmen and was respected for his honesty, judgment and business acumen. Other merchants asked his advice or help arbitrating a trade dispute. His mercantile experience in Kuwait and Basra was well known, especially his dealings with the elite Kuwaiti merchants who had entrusted him with their merchandise, and the ingenuity and leadership he displayed during the two years it took to sell through their merchandise. The townspeople saw him as unbiased and generous, many repeating the story of his kindness to a desperate man in India.

Perhaps because of that, Abdulrahman's *majlis*, the reception hall in his home, became the gathering place for friends and business associates after *Salat Al Isha* (the last evening prayers). In the comfort of my grandfather's home, they sipped their coffee with cardamom or tea, and debated politics after listening to the BBC and the Monte Carlo radio stations. Sometimes they discussed religious matters if it affected their businesses or society, and sometimes they listened to each other recite poetry, particularly of ancient Arab poets. Al Mutanabi was a favorite.

Abdulrahman Saleh Alsuhaimi (seated); & sons, left to right: Khalid, Abdulaziz (standing behind), Sulaiman. Jubail, 1947.

Semm Yubah

Strong resolves come in proportion to men of determination, and noble deeds come in proportion to magnanimous men. Little things are deemed great by little minds, while grave calamities pale into insignificance in the eyes of the great.

My grandfather's *majlis* became one of the three places known for exchanging ideas and latest news. The other two were the Governor's house, and the home of Al Gusaibi, an extremely successful merchant from Al Hasa. *Majlis* can serve many purposes, and some are known as a social club. Abdulrahman's *majlis* served as a makeshift Town Hall, even the local governor attended regularly to offer his opinions about pressing matters and listen to my grandfather and the other citizens voice their opinions.

Word spread of Abdulrahman's diplomatic skill at amicably mediating conflict, and many merchants sought his advice on resolving trade disputes, as did several nomads along with the local townspeople who needed guidance in their personal affairs.

An acquaintance from Jubail once approached Abdulrahman for assistance shortly after moving to Dammam. The young man said his mother had told him to visit Abdulrahman when he was ready to marry but, unfortunately, he didn't have enough money to cover his wedding expenses. Abdulrahman disappeared inside his shop and returned with a pouch for the young man. Inside was enough gold for him to wed, and for his mother to live comfortably for her remaining days.

Abdulrahman told him. "Your father put this money in my custody until you were grown. Your mother asked me to hold it for you until now." Abdulrahman embraced the man and said, "God bless you all, son. Please say Salam to your mother." With the funds the young man married, moved his mother to a better house and secured a scholarship to complete his university education. He later landed a job with Aramco and after a few years left to open his own business to much success, and became a well-known philanthropist and a multibillionaire in Saudi Arabia.

Adel Alsuhaimi

Abdulrahman's unequivocal ability to resolve disputes with accuracy, fairness, and wisdom had earned him the title, Wise Arbiter, by the townspeople. His generosity and willingness to help others with their problems had won their hearts.

He did, however, refrain from arbitrating over any matters dealing with blood feuds or revenge killings, or homicides. He had, after all, descended from a family who had witnessed first-hand what it was like to lose a family member to murder when his distant cousin, Prince Nasir Alsuhaimi, had been killed by the rival ruling family, Al Sulaim, and the Alsuhaimi family had to flee the region and settle in Alhilaliyah to avoid persecution.

Abdullah Saleh Alsuhaimi (nine-years-old) half-brother of Grandfather, Jubail, 1946.

It was an extremely risky undertaking to advise someone on a revenge killing or blood feud. Any advice Abdulrahman offered may have had dire repercussions for his own family. And if there were a credible threat to his family, Abdulrahman would have had no choice but to flee with his family. It would have also meant the end of his business there, and everything that he built over the years. Abdulrahman didn't want to chance any of that and referred any cases dealing with murder to Jubail's Governor.

Yet, Abdulrahman's reputation as a trusted arbiter grew, and the Governor of Jubail, Al Shuwayyer, expressed an appreciation and interest in his talent for arbitrating personal and business conflicts. Al Shuwayyer had been overwhelmed by the number of cases he had, and believed Abdulrahman was a perfect candidate

Semm Yubah

for his assistant, someone to act as a mediator and advisor on local affairs.

Abdulrahman accepted the governor's offer and served as the town's arbiter. After many years, the situation had eased substantially, and the burden of resolving the disputes prevalent in Jubail's society had lessened. It was 1933 now, one year after Ibn Saud consolidated his kingdom of Saudi Arabia and named himself its king. The security of Jubail and its environs had improved, and Abdulrahman and his family and the locals believed that they would live, finally, with greater ease. It was also the same year that rumors spread through town—a dhow was sailing toward Jubail with important passengers—American petroleum geologists who hoped to find black gold on their shores.

CHAPTER 8

The Dream

My grandfather, as I've mentioned, had kept current with the news in the region, trying to gauge the impact it might have on his trade business. Since my grandfather worked closely with Jubail's governor as an arbitrator of local affairs, he had been privy to the latest developments in the region and how it might affect his greater community. Still, as perceptive as my grandfather was, I don't believe he had ever imagined the scope of the transformation that was about to transpire. How could he? It would have been impossible to foresee the metamorphosis that would occur in the region. He couldn't possibly have fathomed that his native land, known for its camel and goat herders, its Bedouins and clans and warring tribes, its famines and droughts and disease would soon become synonymous with wealth and prosperity.

Prior to the thirties, black gold in Arabia had been a dream and only for some. It's true oil had been discovered at Masjid-i-Sulaiman in the Zagros Mountains in western Persia (now Iran) in 1908, and later in Iraq's Kirkuk well in 1927, and it had ignited exploration in the region. Although it's interesting that Austrian geologist Emile Tietze had noted the oil possibilities in the region back in 1879, as international journalist and scholar, Allison Keating states in her book, *Mirage: Power, Politics, and the Hidden History of Arabian Oil:*[98]

> "Tietze's opinion of the adjacent area appears so startlingly ahead of its time that it is difficult to imagine how it was almost totally ignored by the petroleum seekers of the first decades of the twentieth century. Tietze wrote: 'it might be of interest to mention the occurrence of bitumen on the Arabian side of the Persian Gulf... the possibility of a geological connection between the south Persian and the Arabian petroleum areas certainly exist in the same manner as between the bitumen seepages on the Caucasian and on the Turkmenian side of the Caspian Sea.' With notable clarity, Tietze added: 'Any petroleum industry to be established in Persia, should realize the possibility of a foreign, but nearby competition, and therefore reckon with the condition on the Arabian side of the Gulf.'"

Max Steineke in Arab clothing. American Headquarters Building, Jubail, 1935.

But as far the Arabian Peninsula, Bahrain and Kuwait were concerned, it would take close to a decade before anyone would succeed in finding oil in commercial quantities. In 1922 Ibn Saud

---

98 Keating, Allison; *Mirage: Power, Politics and the Hidden History of Arabian Oil*; Prometheus Books; Amherst, N.Y. Pg. 28.

had met with the indefatigable New Zealand mining engineer Frank Holmes (whom I'll discuss in depth later), and they shared the common goal of oil but turning it into a reality was still years away. Discovering oil had been no easy task. The American geologist Max Steineke of California-Arabian Standard Oil Company (CASOC) wrote in the October 1945 issue of his company's employee newspaper, Oily Bird.[99]

> *In almost all cases, the exact origin of oil is indeterminate, but where positive data is available on the subject, they invariably indicate a marine source, that is, close association with sediments that were originally deposited in the sea but later hardened into rocks. Furthermore, the scientists have found that the rocks producing petroleum are composed of a high percentage of small marine shells most of which are microscopic in size. Also, they have found that in many cases organisms similar to those occurring in rocks that have generated oil are now living in the sea and that these organisms living today contain minute globules of fatty substances from which petroleum-like material can be made in the laboratory.*
>
> *We have good evidence that the organisms found in the rocks that generated the Arabian oil lived approximately 150 million years ago. They evidently lived in a quiet sea or a somewhat enclosed basin vaguely similar to the Persian gulf of today except that it was very much larger. As the organisms died they sank to the bottom, forming layer upon layer until they formed a deposit hundreds of feet thick. These layers in turn were covered by thick deposits of mud, sand and shell beds, attaining a thickness of many thousands of feet. As the deposits were laid down, the sea bottom gradually subsided due to earth movements, which allowed a great accumulation of sediments with comparatively little change in the depth*

---

99 Energy 2012, Aramco World, accessed March 2017, <http://www.saudiaramco.com/content/dam/Publications/Energy%20to%20the%20World%20-%20English/Vol-1-Chapter-3.pdf>

and character of the sea. As the overburden of later sediments mounted, the deeply buried ones near the bottom were naturally compressed, and they were also heated to hundreds of degrees in temperature due to the great depth. Because of the great pressure and heat applied to the sediments over a period of many millions of years the greater mass of deposits were hardened into rocks. During this change in the character of the deposits the fatty matter in the micro-organisms comprising a substantial portion of the sediments were changed by chemical processes into petroleum products of various types. Intensely salty water, and often brines, with which the sediments were saturated, may also have aided in the chemical reaction whereby the fatty globules in the minute organisms were changed to petroleum products....

In 1930 Standard Oil Company of California (SOCAL) bought an oil concession from the Bahrain Petroleum Company (BAPCO), and two years later, finally discovered oil in commercial quantities in Bahrain, making it the first Arab Gulf state to find oil and benefit from its revenues and dramatically improve the quality of its citizens' lives.[100]

But nothing had occurred yet that would radically transform the peninsula from an impoverished country into one of the richest in the world. That was about to change. The quest for Arabian oil was set to go into full swing.

Up to 1931, the main income of the Arabian Peninsula had been derived from *Hajj*, the pilgrimage to Makkah (one of the five pillars of Islam[101]), which every adult Muslim was expected to make at least once during his or her lifetime, but the region

---

100 Discover more 2020, BAPCO Website, accessed 2 November 2018, <http://middleeastarab.com/bh/bahrain-history-discovery-oil.htm>

101 The five pillars of Islam are the framework of Muslim life. The first is the Shahada, the testimony of faith; the second is Salat, prayer (Muslims pray 5 times a day for a few minutes); the third is zakat, giving aid to the needy; the fourth is Sawm, fasting during Ramadan; and the fifth is Hajj, the pilgrimage to Mecca.

What are the five pillars of Islam? 2002, Islam Guide, accessed 10 July 2017, <https://www.islam-guide.com/ch3-16.htm>

was experiencing serious repercussions from the Great Depression along with the rest of the world, and income from the Hajj had dwindled since many people were unable to afford the trip. Even though Ibn Saud by 1932 had successfully unified the various factions within the Peninsula and established his kingdom of Saudi Arabia, his country was facing a severe financial crisis.[102] It would take the determination and dogged pursuit of geologists during the 1930s to alter his country's course.

The Road to Black Gold
The discovery of the world's most wanted natural resource had dominated the interest of American oil companies and prompted them to establish a presence in the region, which resulted in a new economic relationship between the United States and the oil-exporting Arab countries. Between the mid-1940 and 1970s, the oil companies known as the 'Seven Sisters' were among the pioneers in the oligopolistic petroleum industry, and controlled a significant share of petroleum reserves.

It is important to mention the prominent figures and events that contributed to establishing a booming petroleum industry in the Arab world if we are to understand the impact it had on the inhabitants of the Saudi Arabia region, as well as Abdulrahman and his family. But first I want to identify some of the oil companies founded in the 20th century that shaped today's Saudi Arabian oil industry.

The Anglo-Persian Oil Company
The Anglo-Persian Oil Company (APOC) was established soon after oil was discovered in the Iranian city of Masjed Suleiman in 1908. Its origins can be traced back to 1901 when wealthy London

---

102 Rasoul Sorkhabi, Ph.D. 2008, The Emergence of the Arabian Oil Industry, GeoExPro, accessed 9 July 2018, <3http://www.geoexpro.com/articles/2008/06/the-emergence-of-the-arabian-oil-industry>

socialite William Knox D'Arcy struck an oil concession deal with the then ruler of Persia, Mozaffar Al-Din Shah Qajar. D'Arcy had attained exclusive rights for prospecting oil for six decades in a vast territory that included Persia (Iran), and hired a geologist to survey its immense deserts for oil.

Despite investing thousands of pounds into the venture, Persia showed no signs of oil, and D'Arcy, whose fortune was quickly disappearing, was forced to sell most of his rights to the Glasgow-based Burmah Oil Company. Burmah Oil founded the Anglo-Persian Oil Company after the successful oil drilling operation in Masjed Suleiman and by 1913 began volume production of Persian oil products.

Gulf Oil Corporation
A major player in the petroleum industry from 1901 to 1984, the Gulf Oil Corporation was first established after the discovery of oil in 1901 on January 10th when oil gushed out of the ground for nine days at Spindletop in the southern end of Beaumont, Texas.[103] However, it was not until the merger of several oil companies–the Gulf Refining companies of Texas and the J.M. Guffey Petroleum– that the Gulf Oil Corporation was officially established in 1907. The 'Gulf' alludes to the Gulf of Mexico and not the Arabian Gulf.

Iraq Petroleum Company (IPC)
Before 1929 it was known as the Turkish Petroleum Company (TPC) formed the exploration of oil in Mesopotamia. The IPC held a monopoly on all oil production and exploration activities in Iraq from 1925 through 1961. Today, its headquarters is in London, and it is jointly owned by some of the biggest oil companies in the world.

---

103 Robert Wooster and Christine Moor Sanders 2020, "Spindletop Oilfield," Handbook of Texas Online, accessed June 2018,, <https://tshaonline.org/handbook/online/articles/dos03>

OTTOMAN EMPIRE 1914

In 1914, as war broke out, the Ottoman Empire consisted of core territory and outlying areas under "nominal" control, <https://www.thenational.ae/arts-culture/how-the-first-world-war-shaped-the-borders-of-the-middle-east-1.785667#2>

SoCal

The company emerged in the Arabian Gulf after purchasing oil concessions from the Gulf Oil Corporation in 1933, which had closed its oil drilling operations in Bahrain.

SoCal was one of the seven sister companies that succeeded the Standard Oil Company established in 1870 by John D. Rockefeller. The Standard Oil Company was the biggest oil refining company of its time but its multi-million dollar enterprise operations had come to a halt after it was declared an illegal monopoly. The sister companies in addition to SoCal included: The Standard Oil of New York, Standard Oil of New Jersey, Standard Oil of Indiana, Standard Oil of Kentucky, Standard Oil Company, and the Ohio Oil Company. In 1936, SoCal had partnered with the Texas Oil Company, also known as Texaco, to benefit from their strong marketing presence in Asia and Africa, and formed CALTEX.

Saudi ARAMCO

A national petroleum and gas company in Dhahran, Saudi Arabia, the company holds the world's largest crude oil reserves and, according to a 2015 *Forbes* report, is the largest oil and gas company in the world.

In 1936 Texas Oil Company (later called Texaco) purchased a 50 percent stake in CASOC (California-Arabian Standard Oil), and in 1944 it was renamed the Arabian American Oil Company, or ARAMCO.

Four years after ARAMCO was established, many other oil companies bought stakes in the company, including Standard Oil (Exxon) and Socony-Vacuum (Mobil). The company later came to be known as 'Saudi ARAMCO' after the Saudi government completed its buyout of assets in 1973 and 1974.

These are some of the most central players in the discovery of oil in the Arabian Peninsula. Now I want to provide the backstory that led to the emergence of Saudi Arabia as one of the world's most important oil producing countries.

The Battle for Oil in Iraq

Toward the end of WWI, western powers became increasingly aware of the importance of oil, not only for its obvious economic and military benefits but also for urbanization and the development of their country's infrastructure, and oil was rapidly taking the place of coal.

The British Empire, despite controlling the Anglo-Persia Oil Company with its vast oil reserves, was still experiencing oil shortages in their homeland. Although Britain had gained control of Iraq (per the secret Sykes-Picot agreement), it had given the key region of Northern Iraq, which included oil reserves, to their ally, the French.

Soon after the signing of the armistice, Britain had double-crossed France by sending in troops to gain control of the oil fields in the northern Iraqi city of Mosul, originally assigned to the French. Britain's failure to abide by the terms of the Sykes-Picot agreement enraged France whose lack of sufficient oil resources had made them dependent on foreign countries. During the Versailles Peace Conference, Britain's Prime Minister David Lloyd George and France's Georges Clemenceau came close to a brawl over it if U.S. President Woodrow Wilson hadn't intervened.[104] Once close allies, France and England were now bitter enemies over control of a natural resource.

In 1920 the two countries reached another agreement, the San Remo Agreement, in which France agreed to give Britain control of the entire Mesopotamia, which included modern Iraq, Syria, and Kuwait. In return, France received the German regional share of the Turkish Petroleum Industry (The TPC was a joint venture from 1912 between Royal Dutch/Shell, the Deutsche Bank, and

---

104 James A. Paul 2002, Global Policy Forum, accessed 7 August 2017, <https://www.globalpolicy.org/component/content/article/185/40479.html>

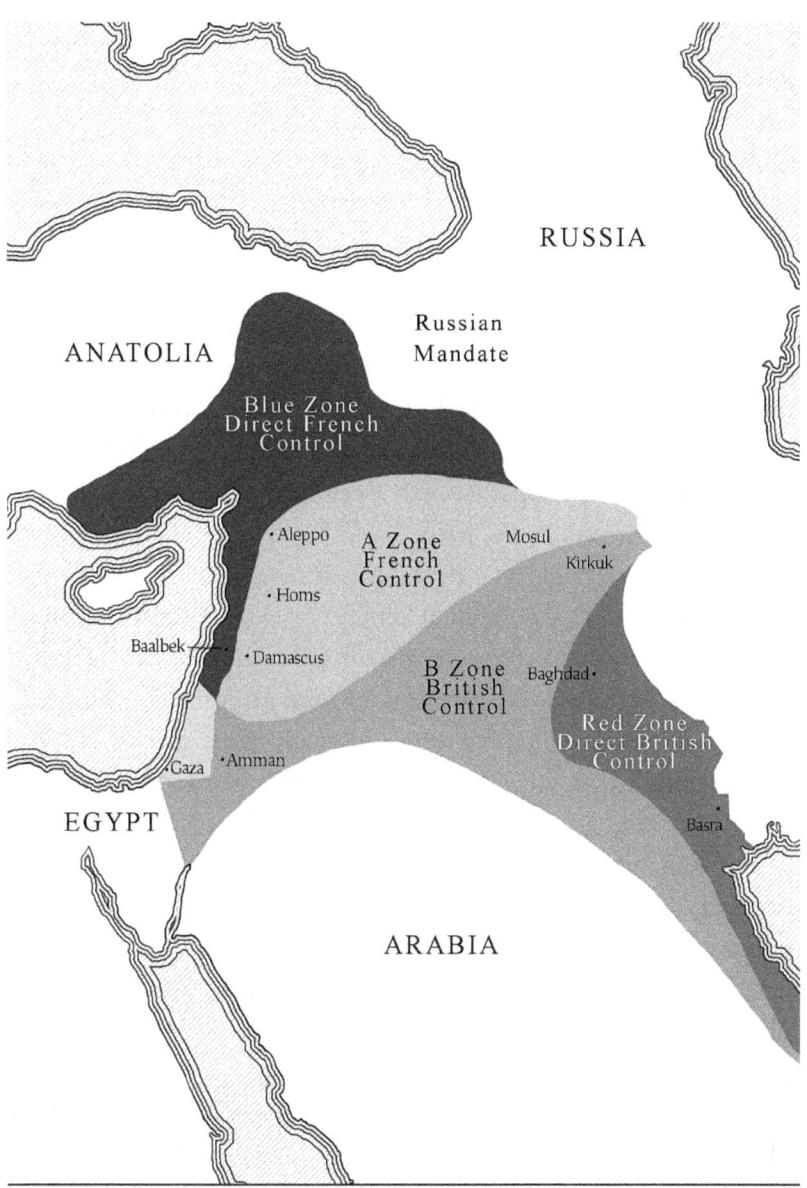

SYKES-PICOT, 1916

Sykes-Picot redrew the map in 1916 into areas of British, French and Russian rule and "buffer" zones under British and French protection, <https://www.thenational.ae/arts-culture/how-the-first-world-war-shaped-the-borders-of-the-middle-east-1.785667#1>

the Turkish National Bank, formed to promote oil exploration and production within the then Ottoman Empire.)[105]

As a result, Britain had gained the upper hand in the control of the region's oil industry. France, however, had not been satisfied and in 1924 formed the *Compagnie Francaise des Pétroles*, to counter the British colonial efforts by securing a sizeable share of Iraq's oil revenues.

Now, both American and British oil companies were in Iraq to carve up oil revenues for themselves, but the agreement between France and Britain had excluded American companies. The signing of the San Remo Agreement provoked strong protests from American oil companies, and Washington began pressuring Britain through sanctions, with the U.S. press labeling Britain's agreement with France as old-fashioned imperialism.[106]

The United States government kept the heat on Britain, claiming the Turkish Petroleum Company's oil concession with the now non-existent Ottoman Empire was invalid. The threat prompted Britain to rethink its policy and eventually they succumbed to pressure from across the Atlantic and promised to give the U.S. a better deal.

American oil companies in Iraq were now told by the U.S. government to form a consortium to insure their chances of gaining oil contracts in the region. Even though oil had still not been discovered in commercial quantities, the prospects for the United States acquiring significant geopolitical influence in the region were strong.

By 1927, oil was discovered by the British exploration team led by D'Arcy in Kirkuk, Iraq, and in 1928, tensions escalated between various parties over control of oil revenues. The famous Red Line

---

[105] The 1928 Red Line Agreement 2018, Office of the Historian, accessed 5 October 2018, <https://history.state.gov/milestones/1921-1936/red-line>

[106] James A. Paul 2002, Global Policy Forum, accessed 7 August 2017, <https://www.globalpolicy.org/component/content/article/185/40479.html>

SAN REMO, 1920

The San Remo meeting of Allied Powers in 1920 changed those boundaries again, producing the colonial compromise of the mandate system, <https://www.thenational.ae/arts-culture/how-the-first-world-war-shaped-the-borders-of-the-middle-east-1.785667#3>

Adel Alsuhaimi

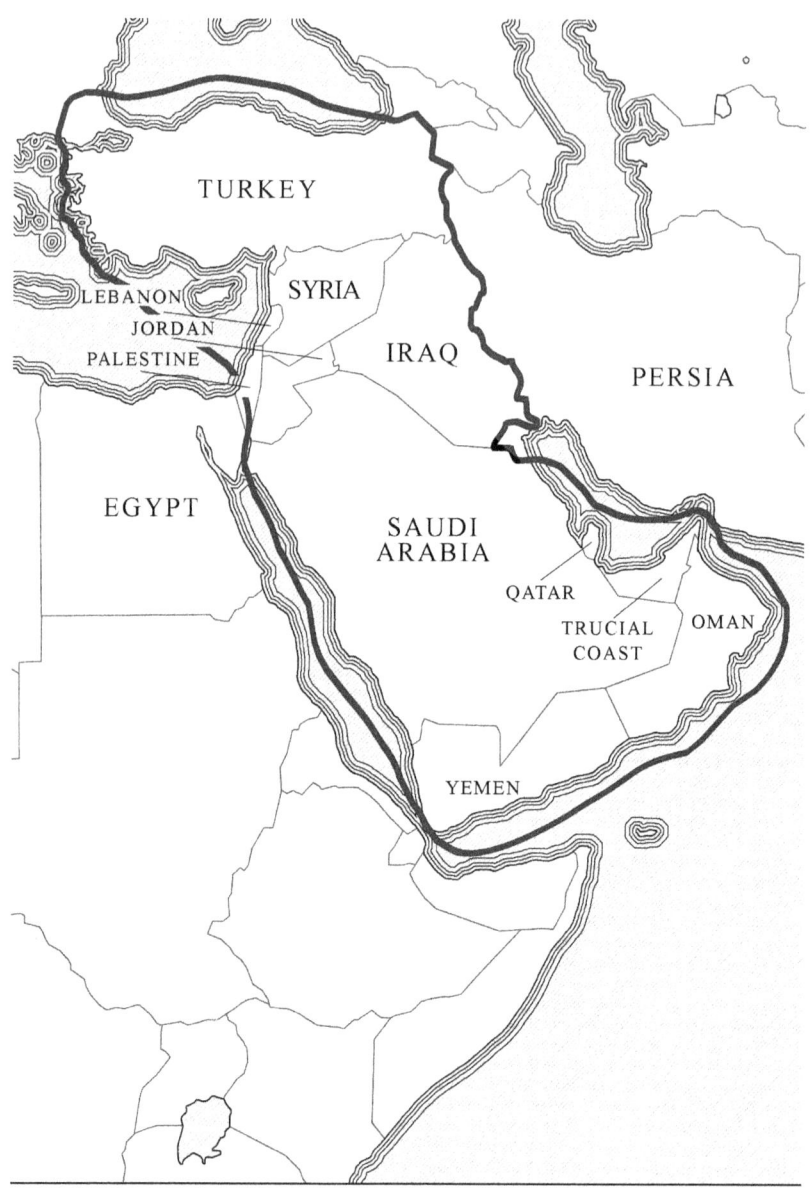

RED LINE AGREEMENT 1928

Red Line Agreement demrking Ottoman Territories (By Golbenkian) Agreement, 1928.

Agreement was made the same year, and "each of the four parties received a 23.75% share of all the crude oil produced by TPC (Turkish Petroleum Company, later called Iraq Petroleum Company), which was allowed to operate anywhere in the Middle East between the Suez Canal and Iran, with the exception of Kuwait."[107] It included a self-denying clause in which none of the signatories were permitted to independently seek oil interests anywhere in the ex-Ottoman Empire. It is said the magnate responsible for making the agreement, Calouste Gulbenkian, a Turkish-born British financier, industrialist, and millionaire, had drawn a red line on the map to delineate the Ottoman Empire when the other parties present had claimed they were uncertain of its exact boundaries.[108]

In the agreement Britain had promised the American oil companies a fair share of the oil industry—under a quarter of the shares. The remaining 5 percent went to Gulbenkian who, in 1911, had been instrumental in forming the Turkish Petroleum Company (later known as the Iraq Petroleum Company), and had become the first to exploit Iraqi oil; his 5% share had made him one of the world's richest men.[109]

By giving Americans a share of the oil revenues in the Red Line Agreement, Britain secured the upper hand in Iraq. The Turkish Petroleum Company, after the signing of the Red Line Agreement, was changed to the Iraq Petroleum Company, one that would always act according to Anglo-American interests.

The company would occupy a monopolistic position with Iraq's oil industry at the expense of Iraqis. Other companies, such as British Petroleum, Standard Oil of New Jersey, Shell and Mobil were set up

---

107 The 1928 Red Line Agreement 2018, Office of the Historian, accessed 5 October 2018, <https://history.state.gov/milestones/1921-1936/red-line>

108 Red Line Agreement," 2020, Encyclopedia of the Modern Middle East and North Africa, Encyclopedia.com, accessed 5 October 2017, <http://www.encyclopedia.com/humanities/encyclopedias-almanacs-transcripts-and-maps/red-line-agreement>

109 The Editors of Encyclopaedia Britannica, Calouste Gulbenkian 2020, Encyclopædia Britannica, accessed 25 January 2020, <https://www.britannica.com/biography/Calouste-Gulbenkian>

and, along with the Iraq Petroleum Company, monopolized Iraq's oil industry. This left nothing for the Iraqi people. In 1959 the Iraqis overthrew the ruling Hashemite monarchy (established by King Faisal—the 3rd son of Hussein, Grand Sharif of Makkah—in 1921 under the British), and in 1972 the Iraqi government nationalized the Iraq Petroleum Company.

Major Frank Holmes, Father of Oil
Major Frank Holmes, a New Zealander mining engineer, had been a pioneer in the exploration of oil in Arabia. Holmes, affectionately called "Abu Naft," (the Father of Oil) by Arabs, had gained global experience working in gold mines. In WWI he was a quartermaster for the British army, and as historian Daniel Yergin tells us in his book, *The Prize: The Epic Quest for Oil, Money & Power*, "…it was while on a beef-buying expedition in Addis Ababa in Ethiopia that he first heard from an Arab trader about oil seepages on the Arabian coast…"[110]

In 1918 journalist Aileen Keating tells us he had written to his wife in England.

> *"I personally believe that there will be developed an immense oil field running from Kuwait right down the mainland coast."* [111]

Two years later he established the Eastern and General Syndicate in London to develop oil ventures in the Middle East. "A promoter par excellence," Yergin says, " with a gift for making people believe in him, he traveled up and down the Arabian side of the Gulf…"[112] with hopes of obtaining an oil concession. He succeeded and secured a deal with Ibn Saud, then the king of the Najd region.

---

110   Yergin, Daniel; *The Prize: The Epic Quest for Oil, Money & Power*; Free Press, Div. of Simon & Schuster, New York, N.Y. 1991; Chapter 15, Pg. 263.

111   Keating, Aileen; *Mirage: Power, Politics, and the Hidden History of Arabian Oil*; Prometheus Books; Amherst, N.Y. Chapter 1 Pg. 57.

112   Yergin, Daniel; *The Prize: The Epic Quest for Oil, Money & Power*; Free Press, Div. of Simon & Schuster, New York, N.Y. 1991; Chapter 15, Pg 263-264.

Semm Yubah

The British had long exerted strong influence in the region, but when Sir Major Percy Cox, the British High Commissionaire who had provided financial support to Ibn Saud to help crush Ottoman influence, heard of Holmes' presence in the region, he was troubled. Cox was not at all keen on Ibn Saud striking an oil concession deal with any company other than APOC, (later British Petroleum), and he dissuaded Ibn Saud. During that same time an Arab-American intellectual, writer, and political activist, Lebanese born Ameen Rihani, was visiting Ibn Saud, and viewed Cox's plans as just more of Britain's imperialism. Rihani encouraged Ibn Saud to sign with Holmes, and Ibn Saud gave Holmes a concession to explore oil in the Al-Hasa region. In return Holmes agreed to pay an annual rental fee of £2,500 to Ibn Saud.

Exploration in the region began, and later Holmes hired Arnold Albert Heim, a prominent Swiss geologist, who had visited Arabia in 1924. After surveying the region for two years, Arnold reported the chances for oil in the region were next to impossible.

As a result Holmes discontinued paying the annual rental fee to Ibn Saud, and secretly put his oil operations on halt; however, he did not officially end the contract.

Bahrain
Disappointed with the lack of opportunity in Al-Hasa on the Arabian Peninsula, and unable to find a bidder for the Eastern and General Syndicate, Holmes focused his sights across the waters, on the small island of Bahrain where he eventually received an oil concession for exploration activities.

In 1925 Holmes had been awarded the concession as gratitude for drilling for artesian water wells for Bahrain's ruler Sheik Hamad Al Khalifa, who had been more concerned with finding water. In Bahrain, Holmes collected oil-rich rock samples that proved essential later. However, at the time the financial woes of his business were intensifying, prompting him to return to London in search of financial supporters for his oil endeavors but he was met with disdain and misgiving.

With no luck in London, he ventured across the Atlantic to the U.S. to seek out in his words, "the really big New York sheiks."[113]

Holmes, who now had produced a detailed and impressive geological report of his oil-rich rock samples, eventually captured the attention of the Gulf Oil Corporation. The company sent their geologist to Bahrain to confirm Holmes's findings and later gave the green light to immediately start oil drilling. By 1927, the Gulf Oil Corporation had agreed to accept Holmes' concessions and kept him on as manager of the Bahrain operation. However, in 1927 things became problematic for the company when the Turkish Petroleum Company underwent restructuring, which led to the formation of a consortium of several oil companies. These included the Royal Dutch-Shell, Anglo-Persian, the French Oil Company, and more—all organized by Calouste Gulbenkian, along with his 1928 famous Red Line Agreement. The Gulf Oil Corporation, a signatory of this agreement, was now forced to comply (with its stipulation of no oil exploration and production activities within the defined territory, independent of the Iraq Petroleum Company), and it affected its operations in Bahrain. Gulbenkian was not interested in oil exploration in Bahrain, and the Gulf Oil Corporation sold its oil concession to the Standard Oil of California (SoCal) for $50,000.

In 1929 SoCal set up a Canadian subsidiary, BapCo (Bahrain Petroleum Company) and, with Britain's approval, carried out operations in the region.

BapCo kept Holmes as head of oil exploration in Bahrain and in 1931 started drilling operations on *Jabal al Dukhan*—Bahrain's

---

[113] Yergin, Daniel; The Prize: The Epic Quest for Oil, Money & Power; Free Press, Div. of Simon & Schuster, New York, N.Y. 1991; Chapter 15, Pg 265 Daniel Yergin 2012, The Prize, accessed June 2017, <http://bit.ly/37IVhCU>

'Mountain of Smoke'—and the following year they witnessed their first gusher—light crude oil with a capacity of 9,600 barrels per day.

By 1934, Bahrain's oil production had risen to 285,000 barrels, sufficient to start exporting. Later, in 1952, an agreement was signed granting the Bahrain government 50 percent concession for every barrel of oil produced, after which Bahrain had an oil production capacity of 11 million barrels per year.

Bahrain's rise to fortune prompted many to wonder what hidden treasures lay 12 miles away across the sea and hidden deep beneath the scorching desert sands of the Arabian Peninsula.

Kuwait

News of Bahrain's success had reached Kuwait. Until 1930, Kuwait earned profitable revenue from its prestigious pearl fisheries, but the price of natural pearls drastically decreased with the advent and mass production of Mikimoto's cultured pearls from Japan. The Emir of Kuwait, Sheikh Ahmed Al-Jaber Al Sabah, was now in dire financial straits and desperate for his country to follow in the footsteps of its Arab neighbor, Bahrain.

The Gulf Oil Corporation, a signatory of the Red Line agreement, kept its eye on Kuwait, which had not been restricted by the agreement, and knew it was free to operate in the country. But Kuwait was still under British influence, and any contract with the American Gulf Oil Company meant going against Britain's interests.

Both the British-controlled Anglo-Persian and the American Gulf Oil approached Kuwait's Emir between 1930 and 1932 for an oil concession in the region. The Emir, hoping for the best deal, decided to play them off of each other but was more inclined to sign with Gulf. Holmes realized then that it would help them both if Gulf and the Anglo-Persian Company united and became one prospective buyer, and they opted to establish a 50-50 joint venture—the Kuwait Oil Company—and offered the Sheik one deal.

On December 23, 1934 Sheikh Ahmad signed an oil concession (covering the entire 15,800 square kilometers of Kuwait for 75 years) to the newly formed Kuwait Oil Company and appointed Major Holmes as his representative in London.[114]

A year later, oil exploration began in Kuwait, and the first oil well spudded in 1936 in Bahra but the well was dry. Kuwait Oil initiated a second location, discovering oil in substantial quantities in the Burgan field in southeastern Kuwait in 1938 with the potential for more than 4,000 barrels per day, and in 1946, it exported its first crude oil cargo.

The Kuwait Oil Company was fully nationalized by the end of 1975. The Kuwaiti government set up the Kuwait Petroleum Corporation (KPC) to unify all four of the country's oil producing companies. Today, the KPC manages operations across six continents and its subsidiary is the fourth largest oil producer in the world.

Arabian Oil and Jack Philby
Another major character was about to take center stage in the quest for oil on the Arabian Peninsula. Jack Philby, a former colonial intelligence officer in the British government's Civil Service, explorer, cartographer, naturalist, and Arabist, was the leading authority on the peninsula, and a devoted friend to Ibn Saud. Philby, deeply entrenched in the Arab culture, had converted to Islam, and had been given the Muslim name, Abdullah by Ibn Saud. Philby would play a pivotal role in helping Saudi Arabia.

In 1932, with Ibn Saud's newly established kingdom of Saudi Arabia still facing tough economic times, the king was desperate to alleviate the dire conditions of his people, and turned to his close friend, Philby, for advice.

---

114 Rasoul Sorkhabi, Ph.D. 2008, The Emergence of the Arabian Oil Industry, GeoExPro, accessed July 2018,, <http://www.geoexpro.com/articles/2008/06/the-emergence-of-the-arabian-oil-industry>

Semm Yubah

Philby loathed British colonialism and had been an outspoken critic of their policy, despite being a former worker in the Indian Civil Service, and had retired from his government position to pursue his other interests. He made his home in northwestern Arabia, a port city on the Red Sea that served as gateway to the holy city of Makkah, in a town called Jeddah, where he became known as a prolific writer and explorer.

In the 1950's Pulitzer prize winning author Wallace Stegner writes about the old city of Jeddah (sometimes spelled Jiddah) in his book *Arabian Discovery*, (the story of Aramco, later serialized in *Aramco World)*[115] as only he can:

In 1933 Jiddah still presented to the sea its ancient, unreal facade. Tightly concentrated, surprisingly tall, it sprang up on the barren shore, squared by the wall that Steve Bechtel's bulldozers would one day push down. Its four- or five-story buildings with their cutout arches of windows and their ranks of ornate balconies might have been made of sticks and pasteboard; or it might have been a child's city of blocks knocked out of plumb. It looked, said one traveler, like a city that had slept on its feet for ages but had been prevented from lying down to sleep properly.

In the old town, in those days, the walls leaned together over alleys barely wide enough for two donkeys to pass; the warped, carved, weathered balconies all but touched. Minarets tilted dizzily and the whole town sagged and slouched on foundations gradually sinking into the unconsolidated coral sand. In its crooked enduring way it looked as ancient as Genesis, and some thought it was.

Around Jiddah the shore could only be Arabia—pale, seared, discharged of color, treeless, spotted with sparse shrubs. The land

---

115 Wallace Stegner 1968, Discovery! The Story Of Aramco Then, Aramco World, accessed May 2018, <http://archive.aramcoworld.com/issue/196801/discovery.the.story.of.aramco.then-chapter.1.contact.htm>

flows down from the distorted rim of mountains to the mirage-like margins of the Red Sea, where beaches grade imperceptibly into coral bottoms and barely covered reefs and the gradually deepening waters mottled in scallops and bays of tan, near-white, emerald, finally blue.

In Jeddah, Philby became a partner in a trading company, and later the unofficial adviser of Ibn Saud, (although they first met back in 1917 in Riyadh). But even before the establishment of Saudi Arabia in 1932, Philby had suggested to Ibn Saud that he explore his kingdom for oil, and introduced him to an American philanthropist, businessman, and millionaire—Charles R. Crane, an irrigation expert.

Ibn Saud, like his counterpart in Bahrain, had been more interested in artesian water wells than oil, and Crane commissioned an engineer, Karl Twitchell, to explore the region for water resources as well as oil and minerals.

In 1931 Twitchell was sent to Jeddah where he checked existing and potential water sources, then set out on a 1,500-mile expedition to the north, a trip that Twinchell's wife described as "extraordinary....There was no sign of life. There wasn't a blade of grass. There was nothing - not even an ant. And sheer silence."[116]

But to Crane's disappointment, Twitchell's 1932 report was not at all promising as far as the likelihood of finding artesian waters. However, his report for oil prospects in the Al-Hasa region was far more optimistic. Excited by the news, Ibn Saud commissioned Twitchell to go to the U.S. and invite American oil companies to start oil exploration activities, prompting a new relationship between the United States and Saudi Arabia, but at the expense of the British.

After Twitchell's U.S. visit, Philby received a letter from an advisor of SoCal, Francis Loomis, for an oil concession settlement

---

[116] Paul Lunde 1984, A King and a Concession, Aramco World, accessed May 2018, <http://archive.aramcoworld.com/issue/198403/a.king.and.a.concession.htm>

with Ibn Saud. SoCal, aware of Twitchell's personal connection with Ibn Saud, hired him as an advisor and commissioned him along with their lawyer, Lloyd Hamilton, to strike an oil concession deal. In February, 1933, Twitchell and Hamilton arrived with their wives in Jeddah via ship and had contacted Philby for a meeting with Ibn Saud. But they found that such an agreement would not happen overnight.

At the same time, the British expressed keen interest in receiving

Mr. Abdullah Sulaiyman, Saudi Finance Minister, & Mr. Llyod N. Hamilton, lawyer & negotiator for Socal, signing the historic oil concession agreement; Khuzam Palace, Jeddha, May 29, 1933.

an oil concession from Ibn Saud. Philby asked British-influenced Anglo-Persian and Iraqi Petroleum companies to commission an oil bid negotiator. The British sent Stephen Helmsley Longrigg, but Philby discovered he was not willing to pay more than £6,000 in concessions. The Americans, on the other hand, were willing to pay a great deal more.

After three and a half months of lengthy negotiations, the Americans won the concession, and were now involved in the exploration of oil on the Arabian Peninsula. Ibn Saud signed an agreement with SoCal, with the company paying an upfront fee of £35,000 along with other payments in multiple installments, and the company was awarded an oil concession for 60 years.

Discovery of oil in Dammam
Following its meeting with Ibn Saud, SoCal set up a subsidiary, California Arabian Standard Oil Company (CASOC) in 1933 to drill for oil in the newly formed Saudi Arabia. CASOC wasted no time and sent a team of geologists to the eastern city of Dammam—Robert P. (Bert) Miller, Schuler B. (Krug) Henry, Art Brown, Thomas Koch, Hugh Burchfield, and Soak Hoover. Among the first geologists were Bert Miller and Krug Henry who travelled via dhow from Bahrain and, dressed in the native clothes of Arabia, arrived on the shores of Jubail, my grandfather's town.

Pioneers at Jubail Headquarters, left to right: Max Steineke, J.W. Hoover, H.L. Burchfiel, A.B. Brown, Schuyler B. "Krug" Henry, W. Burleigh, T.W. Koch, Robert P. "Bert" Miller, Felix W. Dreyfus, R.C. Kerr; Jubail, 1934.

Semm Yubah

It hadn't taking long for the word to spread that American geologists were sailing on a dhow from Bahrain for their city in hopes of finding oil. Wallace Stegner writes:

"On shore were gathered robed throngs of people, throngs who obviously represented more than the normal population of the town. As they stepped out to be greeted by the local Amir and the soldiers who were to form their compulsory escort, they learned that several dignitaries from Jubail and Qatif, the big oasis down the coast, had come to greet them too, as well as many Bedouins from the hinterlands. All apparently were planning a big celebration of welcome.

Miller and Henry, however, had other plans and after paying the proper courtesy calls and drinking the appropriate number of cups of coffee, they spotted a Jabal to the south and learning that it was called al-Jabal al-Barri, piled into the two touring cars that Twitchell had rented from the government in Jiddah and driven across country for their use. If they had hoped to discourage the holiday spirit of the crowds they were

Standing by the car are geologists Hoover & Henry,
Bert Miller is by the second car, 1935.

disappointed. Everyone climbed aboard camels and white al-Hasa donkeys, and streamed after them."[117]

Escorted by Saudi soldiers and guides, they set out for their work and quickly decided that they needed a place of operation, and chose Jubail to set up one of their offices. "It was, by comparison with Qatif and Hofuf, a cool and breezy town, and it had a fair port for the landing of supplies from Bahrain."[118]

When Bert Miller and Krug Henry inspected those nearby rugged hills after their arrival in Jubail, Miller reportedly later said "... we knew then, in just a few minutes, it was like a copy of Bahrain Island."[119]

Abdulrahman had been among the first people gathered to welcome the geologists when they arrived in Jubail to extend his hospitality, offering accommodations and food. The American team had appreciated his kindness, and as a token of their gratitude and good will, they helped him buy and install the very first ice-making machine. In fact, Kansas-born Bill Eltiste—pioneer driller on the Arabian peninsula, rig maker, wildcatter and inventor of the device that helped extinguish one of the oil fires, and who was a very good man—had installed the ice maker at Abdulrahman's house in Jubail. An ice maker was a huge leap forward in life's comforts—it was simply not available then and was considered a supreme luxury—one certainly not available to the locals of Jubail. It was a very big deal, making ice at home in 1937 Saudi Arabia, and my grandfather had spoken highly of the geologists and engineers who had helped our family. My father, Abdulaziz, was 8 years old when Eltiste had installed it and thought it resembled a rocket, at least that's how

---

117 Wallace Stegner 1968, Discovery! The Story Of Aramco Then, Aramco World, accessed 12 June 2017, <http://archive.aramcoworld.com/issue/196803/discovery.the.story.of.aramco.then-chapter.3.beachhead.htm>.

118 Ibid.

119 Mary Norton1988, Well Done, Well Seven, Aramco World, accessed 8 July 2017, <http://archive.aramcoworld.com/issue/198803/well.done.well.seven.htm>

he described it to me. He was very impressed with Eltiste's skills. As a child he believed Eltiste possessed some magical or divine powers, getting a machine to mysteriously produce ice. Eltiste and my grandfather had become fast friends, and their friendship lasted for over 10 years. Eltiste was the man who would later advise my grandfather about investing in a water drill.

The American engineers and geologists also offered to help buy pickup trucks and radios for the Governor of Jubail as well as Abdulrahman and other leading merchants in town. It was a luxury that allowed them to listen to the BBC news and keep track of developments in their region and other parts of the world.

The American geologists and engineers and the townspeople of Jubail developed strong ties, which grew into lasting friendship. Again, Wallace Stegner writes:

> *The Americans were energetic and enthusiastic, knew their geology and went about their work as if they were in Colorado. The Amir of Jubail, the qadi, the guides, the soldiers, were friendly. Cautiously, visitors and residents explored each other's peculiarities. It was surprising to both sides to find that Arabs and Americans laughed in the same places; it was at first a possible irritation and later a basis for respect when the Americans found Saudi Arabs tough, independent, and disinclined to give in in an argument, and the Saudis found Americans more willing to fraternize than the British....*
>
> *They watched carefully to avoid friction with their Arab helpers, and did their level best to be charitable when some Arab customs jarred their sense of logic. They practiced their Arabic on children and soldiers and houseboys and visitors from the towns, drank pots of sweet tea and cardamom-flavored coffee and learned not to use the left hand in eating. Finding Arabs like other people elsewhere, they learned to like some of them better than others, and they made some progress toward knowing themselves and the country in which they worked.*[120]

---

120 Ibid.

Pioneers Robert P. "Bert" Miller & Richard C. "Dick" Kerr standing in front of the Fairchild airplane, Jubail, 1935.

Eventually after surface mapping, aerial reconnaissance, surveying and drilling, they discovered what became known as the Dammam Dome, 8 kilometers away from the region's famous port village and which the locals called Jabal Dhahran.

Camp at Salwah, left to right: Tom C. Barger, Walter H. Hoag, Max Steineke, & T.F. Hariss; Salwah, December, 1937.

Semm Yubah

In 1934, CASOC conducted aerial mapping of the region of the Dammam dome with a Fairchild 71 airplane manned by geologist Dick Kerr. However, oil would not be discovered until they sent the highly skilled and experienced geologist, a big, burly man named Max Steineke, to join the team in Saudi Arabia. A

Steineke takes time to be alone on a sand dune, 1935.

graduate of Stanford University with an AB geology degree, he had considerable experience exploring for oil in California, Canada, Alaska, New Zealand, and Columbia. In 1936, he would become SOCAL's chief geologist, a position which he held until 1946, and the man responsible—along with his team—for discovering oil in well #7 in Dammam, Saudi Arabia.

The process of mapping rocky hillocks went on for many months in the concession region, until Steineke with his team of geologists finally began drilling in Dammam #1, their first well. However, his hopes of having any major breakthrough dimmed in 1935 after the well had passed through the "Bahrain Zone" and showed only slight indication of oil and gas reserves.

Photos 1 & 2: Ten minutes after the explosion, the derrick lurched downward toward the funnel of smoke (Stegner in ***Discovery***, July, 1939).
Photo 3: Close-up of melted rig and fire, Dhahran, July, 1939.

Semm Yubah

After closing the first well, he and his team of geologists drilled a second, Dammam #2 in 1936, but to their disappointment, it contained only salty water. Still Steineke was undaunted and trusted his intuition, and with his team kept their efforts strong. They drilled the Dammam #3, which did show signs of oil. Both Number 4 and Number 5 were dry. Number 6 was never explored because Steineke believed that there was a better site that showed promising signs of considerable oil reserves—Dammam #7.

In December 1936, a deep test site was chosen, since Steineke preferred testing deeper oil zones. In the spring of the following year, a residential community of air-conditioned cottages was developed for the American families of the geologists working there.

Drilling at the deep test site started on December 31, 1937, but a major accident occurred. The oil well blew out, and the rig was catapulted high into the air. This was terrible news for Steineke and his team as well as CASOC impatient and concerned about the money they were losing by the day, and for Ibn Saud who needed an alternate source of income besides those received from the Hajj pilgrimage season. All efforts came to a halt, and Steineke was asked to return to San Francisco.

Steineke was not someone who gave up easily, stalwart in his convictions that there was Arabian oil. While he was in California trying to persuade his company to continue with the operation, he received word that his prediction was, indeed, true when they found what they were looking for in Well #7. He returned to Saudi Arabia and instructed his team to dig deeper. And on March 4, 1938, after three years, Steineke finally saw his vision realized. More than 1500 barrels of black gold were discovered, what Ibn Saud and SoCal had been waiting for so long. By the end of the first week, over 3000 barrels of oil were being produced daily. Success was met with more success, and production reached more than 12,000 barrels per day by the end of the month.

Mr. Harriss & Hoag party moving from Jubail to Musa Llamiyah; Eastern Province, 1936.

The following year, a small oil refinery was built at the eastern port of Ras Tanura located at the tip of a small peninsula, and a pipeline was installed from its port to the Dammam field. Now that Saudi Arabia was producing thousands of barrels per day, export was an inevitable outcome.

On the 1st of May, 1939, Ibn Saud made a special visit to the Ras Tanura port to mark the beginning of the first export of oil cargos. By the end of the year, Saudi Arabia's oil export sales amassed to nearly 4 million barrels. The success of the oil drill headed by Steineke led SoCal to negotiate new terms of the agreement. It successfully extended its concession area by nearly 310 kilometers in return for a payment of £140,000 in gold and an increase of the annual rental fee to £25,000. In addition, £100,000 was also promised the Saudi government if new oil was discovered in the concession area.

Britain and Saudi Arabia: The ending of the colonial relationship

A few years later, after the establishment of ARAMCO in 1944, tensions developed between Ibn Saud and the British, and marked a shift of regional influence from the British to the Americans. The relationship between Ibn Saud and the British had first officially developed with the signing of the Treaty at Darin in 1915.

The British for many years had a significant role in helping Ibn Saud rise to power through military and financial support and also in the establishment of the kingdom of Saudi Arabia.

King Abdulaziz during his first visit to Aramco in 1939 is shown over oil installation by Floyd W. Ohliger; Dhahran, May, 1939.

However, the discovery of oil in Dammam replaced British colonialism with American capitalism, leading to a rise in American influence in the region. But now Saudi Arabia was on the road to becoming one of the world's powerhouses.

CHAPTER 9

WWII and Oil Supremacy

As the thirties were drawing to a close, the world was on the verge of yet another war that proved to be one of the pivotal events of the 20th century, one that left an indelible imprint on the people who survived.

The Great War had demonstrated the need for massive amounts of oil and all its by-products. No one doubted its importance as an asset, and that it was vital to a growing economy, indispensable during wartime, and one of the most powerful fuels of its time. In the years leading up to WWII with political tensions mounting, Saudi Arabia, although still an underdeveloped country, found itself in the middle of a power struggle since it was strategically located between the east and west. And, of course, it possessed vast oil reserves.[121]

Germany and its ally, Japan, with no indigenous oil reserves and thus dependent on foreign sources for its supply, had showed increasing interest in acquiring concessions in the Middle East. Both had sent delegations to Jeddah but failed to secure any.[122]

---

[121] Aramco Publications, accessed 24 November 2017, <http://www.saudiaramco.com/content/dam/Publications/Energy%20to%20the%20World%20-%20English/Vol-1-Chapter-4.pdf>

[122] Wallace Stegner 1969, Discovery! The Story Of Aramco Then, Aramco World, accessed 15 February 2017, <http://archive.aramcoworld.com/issue/196902/discovery.the.story.of.aramco.then-chapter.8.into.production.htm>

Hunger for oil would influence Germany's decision to invade Russia in 1941,[123] as well as Japan's to bomb Pearl Harbor. (Prior to WWII Japan had imported most of their oil and other raw materials from the U.S. but President Roosevelt, in an attempt to curb Japan's imperialistic expansionism, had implemented economic sanctions and trade embargoes—which involved cutting off oil—after Japan, searching for more reserves, had declared war on China, one of America's allies.)[124]

Anarchy soon became rampant in Europe and food was scarce as well as hope for a better tomorrow. Hitler had succeeded in harnessing his country's frustrations over its failing economy, "a weaker and poorer country in 1939 that it had been in 1914,"[125] and just before dawn on September 1, 1939, he ignited the global conflict. With no warning, no declaration of war, Hitler's *Luftwaffe* bombed Polish airfields, his *Kriegsmarine* attacked the Polish Navy in the Baltic Sea, and 1.5 million German troops stormed Poland.[126]

The massive invasion had propelled Britain and France to rush to Poland's defense under the terms of the 1918 Treaty of Versailles, and fight as allies the rising Nazi threat. After three weeks, however, Germany defeated Poland and expanded its hegemony invading Norway and Denmark, then the Netherlands, Luxembourg, and Belgium, and on May 10, 1940, the Nazis invaded France. By June 21st, the French Prime

---

123 Oil - Oil and world power 2014, American Foreign Relations, accessed 24 November 2017, <http://www.americanforeignrelations.com/O-W/Oil-Oil-and-world-power.html>

124 Pearl Harbor 2009, History.Com, accessed October 2017, <http://www.history.com/topics/world-war-ii/pearl-harbor>

125 David Frum 2014, The Real Story of How America Became an Economic Superpower, The Atlantic, accessed January 2018, <https://www.theatlantic.com/international/archive/2014/12/the-real-story-of-how-america-became-an-economic-superpower/384034/>

126 1939: Germany invades Poland, On This Day 2005, BBC News, accessed March 2017, <http://news.bbc.co.uk/onthisday/hi/dates/stories/september/1/newsid_3506000/3506335.stm>

Minister Marshall Philippe Pétain had ceded three-fifths of French territory to German control,[127] and at the end of the war, had been tried for treason and sentenced to death but Charles De Gaulle commuted his sentence to life in prison.[128]

In April, 1941 Hitler had launched his forces further east, infiltrating the Balkan countries of Yugoslavia and Greece, and a few months later, the Soviet Union. When Japan, Germany's ally, bombed Pearl Harbor on Sunday morning, December 7th, 1941 in an attempt to destroy the Pacific fleet, the attack ended the debate about U.S. involvement in the war.

The global military conflict lasted 6 long years between the Axis Powers—Germany, Japan, Italy, Romania, and Bulgaria—and the Allies—the United Kingdom, the United States, USSR, France, Belgium, China, Australia, Norway, New Zealand, Canada, Africa, Denmark, Netherlands, Greece, Yugoslavia, and several other countries. The battles between these two military alliances were waged with greater brutality and intensity than the First World War, and ended with the killing of over 60 million people approximately 40 million were civilians, some historians estimating15 to 20 million[129] were killed in Hitler's concentration camps, and more in Japan's and Mussolini's. The casualties of WWII were nearly three times greater than the 20 million fatalities that occurred during the Great War.

Despite the war consuming the western world, the seaport city of Jubail on the Gulf, the home of my grandfather and family, had remained unscathed. It was far enough away from the fighting in Europe but close to the British Navy stationed in British-controlled Bahrain. Still, my grandfather and the residents of

---

127 Blitzkrieg 2011, History, BBC News, accessed January 2017, <http://www.bbc.co.uk/history/worldwars/wwtwo/blitzkrieg_01.shtml>

128 Henri-Philippe Pétain 2018, History.com Editors, <http://www.history.com/this-day-in-history/marshal-petain-becomes-premier-of-occupied-france>

129 Matthew Day 2013, The Telegraph Article, Business Insider, accessed 6 August 2018, <http://www.businessinsider.com/shocking-new-holocaust-study-claims-nazis-killed-up-to-20-million-people-2013-3>

Semm Yubah

Jubail never dismissed a German threat. The British Navy, after all, had been engaged in intense warfare with Germany and the other Axis countries. If Britain's authority weakened, a German invasion of Jubail, only a few hours from Bahrain, was not improbable. The recent discovery of Saudi oil had made the region a highly coveted military resource.

To prevent an attack by any Axis power, Saudi Arabia did its best to contain talk about the discovery of its oil reserves, as advised by the American companies with concessions there. The U.S. had not entered the war yet, but the discovery of oil in commercial quantities in Dammam #7 well in 1938 had already given Saudi Arabia strategic prominence, and the American companies as well as the Allies were acutely aware of it. When war broke out in Europe, the American geologists living and working in eastern Arabia at California-Arabian Standard Oil Co. (CASOC) had heard about Germany's and Japan's recent efforts to obtain oil concessions in the region. As a precaution, they sent staff into the desert to search for German infiltration but never found evidence of it. There was, however, one incident that occurred later and had prompted concern.

On October 18, 1940 Mussolini had ordered four Italian bomber planes to fly to the British protectorate of Bahrain to destroy its oil refinery and cut off its flow of oil to the Royal Navy.[130] At 3 o'clock the next morning the bombers finally reached Bahrain.

Wallace Stegner, in his book, *Discovery: The Story of Aramco Then*, sets the pre-dawn scene:

> *The night of October 19, 1940. The sky is full of light from a late three-quarter moon, the purity of its cup is broken only by one trailing film of cloud, the stars are pale but very many. Over the Gulf, where sometimes a heavy fish splashes in water still as oil, the lower air is faintly pearly. Bahrain lies afloat, its houses*

---

130 William E. Mulligan 1976, Air Raid! A Sequel, Aramco World, accessed 20 July 2018, <http://archive.aramcoworld.com/issue/197604/air.raid.a.sequel.htm>

Adel Alsuhaimi

dark, the crocked alleys of Manama blackly rutted among the moon-white walls. Only the refinery blazes with light, a hub at the center of lighted spokes of roads, throwing its harder, brighter, five-and-dime glitter back at the softer glitter of the stars and the cooling metal of the moon. Five hundred yards to one side, the gas flares gush flame.[131]

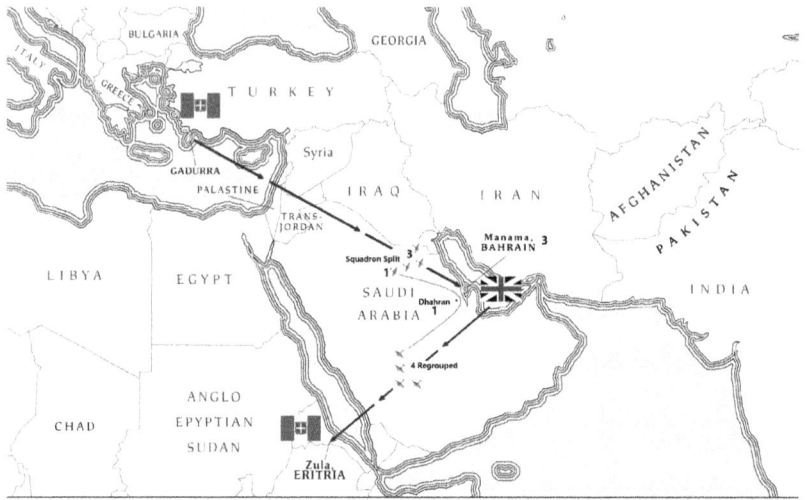

ITALIAN BOMBERS RAID ON BAHRAIN AND SAUDI ARABIA 1940

Italian bombers air-raid route to bomb Bahrain refinery, which supplies the British Navy, 03:00, October 19, 1940.

Somehow one of the planes found itself separated from its squadron and ended up off course—approximately 30 miles west of Bahrain—the pilot flying over Saudi Arabia's Dhahran and releasing his deadly cargo there. The other three remained on target for their mission. Bombs detonated over Bahrain and Dhahran and ignited the sky. Collectively, the four Italian planes had dropped two or three-dozen small 50-pound fragmentation bombs on Dhahran and more than 80 on Bahrain, but, surprisingly, they did

---

131 Wallace Stegner 1970, DISCOVERY! The Story of Aramco, Then, Aramco World, accessed 17 August 2017, <http://archive.aramcoworld.com/issue/197001/discovery.the.story.of.aramco.then-chapter.12.air.raid.htm>

little damage, and did not disrupt the production of oil. My great uncle Mohammad resided in Bahrain at the time but none of my elders had ever discussed the incident with him, or at least none that are still living, so unfortunately, I missed the opportunity of his first-hand account. Interestingly enough, Bill Eltiste, the same pioneer driller who had helped my grandfather install the icemaker in Jubail before the war, had been stationed in Dhahran during the bombings, and it was his job along with a colleague to dispose of all the duds the following day.[132]

By the time the sun rose on October 19th, it had been evident that the Italian planes had completely missed the refinery. (Although Italian radio broadcasters announced the mission had been a success and the refinery completely destroyed.) The pilots had targeted the bright orange gas flares but, unbeknownst to them, the flares had been relocated farther away from the refinery only days before. Still, the aerial bombardment had unnerved enough people and highlighted the need for heightened alertness and increased security, [133]and, as a result, some expats had sent their wives and children back to the states.

In the years following, a team of American geologists maintained a presence in Saudi Arabia to ensure the safety of the concession—an area that covered the eastern region, stretching from the Al Hasa Gulf to the deep interior, as far west as Najd. When Pearl Harbor was attacked, and the U.S. officially entered the war, many Americans left Arabia to serve in their military, and the Americans work force at the oil companies decreased to a skeleton crew of a hundred. Production had to be scaled back, but the Hundred Men, as they came to be known, still supported the allied war efforts with the aid of Arabian oil.

---

[132] Wallace Stegner 1970, DISCOVERY! The Story of Aramco, Then, Aramco World, accessed 16 August 2017, <http://archive.aramcoworld.com/issue/197001/discovery.the.story.of.aramco.then-chapter.12.air.raid.htm>

[133] William E. Mulligan 1976, Air Raid! A Sequel, Aramco World, accessed November 2017, <http://archive.aramcoworld.com/issue/197604/air.raid.a.sequel.htm>

Adel Alsuhaimi

Ibn Saud decided to halt any further oil exploration activities as long as Hitler was on his quest to conquer nations under Germany's Nazi flag, and ARAMCO discontinued its oil drilling activities. Arabian oil was just too much of a temptation.

Saleh's Reunion

As the war raged on, its effect began to ripple across Saudi Arabia, and the ongoing conflicts of warring tribes had only exacerbated it. Transporting food to the heart of the country became difficult. Saudi Arabia had grown dependent on food imports and the war caused a disruption of its supplies, especially after 1943 when rice from India and Burma were cut off. In addition, local crops suffered from severe droughts, and famine became inevitable.[134] Public health declined, with disease—malaria, tuberculosis, smallpox, malnutrition, and other illnesses—continuing to be an Arabian misery.

Group photo of family reunion after relocating to Jubail, 1946, left to right (standing): Grandfather Abdulrahman, his half-brother Ibrahim, his son Abdulaziz, his half-brother Abdullah. Sitting (center): Great-Grandfather Saleh Alsuhaimi; left to right (sitting): grandsons Sulaiman & Khalid.

By 1945, the Najd region had been ravaged by epidemic. So it had seemed biblical that the farmers' ancient enemy would next plague them. Locals referred to 1945 as the Year of the Locusts, having witnessed dense swarms shuttering Saudi Arabia's skies, devouring all the vegetation in its path. My grandfather's hometown of Unayzah and the rest of the Najd region had not been spared, and had experienced the same whirring and rasping sounds, the

---

134 Wallace Stegner 1970, DISCOVERY! The Story of Aramco, Then, Aramco World, accessed 16 August 2017, <http://archive.aramcoworld.com/issue/197002/discovery.the.story.of.aramco.then-chapter.13.the.time.of.the.hundred.men.htm>

Semm Yubah

blackening clouds closing in as the locust ate its weight in plants each day. These "desert locust," travelled great distances, gaining speed as they progressed, even banding together with other swarms, consuming crops and devastating the land, threatening famine in its wake.[135] It is said that "a desert locust swarm can be 460 square miles in size and pack between 40 and 80 million locusts into less than half a square mile."[136]

My great-grandfather, Saleh, had been still living in Unayzah then with his new family. (He had married twice since the death of first wife in 1918, and had other children from his third marriage.) His home had remained Unayzah, except for his brief stay in Kuwait when he had schooled Abdulrahman in the trade. On occasion he had traveled to Kuwait to see his son and for business, and Abdulrahman's had always pleaded with him to move to Jubail, citing Unayzah's unpredictability and unrest as strong reasons for relocating, claiming it was no longer a viable place for him and the family. Saleh had refused, unwilling to even consider his son's requests. Nothing Abdulrahman said could convince him to abandon his beloved Unayzah and uproot his family. He had spent his entire life there—from young boy to old man. He had been married there, raised his children there, and still enjoyed the company of old friends. Even the thought of leaving prompted angst.

Still, the mercurial times of recent years had not been kind, and the Year of the Locusts with its destructive swarms had been one challenge too many. Saleh was no longer in his prime and didn't have the stamina to tolerate hours of manual labor, and his ability to earn a living had greatly declined. The circumstances of

---

135 Richard Hobson and John Lawton 1987, New Battle in an Ancient War, Aramco World, accessed June 2018, <http://archive.aramcoworld.com/issue/198703/new.battle.in.an.ancient.war.htm>

136 Locusts 2015, National Geographic Society, accessed March 2017, <http://www.nationalgeographic.com/animals/invertebrates/group/locusts/>

the changing times had finally forced his hand, and in 1946 when WWII ended, Saleh, despite his reluctance, had agreed at 82 to move, *inshaa Allah*, with his family to Jubail.

Abdulrahman couldn't have felt more blessed. At forty-seven he would once again be reunited with his father. Still he had understood the enormity of Saleh's decision. His father had been an extremely proud man, and it had been difficult to admit he was incapable of working endless hours. Now he would have to depend on his son. He was giving up not just his native home but his role as head of the household.

I realize that there will come a time when I will have a similar scenario with my own family, when age will impose its limits. It is a profound experience—an elderly parent surrendering responsibility to an adult child–one that is universal and crosses divides, making no exceptions for gender, race or creed.

Still, Saleh was practical above anything else, and his pragmatism made him take a cold, hard look at what the future would hold for him and his family if they stayed in Unayzah. His levelheadedness won over nostalgia, and he wrote to Abdulrahman. He would spend his final years with his son and grandchildren, and, of course, now he would get the chance to regale them with his war stories.

In 1891 my great-grandfather, at 25, fought in the Battle of Mulaydah, alongside his tribesmen from Najd and Qasim against Ibn Rasheed, ruler of the kingdom at Ḥāʼil.[137] They lost, unfortunately, and my great-grandfather returned home severely injured, a bullet piercing his belt and lodging deep in his abdomen where it remained until his death. He never wanted it surgically removed, fearful he wouldn't survive the procedure. The injury had permanently impaired his gait. Still, he was proud that it had been earned protecting his homeland and displayed his scar to any willing audience. He had relished recounting his youthful days fighting for

---

[137] Battle of Al-Mulaydah 2012, Encyclopedia Brittanica, accessed 15 December 2017, <https://www.britannica.com/event/Battle-of-al-Mulaydah>

Semm Yubah

Ibn Saud long before the kingdom's unification, and he brandished his sword with theatrical flair to the delight of all his grandchildren. To this day the sword is displayed in a place of honor in the living room of one of his granddaughters.

Abdulrahman, a dutiful son, had withstood the intense heat and flies, the shamals blowing sand and dust, and traveled the distance west across the desert in a rented half-lorry to Unayzah. He packed the family's belongings and transported them back to the safer and more prosperous city of Jubail, and headquarters to the American oil companies.

My great Uncle Ibrahim (Abdulrahman's half-brother by Saleh's second marriage) was sixteen when they made the trip, his first time travelling outside of Unayzah, and the journey had left quite an impression. He remembered clearly the searing sun and desert glare, the endless stretches of sand and sky, the Bedouins weathered faces staring out from low-slung tents, herds of scraggly black goats, the white Hassawi donkeys with their hennaed dots, but he was most impressed with Abdulrahman. He had never seen a more devoted son. Abdulrahman had doted on his father and attended all his needs, making certain of his comfort, not an easy feat given the journey of nearly 700 kilometers of harsh and barren terrain they had to traverse. The trip through the desert had lasted a week in unbearable heat, the truck occasionally getting stuck in the sand, sometimes sinking deep into those muddy sabkhas (a salt flat,

Great-Grandfather Saleh Alsuhaimi attending to family farm, west of Jubail, 1948.

a sticky mixture of briny water and sand that can prove disastrous for heavy trucks in the desert). Every time the truck got stuck–and it did and often–my grandfather and his brothers jumped out and push it to get any traction but they always kept Saleh safely seated in the lorry.

Whenever they'd stop to rest or for prayers or to set up camp, Abdulrahman guided Saleh out of the high lorry cab, making a cradle of his hands as a makeshift step. No one else had been permitted to attend to Saleh, even though Abdulrahman had hired laborers from Jubail to assist with the trip. A rare example of child-parent love, my great Uncle Ibrahim had said to me when I was a boy. This was how Abdulrahman wanted to honor his father. This was how he showed his love.

After the family had settled in Jubail, Saleh adjusted quickly to his new surroundings, and soon discovered that, for the first time in his life, he was free from the demands of work and now had the hours (and energy) to spend as he pleased. It was certainly a new experience for him, and before long, he settled into a routine, developing a habit of hiking the mile and a half to and from the rows of farms outside of Jubail where Abdulrahman's was. Much of the family's food had been grown there—crops of alfalfa, tomatoes, watermelons, cucumbers, potatoes, Alhasa brown rice, and, of course, dates—and Saleh idled his hours caring for them, occasionally basking in a small man-made watering hole next to the farm. It wasn't very deep but even a dip afforded him the chance to cool off before trekking back to the house. Jubail has been blessed with groundwater deep beneath its surface, and since the farms' productivity depended on water irrigation, wells had been built by hand adjacent to them. Most of the water from the wells tasted brackish and bitter but there were no viable alternatives. Clean, sweet water was scarce. But all water was considered God's property, and according to Islamic law, ownership was possible only when it was contained by a vessel.[138]

Two years after Saleh had arrived in Jubail, he beamed with pride witnessing the momentous event for the Alsuhaimi family—the installation of a modern-day water well next to their farm.

An Investment Worth Its Weight

After WWII had ended, revenues from oil exports skyrocketed with numerous countries in dire need of oil to redevelop their damaged infrastructures, and oil exploration and drilling activities resumed in Saudi Arabia, and with that came an influx of Americans working in the region. Aramco introduced an ambitious expansion program that required more supplies and equipment—machinery and parts, transportation trucks, building materials and food supplies and more contractors, managers, engineers, suppliers, and workers. Perhaps it was out of self-interest, the desire to keep their new neighbors friendly toward the U.S. as well as good will, but they had also started talks with the locals about cultivating their entrepreneurial and technical skills. In 1948, a team of Aramco's geologists suggested to Abdulrahman that he purchase a water well drilling rig that was being auctioned by the British stationed in Abu Dhabi.

My grandfather, an astute businessman, thought investing in the rig might turn into a profitable venture, and Aramco employee and his friend, Bill Eltiste thought so too. Aramco's technicians and drillers, after all, promised to refurbish the rig, supply the required materials and parts until it became fully operational, and would train him in its operational procedures.

For Abdulrahman, it was an opportunity of a lifetime and an ironic repetition of history. His father had spent his entire life in Unayzah digging water wells by hand. Abdulrahman and Saleh

---

138 Hamad M. H. Al-Sheikh 1997, Second Expert Consultation On National Water Policy Reform In The Near East, Cairo, Egypt, 24-25 November 1997, accessed February 2018, <http://www.fao.org/docrep/006/ad456e/ad456e0e.htm>

had traveled to Kuwait all those years ago searching for a more sustainable way to make a living. Now Abdulrahman would return to the business of water wells but with the aid of technology and modern equipment.

My grandfather, however, had needed additional investors if he hoped to purchase the rig and had invited two other merchants in Jubail to become joint partners. An agreement had been drawn between Abdulrahman and Aramco, and the rig was sent to Jubail from Abu Dhabi, more than 850 kilometers away. Aramco was true to its word, making sure the rig was equipped with the necessary parts and supplies, and was in proper working condition, and then they proceeded to teach my grandfather how to run it.

Aramco had gone to great lengths to ensure that Abdulrahman and other locals became highly skilled technicians, and they committed to their training until they felt the Saudis were proficient enough to operate the rig without their support. My grandfather and the other townspeople had been grateful to the Americans for sharing their engineering know-how and expertise, and would remain indebted to them for these life-changing skills.

To his dying days my grandfather referred to that period with the Aramco men as a generosity of heart and spirit. Many years later my grandfather told us the story of the Americans in Dhahran camp during the late fifties and early sixties. By then, my grandfather had moved 15 miles south of the camp to Dammam. Most westerners resided at the Dhahran camp, and for Christmas my father, Abdulaziz, and his brother, Sulaiman, had brought them presents as a token of their appreciation and gratitude for what they had done for Abdulrahman and the entire Jubail community. Dhahran had also been home to the American consulate then, and dignitaries visited my grandfather during Eid al-Fitr—the Muslim high holiday marking the end of Ramadan and a month of fasting—to wish them *Eid Mubarak,* Blessed Holiday, *As-Salam Alaikum,* Peace be unto you. Their visits always followed those of the Emir

Semm Yubah

Santa Claus riding a camel and giving presents to children, 1950.

and Governor who had stopped at other prominent households then too. Islam had been moderate then—no fanaticism, no extremism—and it was a very joyous occasion.

In 1962 I was six when the convoy of cars had stopped in front of our house in Dammam after morning prayers. My grandfather had escorted the Americans into his *majlis*, and my cousins and I served trays of chocolates and sweet biscuits and carafes of coffee with cardamom to the seated men. We had been informed beforehand that our guests had helped us many years ago, and we were told to be extremely gracious. I remember the Americans flanking my grandfather, testing their Arabic on him, and two of my uncles having to translate the Americans' Arabic. My grandfather had a great sense of humor and enjoyed joking with them. It was heartwarming to see.

Even with their different language and culture and religion, they still found common ground. They had been pioneers together, and my grandfather never forgot how the experience had changed his life.

By 1950, the water well digging rig was fully operational and declared a major success. Unfortunately, it had absorbed a significant proportion of the company's cash, and Abdulrahman's two partners hadn't wanted to invest any more money into the project and opted to dissolve the partnership. Abdulrahman accepted their wishes and bought their shares, becoming the rig's sole owner.

By now it had become an asset for the community and fulfilled its promise to provide Jubail a brighter future. Modern-day machines replaced centuries-old crude methods of acquiring water. The drilling rig had the capability of tapping an abundant supply of water deep below the earth's surface, an essential resource for any farmer. The farmer had always contended with deplorable conditions: the infertility of the land, the threat of famines, epidemics and disease, locusts, tribal wars and, of course, hand-made water wells. Through the years farmers learned to adapt and improvise, getting by with

Father Abdulaziz standing near water well drilling rig site, Ras Tanura refinery, circa early 1960s.

Semm Yubah

whatever God handed them, making peace with the severe terrain, spending back-breaking hours digging wells by hand and carting the water to crops. But their circumstances greatly improved with the installations of the water drilling rigs, making irrigation easier and faster. Finally farmers could sustain a decent standard of living.

My grandfather had not only been a perceptive businessman but a lucky one, and his good fortune continued. As fate would have it, Aramco needed oil rigs *and* water drilling rigs for its core sampling and pre-oil exploration activities, and hired Abdulrahman's drilling services, paying him a substantial sum. The family business flourished, and the water well drilling rig turned into a lucrative business for Abdulrahman and the family, which gave him the capital to invest in other ventures.

With the business prospering Abdulrahman decided it was time to expand the drilling company, and wanted his eldest son, Abdulaziz, to assume operation of the rig. He trusted his son's

Father Abdulaziz Alsuhaimi & Geologist Dan Wells representing Aramco, 1960s.

workmanship, having trained him as a trader from an early age. Abdulaziz, my father, had been 19 then, slightly older than my grandfather had been when he had set out on his journey with Saleh across the great Nefud. Abdulaziz worked both in the family shop and at the rig, dividing his time between helping with the trading activities and overseeing the water drilling rig's operations.

By the mid 50s, the foundation for the Al Suhaimi Drilling Services had been firmly established, and his son, Abdulaziz, became quite the visionary, inheriting his father's business acumen, and over the years he became instrumental in the company's successful growth. It was Abdulaziz who would encourage his father to make their next big move.

CHAPTER 10

The Boomtown of Dammam

It was as if the Gulf seaport of Dammam had morphed overnight—from humble fishing village to thriving metropolis, but in reality it took years, and its growth reflected the changes taking place in other parts of the country. In the early 1920s, the Al-Dawasir's, a Najdi tribe from Budaiya in the northwestern section of Bahrain, had migrated to the area to escape the escalating political tension and social unrest in Bahrain. With Ibn Saud's consent, they had settled on the peninsula's Gulf coast, midway between the towns of Qatif and Al Khobar, on the southern rim of the Tarut Bay. It had been an unassuming stretch of land, but they found it suitable for fishing and pearling, and a small village evolved which they had called Dammam. I had been told that the origin of its name stems from the onomatopoeic sound—the "damdamah"—of the local fishermen's drums. My grandfather said the fishermen gathered nightly around a bonfire after a hard journey at sea and played the drums along with the *rubaba*, the Bedouins'—and my grandfather's—beloved one-string cello. Some believe the drums had been sounded to alert the town when the fishermen's ships were spotted homeward bound. Still, others claim its name was derived from the Arabic word, *dawwama* (whirlpool), and refers to a nearby troublesome waterway that the dhows made a point to avoid.[139] Whatever the origins of its name, the city had undergone a unique metamorphosis that was triggered by the discovery of oil in Dammam's famous well #7 in 1938, and the change extended into the next two decades.

After a period of stagnation during WWII, urban development had accelerated, particularly in the fifties, and the modernization of Dammam eventually improved the quality of life for its residents.

Formal Portrait of Aramco's Board of Directors meeting, Dhahran, October 1959. Left to right: Paul H. Arnot, Armaco V.P.; Robert S. Hatch, Aramco V.P.; L.M. Snyder, Aramco V.P.; Howard M. Page, Director, Standard Oil Co. (New Jersey); John Noble, Tapline President; Harvey Cash, Texaco V.P.; J.H. McDonald, Aramco V.P.; Norman Hardy, Chariman of the Board, Aramco; T.C. Barer, Aramco V.P.; George L. Parkhurst, Director and V.P., Standard Oil Co. of Calif.; H.E. Shaykh Hafidh Wahbah, Saudi Arabia Ambassador-at-large; H.E. Abdullah H. Tariki, Director General of Petroleum and Mineral Affairs, Saudi Arabia; Robert I. Brougham, Aramco V.P; Robert Siegel, Executive V.P. (Middle East) of Mobil International Oil, Socony Mobil.

---

139 Dammam History 2015, The Saudi Network, accessed January 2017, <http://www.the-saudi.net/saudi-arabia/dammam/dammam_history.htm>

Semm Yubah

Ibn Saud, who has long dreamed of his kingdom becoming a highly industrialized and commercial state, had designated the increased oil revenues for the improvement of his country's infrastructure, and developing Dammam became a priority, where the oil company, Aramco, was based.

Mud-brick homes with palm frond roofs gave way to modern-day housing and concrete buildings; landscaped and paved streets replaced dirt roads. Locals now heard—to some people's dismay—the honking of car's horns along with the braying of donkey-hauled carts and the bleating of camels laden with wares. Public utilities were installed; hospitals, schools and harbors built; Dammam's King Abdulaziz Seaport was launched, becoming a magnet for countless shipping companies and the new center for trade.

King Ibn Saud realized the camel had become an outmoded means of transportation and wanted a 340-mile railroad built from Dammam to Riyadh, and construction had begun in 1947 once an agreement had been reached between the King and Aramco, with Bechtel Construction Company contracted to build the line.[140] By October 1951 the railway was completed, and the line linked the Gulf Coast port of Dammam with the interior of the country, cutting through the desert to Dhahran, Abqaiq, Hofuf, and Al-Kharj, and finally to the city of Riyadh, home of the King.[141]

The building of the Ras Tanura Refinery in 1945 had also influenced the city's rapid urban development. Only 45 kilometers north of Dammam, the refinery was built on the tip of a peninsula. The decision to build the refinery had originally been met with ambivalence over Germany's wartime threats, but once the project had been given the green light, construction commenced with the use of U.S. steel. They had planned to produce fuel for the Allies'

---

140 Dammam–Riyadh Line, World Heritage Encyclopedia, accessed 4 October 2017, <http://self.gutenberg.org/articles/Dammam–Riyadh_Line>

141 William E. Mulligan 1984, A Kingdom and a Company, accessed 22 September 2018, <http://archive.aramcoworld.com/issue/198403/a.kingdom.and.a.company.htm>

land and sea efforts in the Pacific, but before it was fully operational the war had ended, and it wasn't until 1947 that Ras Tanura Refinery completed its first full year of operation.[142] Since then it has expanded to become Saudi Arabia's biggest refinery and to this day remains a key asset and their oldest refinery.[143]

It was quite an auspicious occasion when King Ibn Saud had visited. William E. Mulligan, who worked for Aramco at the time and resided at the company's camp in Dhahran (just south of Dammam), wrote about the Royal visit.[144]

> *The opening of the refinery also sparked another visit by King 'Abd al-'Aziz; though he didn't actually come until 1947, he came specifically to see the refinery. And when he did, he underlined the changes that had already taken place in Saudi Arabia since his first visit in May, 1939. Then, he and a retinue of 2,000 had driven 320 miles (520 kilometers) from Riyadh in a great caravan totaling 500 automobiles. Now, in January 1947, the aging king and his entourage arrived in a fleet of six airplanes.*
>
> *In some ways, though, the king was just the same and to many who had been there for the first great visit, there were similarities. One was a tent city erected on the site of today's University of Petroleum and Minerals; though he had been expected to stay at a new guest house—completed just in time—the king announced that he was moving to the tents, where, evidently, he felt less confined, closer to his friends and more available to his subjects....*

---

142 A Billion Barrels Ago... 1962, Archives, Aramco World, accessed 9 June 2017, <http://www.saudiaramco.com/en/home/about/history/1940s.html>

143 William Tracy 1966, Island Of Steel, Aramco World, accessed 2 May 2017, <https://www.meed.com/analysis/meed-at-60/ras-tanura-refinery/5015513.article>

144 William E. Mulligan 1984, A Kingdom and a Company, Aramco World, accessed 29 June 2018, <http://archive.aramcoworld.com/issue/198403/a.kingdom.and.a.company.htm>

Semm Yubah

Ras Tanura Refinery official opening in 1947 (following the completion of construction at the end of WWII in 1945).

One of the most agreeable events on the program was the audience King 'Abd al-'Aziz granted the women and children of the Aramco community. The king met and talked through an interpreter with each of the women, several of whom brought along babes in arms. It was a photographer's dream and in a precedent-shattering event David Douglas Duncan, then of Life, obtained a dramatic picture over the king's shoulder of the king chuckling over the antics of the children assembled before him where they were served cookies and juice.

Aramco, the first to use the refinery, had championed Saudi Arabia's efforts to become internationally recognized as a reputable producer and exporter of oil. Unfortunately, King Abdul Aziz Ibn Saud never lived to see the long-term dramatic effects of Saudi oil revenues in a post-war world. On November 9, 1953, the founder and king of Saudi Arabia died at the age of 78. In keeping with religious tradition, the king had been buried in an unmarked grave facing Makkah in the Al-Oud public cemetery in Riyadh.

Prize-winning foreign correspondent and foreign affairs columnist for *The New York Times* C.L. Sulzberger wrote:

> *The death of Ibn Saud is the end of a saga that does not properly belong to this century. He seemed, indeed, to be not a modern or even a medieval man, but one of the last great figures of the Old Testament, a desert prophet who, despite infirmities and age and the incongruities of his airplanes, besides his camels and his Mercedes Benz, besides his slaves, remained always a powerful and vigorous force.*[145]

Ibn Saud's eldest son, Saud Ibn Abdul Aziz, succeeded him as King, and is credited with upgrading the government structure and taking it to the next level. He had surrounded himself with a group of highly educated professionals (His Minister of Oil had been educated in Egypt and the U. S.) and other experts—engineers and scientists, etc.—who assisted in facilitating his ambitious agenda for the country, and soon we saw the construction of hospitals, schools, clinics, and the implementation of other community services. He had also established the first university in the Najd region in the capital city of Riyadh.

With the easternmost region of Saudi Arabia undergoing an enormous transformation, the new King believed his country would be better served if his government maintained a physical presence in that area, closer to the headquarters of the American oil company, Aramco, and the Gulf's major seaport of Dammam. Prince Saud Ibn Jalawi had always ruled the eastern region in the King's service from the heart of the Al Hasa oasis, in the city of Al Hofuf, 165 kilometers west of the Gulf coast. The Prince had governed from there since 1938, upon the death of his father, Abdullah bin Jalawi, cousin to Ibn Saud and his close companion, who had also fought at his side during the 1902 takeover of Riyadh from their arch rivals, Al Rasheed.

---

[145] Archives, NewYork Times, accessed 12 June 2017,, <http://query.nytimes.com/mem/archive-ree/pdf?res=9403E7DB1139E23BBC4852DFB7678388649EDE>

Semm Yubah

Aramco staff & guards inspecting TAP Line pipelines transporting Saudi Oil to Saidon in Lebanon for export to Europe, 1950s.

At the new King's behest, Prince Saud Ibn Jalawi relocated his palace in 1956, the year I was born, to my hometown in the northeast. Dammam was just 12 kilometers north of Dhahran where Aramco had set up their residential community. The King realized having Aramco in close proximity would foster better communications and stronger relationships between them, and help utilize the 23 years of oil concession agreements started in 1933. Besides, Dammam had been experiencing an unprecedented influx of American and other foreign companies, most of them involved with oil export and transportation, and it seemed a logical move.

King Saud Ibn Abdul Aziz had presided over the country for little over a decade. On his watch, in 1960, Saudi Arabia had become one of the founding members of OPEC, and he had witnessed the balance of power shift from the multinational oil companies back to the oil-producing countries. (Although Saud had succeeded the throne as Ibn Saud's eldest son, he was considered an ineffectual monarch and a spendthrift by some of the other royal family members, and in 1958 they forced him to relinquish some of his authority to his younger and more competent brother, Faisal. In 1960 Saud managed to reclaim the throne but by 1962 he was

An Aramco plane stops at TAP Line station airstrip, circa 1950s.

regarded as merely a figure head, and two years later he went into exile, leaving Faisal as King of Saudi Arabia.)[146]

The fifties had been quite a transformative time for Saudi Arabia, and lives were dramatically changed for the better. In 1952, my grandfather still resided in Jubail, and his family continued to grow. In addition to Abdulaziz, he and Norah now had four daughters and two more sons—Khalid, born in 1940, and Sulaiman in 1943. During the 40s, Jubail's first school had opened under the management of Saudi Arabia's Ministry of Education, offering six years of elementary education and later an additional three. Both Khalid and Sulaiman had completed their elementary education there and began their intermediate schooling but Khalid had to withdraw during the middle of his second year when he had to move to Dammam along with my father, Abdulaziz; Sulaiman had left that same year to help Abdulrahman with the family business in Jubail. (Khalid went on to complete his education in Britain in 1966; Sulaiman had been schooled on the job, working with the Americans at Aramco.)

---

146 Wayne H Bowen 2015, The history of Saudi Arabia, accessed 15 November 2017, <http://bit.ly/3aekIIf>

Semm Yubah

By the early fifties, while Dammam's economy was burgeoning, Jubail's was in a downward spiral. Business had not been good for Abdulrahman and the other merchants. Trade waned once merchants had turned their focus away from Jubail to the more dynamic coastal seaport to the south. Dammam was no longer the small, sleepy village dependent on fishing and pearling for its survival. Oil had turned Dammam into a boomtown.

A large number of Jubail's established business owners had already jumped at the chance to set up shop there with an increasing number of merchants planning on following suit, hoping to tap into Dammam's boom expansion and benefit from the burst of commercial activity.

Considering that my grandfather had always been intuitive and observant, especially when it concerned matters of business, I was surprised to learn that he hadn't been the first in the family to investigate Dammam. Although now, in retrospect, I realize why. My grandfather had been a lover of nature. He felt more at peace in the wide open spaces of the desert with its majestic dunes and vast sky. In Jubail he had been only a short stroll away. The desert was his sanctuary, and I don't think he was ready to relinquish that. At least not yet.

My grandfather, who had trusted his intuition and followed his instinct his entire life, had cultivated the same traits in his children. Once or twice a month his eldest son, Abdulaziz (my father), had to travel the forty-eight miles south to the city of Qatif to sell and buy goods for the family business. While there, he always conversed with other merchants to keep abreast of the latest developments. Each time, he heard the same story and from a variety of vendors—wealth and unimaginable opportunities awaited just twenty-three miles to the south. By this time Abdulaziz was newly married to Madawi (my mother, and the daughter of my grandfather's best friend and next door neighbor, Mohammad Alkadi), and had been on the lookout for an opportunity to expand the family business, especially since he would soon be starting a family of his own, and decided to assess the situation for himself.

Algosaibi brothers, Ford Car Agency Grand Opening, Dammam, 1952.

After work one day, he drove his Ford pickup south along the coast and had been shocked by the scale of expansion in the Gulf city. He returned several times to further explore Dammam *and* to be fully prepared to answer the barrage of questions his father would surely ask once Abdulaziz urged him to move their company there.

After listening to his son's account, Abdulrahman made his own trip south and had been equally impressed. If experience had taught him anything, it was that timing was everything, and even a small delay might jeopardize an opportunity. Upon his return he apprised his son of his plans, and sometime between 1952 and 1953, Abdulaziz, together with his new wife and younger brother,

Semm Yubah

Khalid, were sent to live in Dammam and set up shop for the family business. They rented a house but were instructed to research suitable accommodations for the eventual arrival of the extended family.

The benefits of such a move were vast, still Abdulrahman was circumspect about it. He was in his fifties by then and although in fairly good health and had long ago adjusted to his monocular vision, his remaining eyesight was deteriorating. He had always relied on his eldest son's help with their water drilling enterprise as well as their trade business. Now the burden of running both would fall to him, and he wasn't sure how he would manage. Still, he approached the challenge as he did most, analyzing details, and maximizing his time, and, surprisingly, productivity excelled. Somehow this new venture had vitalized him.

During the first few months that my parents and uncle had lived in Dammam, Abdulrahman visited often. My grandfather had been intrigued by the developments of the thriving city but dismayed by the cacophony of noise that accompanied progress. By comparison, Jubail had been a placid place, almost serene. My grandfather's workday there commenced predawn to the sound of birds (not cars) and the call for *Fajr*, early morning prayers.

Great-Grandfather Saleh (second from right), with Khalid (right) Sulaiman (center), and cousin Sulaiman (far left), Dammam, 1956.

After prayers, he strolled through the neighboring desert, savoring its wind-carved dunes and capacious sky, then to work, breaking at noon to face Makkah once again for *Dhuhr* prayers, then home for lunch and a short nap before work. (The customary nap provided a needed respite from working in the brutal sun.) But the conveniences of modern living in Dammam had intruded on my grandfather's ritual whenever he visited. Electricity, considered life-changing ever since the first public power generator had been turned on in Taif in the late 1940s,[147] was now operational in Dammam and became my grandfather's nemesis.

My father's rented house had been adjacent to a carpenter's workshop, and the carpenter used his new electric saw whenever Abdulrahman napped. My grandfather rarely complained but he did to my father about this. Later, he joked that he could never sleep in Dammam with the incessant buzzing, and then he couldn't sleep in Jubail without it.

Abdulrahman's visits had been spent gauging Dammam's activity, analyzing its seaport facilities, collecting data by strolling near Aramco's headquarters and camps. He frequented the business district, conversing with local purveyors, evaluating the rate of the city's progress, and back in Jubail, he weighed the benefits and disadvantages of the move.

Soon, travel arrangements were underway for the entire family. It took Abdulrahman two years to transport everyone but the move to Dammam had been executed without a hitch, and a new chapter for the family commenced.

Around the same time, my grandfather's dearest friend, Mohammad Alkadi and his wife, Muneera, with six of their seven children had moved to Dammam too, to be near my grandfather and his family, and of course, their adult child, Madawi, who had

---

147 Foundations 1982, Aramco World, accessed March 2018, <http://archive.aramcoworld.com/issue198206/foundations-the.pillars.htm>

Semm Yubah

married my father. Abdulrahman and Mohammad would remain inseparable for the duration of their lives.

In those early years in Dammam, my family had moved four times to accommodate the expanding family.

The family's first house had been a modest rental (1952-53) located close to the Prince's palace and the busy open market *and* next door to the carpenter. With the family increasing, Abdulrahman decided they needed to build their own house, and they commenced construction in 1953.

Great-Grandfather Saleh resting and sipping a cup of Arabian coffee, Jubail, 1948.

Saleh was in his 90s by then and quite frail, and had remained in Jubail with Abdullah and Ibrahim, his two younger sons from his later marriages, until construction of the family's new house was completed. As the eldest son, Abdulrahman had been responsible for the financial and physical well being of his extended family whether they resided in Dammam or Jubail, and he made certain that his father's needs were met. Still, he was anxious to bring him to Dammam as soon as possible.

When the new house was ready, Abdulrahman sent for his father. Five years later, his younger half-brothers, Ibrahim and Abdullah, along with their families, joined them in Dammam but had separate houses a short distance away. Our new home (1954-61) had been built on a flat piece of land outside the city center, not far from the railroad station. It was less than half a mile away from our home but the train was visible from our doorsteps, and whenever it approached the station, we heard its whistle echo in the house.

The new place was a two-story Mediterranean-style house with decorative arches and stone benches at the various entrances, and at its center was an outdoor courtyard (the *Hawi*) with a covered walkway (the *sabat)* along its perimeter. Each room had access to the courtyard, which provided ample ventilation for the entire house and enough space for us children to claim as our own.

On one side of the main floor was the *majlis*—the men's reception area—as well as the dining room and buffet for male guests; the other side of the house was designated for the family and included the kitchen, dining area, family room, children's playroom, Abdulrahman's and Nora's bedroom, and adjacent to theirs, Saleh's. There was a private entrance to the house for family members, and a separate one for male guests, and each entrance had a designated stairway to the second floor of bedrooms. The visitors' bedrooms, however, had no access to the family's side of the house. At the inside perimeter of the upstairs floor was a hallway that overlooked the house's open central courtyard, the children's favorite place.

That central courtyard was large enough for us to play everything from ball to tag to riding bikes, at any time of the day, and provided the adults peace of mind since it was enclosed with no exit to the street—and the adults could easily observe us and call to us from any window in the house. There was also an outside play area by the front door entrance, a 30 by 30 foot sandbox where my grandfather sometimes sat with us in the late afternoon when the sun wasn't as strong. Sometimes I waited there for his return from the mosque, and he recited some verses of the Qur'an.

Life in this house had seemed joyful in its simplicity. The day commenced with breakfast with my siblings and cousins, and I can remember the distinct scent of freshly baked *Fatir*—Arabian flat bread made from barley that we used to scoop our food—wafting toward where we waited for our fried eggs and heated milk with ginger. Our dining area, adjacent to the kitchen, was a simple rectangular room where we sat cross-legged on a round woven carpet reserved only for meals. Plates and cups were set directly on the rug without a tray. But in winter our food rested on an elevated steel tray bedded with a thin layer of clean sand, and in one corner

Semm Yubah

of the room, a pyramid of lit coal kept us warm, the smell of burning coal mingling with the aroma of freshly cooked bread.

After ablutions, we'd play until noon when we were called to wash again for lunch. My grandfather, father and uncles returned from the office at this time for lunch, too, and a nap before work, and we were not allowed to play until they woke an hour later with the call for afternoon prayers.

Abdulrahman S. Alsuhaimi seated with grandsons Adel, the author (left) & Mosaad (right), Dammam, 1964.

As the first-born male child of Abdulrahman's eldest son, I became the focus of the adult family members of the household, (and I might add, the likely subject for their childrearing experiments) but I had also been the recipient of many privileges. Sometimes my grandfather allowed me at the age of five to escort him to the evening gatherings at the *majlis* of his best friend and my maternal grandfather, Mohammad Al Kadi. The events at his *majlis* had been known for their light-hearted discussions and story telling, and I looked forward to attending them.

Hand-in-hand we'd stroll to Mohammad's house, my grandfather's thobe rustling, the scent of his oud drifting down,

Grandfather, on mother's side, Mohammad Alkadi visiting Jubail farm lands, circa 1960s.

the stars high in the moonlit sky, the air peaceful in its stillness. To my child's mind, it was equally magical and mundane, which made it all the more reassuring that this was how life would always be, or so I thought. Sometimes I was permitted to accompany my father to the men's *majlis* for luncheons and special business events. They were impressive to me, even at five, and educational, too, and although I was expected to behave and allowed to be a child, I occasionally got into mischief. Once I broke my arm after jumping on the sofa in the *majlis* and falling off, and had to wear a cast for a month. Another time was at a luncheon at one of my Father's friend's *majlis*. The room had been packed with male guests, and my father sat on the Persian carpet with me on his lap while he conversed with an elderly man next to him. No one noticed when I grabbed the small white braided rope lying on the floor and wrapped it around my hand. A few minutes later our host announced lunch was served in the adjacent dining room. My father and I rose along with the old man and immediately his pants fell to the ground. There was an uneasy moment of silence before the man burst into laughter, "Look, what your son did." I would hear the story of how I removed the man's belt and pants repeated many times throughout my young life.

Years later as a grown man with children of my own, I had revisited that first house and was amazed to discover how small

Semm Yubah

and unassuming it actually was. It had always loomed grand in my child's mind, but it had given me some wonderful memories, and those still hold a prominent place in my heart.

Each house my family owned in Jubail and Dammam had an adjacent makeshift barn, a small fenced-in outdoor area with a roof to shade the two cows we kept for milk, and the two dozen hens we raised for their eggs. The children collected the eggs only when asked. Otherwise the chore, along with milking the cow, had fallen to the women of the household: my mother, aunts, and grandmother.

The hubbub of Dammam's sprawling city spoiled the tranquility that my grandfather and father had been used to and sought in a home, and they both longed to return to nature. My grandfather in particular felt boxed in by the city, and it prompted the family's next move. In 1961 my grandfather had found his paradise slightly southwest of Dammam where the sand dunes and desert began.

At the crest of a hill, four Mediterranean style buildings stood on an expansive rectangular plot—a house for Abdulrahman, another for his brother, Mohammad, and a house (similar to their last one) for Saleh and the other family members. A fourth building had been constructed specifically for the *Majlis*, the men's reception hall. At the other end of our plot of land was a sizable construction plant for the family business. Throughout the walled compound there were groves of date palms and oleander, tamarisks and acacia trees, and we had a swimming pool. My grandfather felt content here, waking to the Bul-Bul's chirps, catching the showy Hoopoe bathing in sand, or spying skylarks soaring the skies. Sometimes, he gathered the grandchildren for jaunts to the desert where he seated himself at the base of a sand dune and watch us slide down its steep side. An hour and a half later, my father arrived with the truck to transport us back home.

Adel Alsuhaimi

All the security of my life seemed to disappear when we first moved here, and I enrolled in school at age six. I remember the terror, seeing a classroom filled with strange faces. I had always spent my days in the shelter of family. Still, like children everywhere, I adjusted quickly, and a few weeks later my fear gave way to curiosity, and I formed friendships with other students, some the grandchildren of my grandfather's acquaintances. But it did occur to me, at least in some abstract form, that life might not always be as straightforward as it had been in my grandfather's other house.

In this house, Abdulrahman had witnessed his father's final days. Not long after they made the move, Saleh passed away in 1961 at nearly 97 years of age (102 according to the Islamic *Hijri* or lunar calendar).

Throughout his life, my grandfather has been shadowed by the premature death of his mother, her absence following him since his teenage year. But even though Saleh had survived to very old age, his death didn't sting any less. One is never prepared for the loss of a parent, no matter how old, and Abdulrahman had been no different but took solace that Saleh had been surrounded by those he loved. In keeping with tradition, the family cleansed and perfumed Saleh's body with herbs—*hunoot* and *duhn aoud*—and wrapped his body in a white seamless cotton cloth and buried him according to Islamic law, in a public cemetery without any kind of marker since all of us are equal in death.

Grandfather's brother Mohammad Saleh Alsuhaimi in his shop, Bahrain, 1958.

Semm Yubah

Later in 1963 my grandfather's brother, Muhammad, returned to live with us after 35 years living in Bahrain, and I think their reunion had made my grandfather's grief a little lighter.

Eighteen years later, our family once again expanded their living quarters to adjust to the growing family. With new zoning restrictions they were no longer permitted to have a plant in a residential community and after they built a new construction plant outside the city they demolished the old one within the compound, and built their new and fourth house (1979-1999), larger but similar in style to the other.

My grandfather's health had diminished by the time we moved into this new house. He was suffering from diabetes, and his vision had greatly deteriorated to the point of needing assistance. My sister often squired him to the palm trees that studded our housing compound where she relayed which palm trees bore dates and which were ripe for harvesting. It was not uncommon for him to ask one of us what the sky looked like. Was there a cloud masking the sun or any sign of rain? Had any grass sprouted in the desert around Dammam? He loved the desert so much. We'd take him camping for almost a month seventy-five miles north of Dammam if the rain season was encouraging with my maternal grandfather and his dear friend, Mohammad Alkadi and his family joining us. They'd sit, shoulder to shoulder, watching their grandchildren play.

By 2000 the family became so large that keeping the extended family on one tract of land had become almost impossible. So Abdulrahman's brothers built their own house in a different area of metropolitan Dammam.

To this day Dammam remains my family's permanent home. All those years of migrating from place to place for my grandfather had finally come to an end.

CHAPTER 11

A Thriving Business; Time to Hand Over Reigns to Abdulaziz

Even with Abdulrahman in poor health, he advocated to once again advance the family business since the entire extended family had finally settled in Dammam. His water drilling rig business had experienced steady growth, despite some temporary shortages of labor and capital. The King Abdulaziz Seaport had continued to promote ample opportunities. And in the sixties, Abdulrahman's two younger sons, Khalid and Sulaiman, had joined my father in the operation of the family business.

Father Abdulaziz, standing far right, during a business trip to the Far East, 1968.

Semm Yubah

The family branched out into other areas and made a series of real estate investments and extended their diversification to include manufacturing and technical services—geophysical testing, construction and plant maintenance, road marking and signage, etc.—and the import of oil field supplies, and other business sectors. They maintained their own factory for construction materials, and now competed for government contracts and companies in Saudi Arabia and foreign countries. Later, they invested in utility companies and cement plants.

The addition of Khalid and Sulaiman had given them an understanding of a new era of marketing. Khalid had acquired the skills to analyze global economic trends while studying in Britain. His ability to interpret Dammam's changing economic climate—and by extension Saudi Arabia's—and predict business trends had resulted in successful partnerships with foreign companies. His orchestration of four major joint ventures later accounted for approximately 70 percent of the family's entire business's revenues and wealth. And Sulaiman had been involved in the everyday operation of the family business and acted as translator for my grandfather with foreign businessmen and dignitaries.

Alsuhaimi Drilling Services mobilizing to desert locations, circa 1960s.

Adel Alsuhaimi

My father, Abdulaziz, continued managing the drilling division of the business besides overseeing our real estate investments. Demand for the family's well drilling services increased and business expanded to the regions of Yemen, Al Hasa, the Gulf islands and other remote desert locations, making logistics and planning more complex.

Abdulrahman, despite his diminishing health, maintained his involvement with the family business as well as the community, acting as the close adviser to the Eastern province's ruler, Prince Saud Ibn Jalawi. My grandfather had always considered his community service more his social responsibility than a burden. He had been known for his unbiased judgment, honesty, and empathy, particularly with local affairs and was held in such high esteem that whenever he attended an event at a local *majlis*, people cleared the way for his path. My grandfather felt quite uncomfortable with such attention and shunned any limelight and, as a result, whenever he attended a social function he made it a point to arrive long before any other guests.

By 1980, the Saudi government had completed the final phase of buying Aramco, marking another milestone for the country. They had purchased twenty-five percent of the company's assets in 1973, and the following year, a staggering 60 percent, and by 1980 acquired a 100% stake, finalizing the Saudi government's control in the oil company. The company was re-named Saudi Aramco, and in 1982, the historic oil well, Dammam #7, which put Saudi Arabia on the road to becoming a global political power, was taken out of service

Mr. Weathers congratulates Desco Chairman, Abdulrahman Alsuhaimi, at opening ceremony, December, 1965.

Semm Yubah

after 45 years. During its operation, the rig had yielded 32 million barrels of oil with an average of 2000 barrels a day. During 1999 it was renamed the Prosperity Well. Indeed, Aramco had helped the famous warrior, Ibn Saud, utilize his country's natural resources to develop a highly successful petroleum industry to become the world's largest exporter of crude oil. Black gold had been a game changer for Saudi Arabia.

By the mid 80s, oil prices collapsed and the Saudi economy slowed down and so did our business, and the second generation—myself, my brothers and cousins—began assuming positions within the

Signing contracts for the Al Khobar Municipal Water and Sewage Project. Seated right to left: Abdulrahman Mansour, Muhammad Sukkari, Shaykh Hamad Al-Mubarak, Commission Chairman; J. Binkhorst & F.E. Paterson. Standing right to left: Zamil Bakeer, Charles Bullen, Abdulrahman Ash-sha'wan, Muhammad Al-Khuzayyim, Abdulrahman Alsuhaimi, Abdul Rahman Khatib & Jaseer Dajani; Al-Khobar, June, 1963.

family organization. The timing couldn't have been better. The combination of our new skills and ideas coupled with my father and uncles' vast experience created a synergy and we developed strategies to reinvigorate profits. By 1991 the family businesses completely recuperated from the drop in oil prices, and a new positive trajectory ensued. The family business expanded to include water pump trading services, manufacturing and assembly, and other services related to sewage and water pumps, which greatly supported our drilling sector. More importantly, the family business no longer depended on government contracts. Since the 1990's our customer roster expanded to include a very diversified array of clientele—private and publicly owned businesses, and government ministries and foreign companies operating within the kingdom. Travel and tourism services were also added along with horticultural farming and training and certification, as well as real estate development projects.

My grandfather didn't get to see his business flourish in the nineties. The young boy from Unayzah, who had traveled by camel with his father through the vast Al Nefud desert to Kuwait and Jubail and finally to Dammam to become a prosperous and esteemed businessman, a visionary and a risk-taker, died in 1983 at the age of eighty-four.

I was twenty-seven during that summer of '83, newly married, and had recently transitioned from the world of academia to business. The Iran-Iraq war, which had been raging for three years, had intensified, grabbing everyone's attention including my grandfather's. Most had voiced their support for Iraq but my grandfather held a different interpretation of the regional conflict, and had not been enthusiastic about engaging the Iranians. He had witnessed enough death and destruction in his lifetime, and hated war, no matter how justifiable the cause, realizing its consequences

Semm Yubah

The final activation of the Aramco—Desco tie-in electrical line from the Dhahran Power Plant to Dammam. Abdulrahman Alsuhaimi, Chairman of the board of Desco is seen here turning on the power as Aramco's Saleh Sowayigh looks on; August, 1963.

Desco-Aramco agreement was signed Saturday morning in the office of L.M. Snyder, V.P. and General Manager, Operations. Signatories were (left to right): Snyder, Aramco Treasurer; E.G. Voss and Desco Board Chariman Abdulrahman Alsuhaimi; Sa'ad Al-Mojil, Vice Chariman of Desco. Others present at the ceremony (standing left to right): Mohammed Ba Bitain, Desco Director-Delegate; Zafer H. Husseini, Acting Banking Administrator, G. O. Treasurer's Dept.; Stauffer, Coordinator, and ABD Al-Rahman Khatib, liaison representative, Technical Assistance Div.; & L.E. Goodyear, Law Dept., February, 1962.

were often uncontrollable. The cost that war exacted, he often told us, was much too high. History has certainly proven him right far too many times.

In the early day of that August, my bride and I had just moved into our own new house, the latest addition to the family compound that was located directly across from the palm garden, near the men's main *Majlis* and my grandfather's house. We were thrilled to finally be in our own home and anxious for our new furniture to arrive, and had been busy planning a feast to celebrate the occasion with my grandfather as our guest of honor. He had been extremely generous and kind to us, and we owed so much to him. It was, after all, because of him that I and every member of my family received the best in education, a beautiful home, a new car, and all the other modern conveniences of life that prosperity affords. We had been more fortunate than most, blessed with a comfortable

Sheikh Abdulrahman Saleh Alsuhaimi, DEPCO Chairman, & Mr. D.R. Young signing the DEPCO Power Plan Agreement, December, 1972.

Semm Yubah

and easy life as a result of Abdulrahman's hard work and sacrifice as well as his good luck. Needless to say, we were exceedingly grateful to him and my father. My grandfather had always supported his children, particularly his eldest son, my father, and had made sure all of his grandsons were well educated, and that we understood the value of hard work. The rearing of his granddaughters, whom he loved just as deeply, had been left to the care of their mothers and grandmother, along with the other elder women of the household. This may seem odd to those raised in the west, but this was the norm in Saudi Arabia in those days.

The morning I learned of my grandfather's death I had risen early, and the air was already hot and muggy, typical weather for August. Outside, across from my living room window, the palms stood serene against an azure sky. I answered the phone on the first ring wondering who was calling at such an early hour. As soon as I heard

Grandfather (left) at winter camp with Mosaad, 1975.

my father's voice waver, I knew. The previous night right before midnight my grandmother had phoned him to say Abdulrahman had become gravely ill. My father rushed to their house after instructing my younger brother, Basim, to meet him with the car, and together they eased my grandfather into the back seat. My brother drove while my father sat cradling my grandfather's head on his lap. At the hospital, the on-duty physician examined my grandfather and shortly past midnight pronounced him dead. My father had waited until morning to inform the rest of the clan.

It did not seem possible that my dear *Yubah*[148] was no longer with us. Only a few days ago he was asking me about the color of the sky. Had the nearby dunes changed shape yet? I wasn't sure how to make sense of the days without him.

As a matter of routine I had discussed any family and business matters with my father but I always sought my grandfather's counsel afterwards for a definitive take on the issue at hand. We didn't always see eye-to-eye but I usually realized afterwards the wisdom of his (and my father's) words. Inevitably his advice had a stabilizing effect, especially when I was ambivalent about a particular course of action regarding my career or family or concerned about the politics or economics of the region.

I remember when my father had decided to send me to England during the summer holidays to learn English. At 15 I hated the idea of giving up any free time at the beach but I went at my father's request and after my grandfather reminded me that this trip was a privilege, as well as an opportunity. When I arrived I was immediately impressed with Exeter, the ancient city that sits on the Exe River in Devonshire in southwest England where I spent the summer. A German family hosted me, and they were gracious and kind-hearted during the three months I lived with them while studying English. It was an invaluable experience that not only

---

148 Arabic for Grandfather.

Semm Yubah

improved my English but also exposed me to another culture and widened my worldview. My father and grandfather had been right.

All of us had felt the void when my grandfather had died. He had been the foundation of the Alsuhaimi Family, and it was inconceivable of anyone taking his place.

After the washing (*ghusl*) and shrouding *(al-Kafan)* of the body, and the recital of *Salat al-Janazah*, the funeral prayers during the burial ceremony, we returned home to the Majlis to find it swarming with people (some we knew, and many we didn't). They had arrived to pay their final respects to my grandfather and offer condolences to our family. Among the attendees were those Abdulrahman had helped over the years in their time of need. The sheer number of people took me aback. The scene was surreal but it was clear he had touched the hearts of many, the line of people stretching down the hallway and stairs and out to the street. Cars were forced to park at least three blocks away, many deciding to walk the distance to my grandfather's *majlis*. The rush of visitors continued for two days and eased only on the third. So many told us they had been appreciative of the kindness my grandfather had extended them and told us how he had helped them, something he never shared with us, out of respect for their privacy.

My grandfather had been such a dominant and positive force in all our lives, and it would not be easy for Abdulaziz, my father, to assume his new role as the head of the family household. He was more than aware that no one could replace Abdulrahman but he strove to keep the family together and provide a positive role model for all of us. And all of us kept engraved in our heart, the words of my grandfather: "Family must prevail above all other matters."

I cannot claim that I have been as successful with my own children as my grandfather and my father had been with me and my siblings, but I've tried to, at least, attempt to be a good parent and follow their example. What my grandfather and father did for me, my brothers and sisters cannot be matched. Not yet anyway. I hope though, that the grandchildren and great grandchildren and future generations will learn from the experiences of Abdulrahman's life. The lessons of his life are timeless.

Grandfather (right) & brothers Mosaad (center), Basim (left) having a coffee break en route to desert winter camp, 1975.

Like many who have lost a loved one, I, too, wish for one more time with mine and long to have the chance to talk to my grandfather again. If I could have one wish granted it would be to sit beside him in his *majlis* and ask an endless barrage of questions about his life. He wouldn't mind I'm sure, especially when he'd learn that it would help teach the new generations of family about all the hardships and challenges that he and his father and mine endured.

And I would say him, oh dear *Yubah*, you have done so well, we cannot thank you enough.

EPILOGUE

The Grand Sons; Adel, Brothers and Cousins

My grandfather died in 1983, fifty-one years after the Arabian Peninsula was unified under King Abdulaziz Ibn Saud and became known as the Kingdom of Saudi Arabia. The country has come a long way since he first journeyed through the desert with his father. Abdulrahman had lived long enough to see his country's transformation from an unmapped wilderness—where nomadic

Adel & project staff inspecting a potential project site
south of Dammam city, December, 2005.

tribesmen, the Bedouins, roamed deserts by camel, bandits preyed on caravans, and tribal warfare and revenge killings were commonplace—to a prosperous metropolis spurred by the discovery of oil, with advances in transportation, health, education, housing, and employment. Although my grandfather was a forward-thinker who had been transformed along with his country—from the proverbial rags to riches—he had also become in his final years much more nostalgic and contemplative. Like many of his generation, he longed for the simpler times of yesteryear, and the solace and simplicity of the desert, free of the congestion and crowds, where he could still spy the stars in the silence of a night sky. He had been grateful for those later years when he was given another chance to live so close to nature. The desert with all its travails had shaped him, it was a part of who he was, and he worried that his grandchildren and great grandchildren and his future generations would miss out on that life-changing opportunity. I think he was concerned that urbanization and the comforts and privilege that prosperity brings might compromise the essence of who they were. Perhaps he understood deeply the implication of what Wilfred Thesiger wrote in 1959 in his book, *Arabian Sands*. "All that is best in the Arabs had come from them in the desert…"

Today, Saudi Arabia's economy is one of the largest in the world, and the country is the world's largest oil exporter, deriving nearly 90 percent of its government revenue from oil, and it's also the 12th largest oil and gas consumer.[149]

Since the start of the 21st century, Saudi Arabia has undergone another wave of modernization, and the average household income for Saudi nationals saw a significant increase. According to the McKinsey Global Institute's Report (*Saudi Arabia Beyond Oil: The*

---

149 Mimi Kirk 2017, The Saudi City That's Shunning Oil, Bloomberg CityLab, accessed December 2018, <https://www.citylab.com/equity/2017/03/the-saudi-city-going-oil-free/519531/>

Adel & H.E. Eng. Ali Alnuaimi, Saudi Minister of Energy, in H.E. Riyadh office, June, 2006.

Investment and Productivity Transformation, December 2015) approximately "1.7 million Saudi jobs were created and $450 billion was invested in health, education, and the country's infrastructure."[150]

New schools, universities and hospitals have been built along with a new financial district in Riyadh, and on the Red Sea there is the King Abdullah Economic City, KAEC, (pronounced "cake") which, when completed, will be about the size of Washington, DC,

---

150 McKinsey Global Institute 2015, Saudi Arabia Beyond Oil: The Investment And Productivity Transformation, accessed February 2017, <https://www.mckinsey.com/~/media/McKinsey/Global%20Themes/Employment%20and%20Growth/Moving%20Saudi%20Arabias%20economy%20beyond%20oil/MGI%20Saudi%20Arabia_Executive%20summary_December%202015.ashx>

and house 2 million residents.[151] KAEC is one of seven similar grand economic cities that the late King Abdullah Al Saud had initiated to rekindle economic activity in Saudi Arabia's remote regions: Ha'il and Turaif in the north, Najran in the south, Rabigh and Jazan in the southwest, Arar in the northeast. According to KAEC's CEO, Fahd Al-Rasheed, the new generation of Saudis (more than 50% of Saudi citizens are under age 25) expects a city that matches the modern lifestyle they have grown used to while studying abroad.[152] Also, a new high-speed railway, (known as the Haramain Project) linking the holy cities of Makkah and Madinah, which will be able to move more than 166,000 passengers per day, will commence operation in September, 2018 , improving transport between the two cities during the annual *hajj* pilgrimages,[153] cutting travel time to two hours instead of six by bus.

In addition to the cities planned during the reign of King Abdullah, there is the Neom[154] project, part of Crown Prince Mohammed bin Salman's ambitious visionary plan (Vision 2030) to help diversify the economy, decrease the country's dependence on oil and modernize Saudi society. Neom is a futuristic $500 billion mega-city in the northwest on the coast of the Red Sea, that will be powered by renewable energy, appeal to investors of new technologies including robotics, and cover an area of 26,000 square kilometers, linking Saudi Arabia, Egypt and Jordan.[155]

---

151   Mimi Kirk 2017, The Saudi City That's Shunning Oil, Bloomberg CityLab, accessed December 2018, <https://www.citylab.com/equity/2017/03/the-saudi-city-going-oil-free/519531/>

152   Sylvia Smith 2015, Saudi Arabia's new desert megacity, accessed September 2017, <http://www.bbc.com/news/world-middle-east-31867727>

153   Saudi high-speed rail line to start operating in September 2018, Arabian Business, accessed November 2018, <http://www.arabianbusiness.com/transport/396864-saudi-high-speed-rail-line-to-start-operating-in-september>

154   Neom is a combination of "neo," or new, and a derivation of the Arabic word "mustaqbal," or future.

155   Holly Ellyatt 2018, Middle East Money, CNBC, accessed August 2018, <https://www.cnbc.com/2018/05/10/saudis-500-billion-mega-city-neom-is-attracting-overwhelming-interest-from-investors.html>

Still, Saudi Arabia reaps benefits from its black gold. According to the McKinsey Global Institute's Report of 2015:

"The sharp increases in oil prices, which rose from about $30 per barrel in 2003 to a sustained peak of about $110 per barrel in 2011 to 2013 before dropping back in 2014, fueled a doubling of GDP during the decade. At a time of growing indebtedness across major developed and emerging economies since the 2008 financial crisis, Saudi Arabia has been a rare exception: the Kingdom eliminated national debt and increased reserve assets to $732 billion, the equivalent of almost 100 percent of GDP in 2014."

Yet while the region has provided economic and career opportunities for many, it still has challenges to face—human rights issues and political instability (especially after the Arab Spring of 2011)—as well as a number of other concerns that present major obstacles for the people today. But Crown Prince Mohammed bin Salman is already laying the groundwork for economical and cultural reform, while modernizing Saudi society in the process, and vowing to restore the kingdom to a "more moderate Islam." With Vision 2030, he provides an ambitious national blueprint for a radical transformation of the kingdom. Still, the obstacles he has to overcome are many.

Youth Unemployment and Labor Rights

Youth unemployment is among the kingdom's biggest challenges. The country's unemployment rate is currently at 12.8 percent.[156] According to a 2011 report,[157] two-third of the entire Saudi

---

156 Marwa Rashad, Stephen Kalin 2018, Saudi Arabia needs 1.2 million jobs by 2022 to hit unemployment target, Reuters, accessed November 2018, <https://www.reuters.com/article/us-saudi-labour-jobs/saudi-arabia-needs-1-2-million-jobs-by-2022-to-hit-unemployment-target-official-idUSKBN1HW1CO>

157 Caryle Murphy 2011, Saudi Arabia's Youth and the Kingdom's Future, Woodrow Wilson Int'l Center for Scholars, accessed March 2017, <https://www.wilsoncenter.org/sites/default/files/Saudi%20Arabia%E2%80%99s%20Youth%20and%20the%20Kingdom%E2%80%99s%20Future%20FINAL.pdf>

population is under 30 years of age, and around 37 percent are 14 years old or younger, which places a lot of pressure on the government to provide employment for nearly 2 million Saudis in the next decade.

Although the late King Abdullah had introduced educational reforms with Vision 2030, the skill sets of Saudis fall considerably short of the standards required by the private sector. Many blame the ineffective education system, which leaves students ill prepared for the job market, as the primary cause.

To make matters worse, Saudis prefer higher-paying jobs in the public sector rather than the lower-paying ones in the private sector. According to Reuters, "Some 10 million foreigners are working in Saudi Arabia, doing many of the strenuous, dangerous and lower-paid jobs largely shunned by the 20 million nationals."[158] Changing societal attitudes towards employment will take time, and remains one of the greatest challenges for the Saudi government. Still, the Crown Prince has already tackled joblessness, implementing impressive plans to increase employment. According to a senior labor ministry official, Saudi Arabia aims to create 1.2 million jobs by 2022 by focusing on the retail sector in order to reduce unemployment to 9 percent.[159] The government also plans to cut the jobless rate to 7 percent by 2030, increase the percentage of women in the workforce from 22 to 30 percent,[160] as well as decrease the wage gap between women and men.

---

[158] Marwa Rashad, Stephen Kalin 2018, Saudi Arabia needs 1.2 million jobs by 2022 to hit unemployment target, Reuters, accessed November 2018, <https://www.reuters.com/article/us-saudi-labour-jobs/saudi-arabia-needs-1-2-million-jobs-by-2022-to-hit-unemployment-target-official-idUSKBN1HW1CO

[159] Marwa Rashad, Stephen Kalin 2018, Saudi Arabia needs 1.2 million jobs by 2022 to hit unemployment target, Reuters, accessed November 2018, <https://www.reuters.com/article/us-saudi-labour-jobs/saudi-arabia-needs-1-2-million-jobs-by-2022-to-hit-unemployment-target-official-idUSKBN1HW1CO>

[160] Ibid.

Labor rights are another major issue. Expatriate workers face discrimination in the job market. Two-thirds of Saudis are employed by the state, while expats account for about 90% of the private sector jobs."[161] The wave of rampant nationalization to help local Saudis find work has been done at the expat's expense. The government's implement of the Nitaqat system, a mass Saudization program that aims to improve the representation of Saudis citizens in the private sector by providing them with jobs has made it more difficult for expatriates looking for work. Also, low income and unskilled expat workers have had the added burden of contending with poor working conditions, inequities in wages, and delays in payment. And, according to a January 2018 McKinsey Report, expats are more likely to be the ones displaced, "with 41% percent of the existing work activities in Saudi Arabia's labor market automatable."[162] Saudi Arabia has, however, begun to take steps to rectify these conditions and is proceeding in a manner in line with world standards.

Education

Education is another debated topic in the country's public sector, and many Saudis find the curricula of schools lacking. A report by the Center of Universal Education at the Brookings Institution surveyed Saudi parents who claimed their children had failed to acquire a basic education after spending four years in primary schools.[163] Historically, primary and secondary education has been

---

161 Ahmad Al Omran 2018, Saudi Arabia raises the alarm over rising unemployment, Financial Times, accessed August 2018, <https://www.ft.com/content/df579534-47c3-11e8-8ae9-4b5ddcca99b3>

162 Jan Peter aus dem Moore, Vinay Chandran, and Jörg Schubert 2018, Are Middle East workers ready for the impact of automation?, McKinsey & Co., accessed November 2018, <https://www.mckinsey.com/featured-insights/middle-east-and-africa/are-middle-east-workers-ready-for-the-impact-of-automation>

163 Ghanem, Hafez; Jalbout, Maysa; Steer, Liesbet; Greubel, Lauren; Parker, Adam; Smith, Katie; Arab Youth: Missing Educational Foundations for a Productive Life? The Center for Universal Education, Brookings Institution, November 19, 2013. <https://www.brookings.edu/interactives/the-arab-world-learning-barometer/>

"biased toward religious subjects at the expense of STEM (science, technology, engineering and mathematics) subjects."[164] And, in a 2018 interview with *60 Minutes*, the Crown Prince plans to eradicate any extremism in the education system and stated that Saudi Schools have been infiltrated by the Muslim Brotherhood organization. "No country in the world," he said, "would accept that its educational system be invaded by any radical group."[165]

Political Instability
Although Saudi Arabia is a very stable country, concerns over political instability are on the rise, and some fear that local dissatisfaction over lack of jobs combined with the country's current foreign policy might foster public unrest and culminate in a rebellion. (Indeed, in 2011 and 2012, Kuwait witnessed high-profile protests outside its Parliament.) And there is always the concern that the mounting frustration over unemployment might lead some disgruntled young men to join extremist groups.

Several factors have added to the country's instability: fallout from the 2015 stampeding incident during the *Hajj* which was instigated by the Iranian Revolutionary Guards and resulted in hundreds of pilgrims' death; the drop in oil prices; the majority of population who are under 30 in need of sustainable employment; and territorial disputes with neighboring countries. All of these have contributed to the erosion of confidence, both locally and internationally.

Nonetheless, Saudi Arabia continues to occupy an important position in the economic sphere; Saudi Arabia, UAE, Kuwait and, Qatar as members of the OPEC, have considerable political power in the region.

---

164 Ghafar, Adel Abdel, "A New Kingdom of Saud?" Brookings Institution, February 14, 2018; originally appeared in The Cairo Review of Global Affairs;<https://www.brookings.edu/research/a-new-kingdom-of-saud/>

165 Norah O'Donnell 2018, 60-Minutes, CBS News, accessed July 2018, <https://www.cbsnews.com/news/saudi-crown-prince-talks-to-60-minutes/>

Economy

The economic contribution of the Arabian Peninsula countries in the world is very high. Oil exporting countries, such as Saudi Arabia, UAE, Kuwait, and Qatar, earn significant revenues as members of OPEC, allowing them to gather considerable funding for government spending on infrastructure development and GDP growth. In 2014, ARCADIS built various asset consultancy firms; since Saudi Arabia is regarded as one of the fastest growing markets in built asset performance, it is expected to increase 70 percent over the next decade with the help of these consultancy firms.

Oil, since its discovery in the region, has been the reason behind much of the stability of the Saudi economy. The government took active steps in 1970 with the introduction of its five-year infrastructure development initiatives that helped morph the former agricultural-based society into a bustling modern economic giant. Ever since, it has been on a rollercoaster ride with the development of large-scale real estate and infrastructure projects. The Crown Prince's sweeping reform, Vision 2030, will reduce dependence on oil and diversify the economy and create private sector jobs.

Women's Rights

The country's laws subjugate women in terms of their right to vote in the Shura Council elections. After there were protests for women suffrage in the country, the government in 2011 (under the late King Abdullah) allowed women to participate in municipal elections and become members of the Shura Council (the Consultative Assembly of Saudi Arabia.) While it has been argued that the previous laws restricting women from participating in elections and becoming a member of Shura Council were in favor of Islam, the right of women to have a political voice was enshrined in Madinah during the time of Prophet Muhammad (PBUH).

Also there is a bias against women in the Saudi judicial system. Widows and divorced women face discrimination in the law, receiving unjust treatment by judges and law enforcement. Alimony payments, for instance, go unpaid by spouses who ignore court rulings. Violence against women is not reported for fear of reprisals or being disgraced by the family at large.

On May 4, 2017, King Salman bin Abd Al-'Aziz issued a royal decree easing guardianship requirements for women in the country. (Guardianship laws that require women to seek permission from their father, husband, brother or son to enroll in higher education, seek employment, travel or marry.)

By mid 2018, the ban on women driving was lifted.

And the Crown Prince Mohammed bin Salman has curtailed the religious police's power to arrest women for not covering up. "The laws are very clear," he said, "and stipulated in the laws of Sharia: that women wear decent, respectful clothing, like men. This, however, does not particularly specify a black *abaya* or a black head cover. The decision is entirely left for women to decide what type of decent and respectful attire she chooses to wear."[166]

On the whole, Saudi Arabia has many women's right issues that are now being addressed by the young ruling elite for effective solutions to ensure women have a bright and stable future.

Indeed, when the Crown Prince was asked in an interview[167] if women were equal to men, he said, "Absolutely. We are all human beings, and there is no difference."

Environment

Saudi Arabia has introduced a number of laws in 1985 to manage its various environmental issues, such as reducing noise, air, and water pollution. Air pollution, the abundance of plastic trash, and municipal waste are perhaps the biggest environmental challenges and threat to the Saudi populous. The spread of chemicals from

---

166 Norah O'Donnell 2018, 60-Minutes, CBS News, accessed July 2018, <https://www.cbsnews.com/news/saudi-crown-prince-talks-to-60-minutes/>

167 Ibid.

crude oil refineries turns into harmful greenhouse gases, resulting in air pollution. and have the capacity to increase the temperature in the country, which is destructive for vegetation. Unfortunately, these laws were never seriously enforced and are still challenged by the industry, making its effectiveness insignificant.

The country also faces a problem of desertification and, according to the United Nations Convention to Combat Desertification, 98 percent of Saudi Arabia's land mass is desert (and infertile for growing crops). Less than 2 percent is fertile for vegetation, leaving fewer opportunities for export. The Saudi government has built nearly 30 desalination plants of various sizes throughout the Kingdom to counter the problem, but it also creates another environmental risk—water salt concentration pollution for nearby beaches.

Managing these environmental issues continues to be a huge challenge for the Saudi government as well as a very expensive one. However, the government is eager to resolve these environmental crises.

Healthcare

Saudi Arabia's healthcare system is highly advanced and robust, providing citizens with quality care nearly free or at reasonable rates. Hospitals and clinics are fairly abundant both in city and out-of-town areas. Furthermore, medical facilities are state-of-the-art, with cutting-edge equipment to provide effective and accurate medical treatments.

Despite these benefits, many serious epidemics and diseases are common amongst the Saudi population. The MERS, also known as the Middle East Respiratory Syndrome, led to fatalities in June 2012. In 2015[168] it was noted that health authorities closed an emergency ward of a major hospital after more than 40 people contracted the disease.

---

168 Helen Regan 2015, Saudi Arabia Is Reporting a Surge in MERS Deaths, Time, accessed June 2018, <http://time.com/4014376/saudi-arabia-mers-fatalities/>

Other diseases have also been problematic, such as the Rift Valley Fever, Dengue Fever and Cerebral Malaria. So although the Saudi healthcare system is robust, it does open questions pertaining to the speed at which it can get identify the root cause of epidemics and respond with effective solutions.

The Need for Accountability
The style of government of Saudi Arabia is an absolute monarchy – a system that puts all control in the hands of the King; concerns and interests of the ruling family are above everyone else. Over the years, the Saudi ruling family has relegated the laws of its regions' dominant Islamic caliphate system to punishments, while its economic system, although successful in terms of GDP growth and infrastructure development, has largely been based upon capitalist principles, causing a divide between the rich and the poor.

More importantly, there is little accountability. Plagued by corruption, the Saudi government is frequently criticized by various experts for its lack of accountability. It is no surprise that too much power can and will corrupt individuals.

The Consultative Assembly of Saudi Arabia, also known as the Shura Council, is derived from the Islamic tenet of 'consultative decision making.' For example, the Shura Council played an important role in the government of the Rashidun caliphate where decisions on key issues were openly discussed.

However, the Shura Council in Saudi Arabia has limited powers. The 150-member body can only *propose* laws to the king, who has the power to approve or reject it. The Shura Council in the Saudi government was first setup in 1926 under Sultan of Najd & Hejaz Ibn Saud; however, its powers were restricted following the political pressures of the royal family members, and became unofficially ineffective until King Fahad restored it back to power in 2000.

There is a dire need to have a representative leadership that gives due consideration to its people and manages its affairs by implementing solutions to meet the needs of citizens, and the Crown Prince has promised transparency and openness.

Saudi Arabia Vision 2030

The Crown Prince Mohammed bin Salman has already started his ambitious and progressive reform initiative, Saudi Arabia's Vision 2030. Among its many projects are plans to diversify the Kingdom's economy away from oil; develop public service sectors such as healthcare; education; infrastructure; housing (urban design and environment); recreation and tourism; reinforce economic and investment activities, increase non-oil industry trade between countries through goods and consumer products; and increase government spending on the military.

In addition the Crown Prince intends to implement other initiatives to raise the awareness of the importance of women's participation

Adel Alsuhaimi with US Consulate & Ex-Im Bank guests at family reception hall, September, 2009.

in the labor market, develop legislation to integrate women into all sectors of the labor market, provide childcare for working women. He also plans to develop services for expatriate workers while promoting the integration of expatriates within the culture of the Kingdom and increase citizens' awareness of other cultures.[169] He also wants to develop physical education classes for girls in school, promote diversity and female inclusion in sport, develop sports in school for students with special needs and sport activities at the university level, and create and host world class sporting events.[170] The 2020 target is to redesign 23 sports facilities, and promote a Paralympics in KSA.[171] In his push to modernize the country, the Crown Prince intends to support cultural events, by offering a variety of cultural venues—libraries, theatres, opera houses and art galleries and museums and the opening of hundreds of movie theatres—as well bringing film production to the kingdom.

"We have all the means to achieve our dreams and ambitions," the Crown Prince has said. "There are no excuses for us to stand still or move backwards."

Indeed, the Kingdom of Saudi Arabia is undergoing another transformation.

---

[169] Quality of Life Program 2020, Delivery Plan Pg. 113, Vision 2030, accessed November 2020, <http://vision2030.gov.sa/en/qol>

[170] Ibid, Pg. 116.

[171] Ibid, Pg. 123.

ACKNOWLEDGMENTS

To my parents Abdulaziz & Madawi (RIP), for their remarkable achievement of bringing up ten children. They instilled in us self-esteem, confidence, the highest ethics, respect for God, and a strong belief of the Almighty's guidance and mercifulness. They never spared any effort to keep us safe, educated, respectful, and comfortable; making sure that we upheld family in the highest regard.

To my wonderful wife of forty years who is always patient and loyal, supportive and caring for me, our children, and grandchildren. Her selflessness when she abandoned a career to marry me, have children, and care for all of us full-time deserves the utmost appreciation and admiration. All of us are indebted to her for life.

To my brothers and sisters who all have been there for me. My youngest brother Yousef and sister Nadia stand out for their staunch support and empathy.

To my Uncle Abdulrahman M. Alkadi for his loyalty and continued support. His care and guidance since my early years is appreciated.

To my life-long friends and close relatives: my best brothers-in-law, Abdulrahman A. H. Alsaadi and Adnan A. R. Almansoor; my best friends, Mohammad A. R. Albassam and Yousef S. Alroug. Their friendship and loyalty are priceless.

To my editor Barbara De Santis whose immaculate editing and research contribution were very valuable in turning my original manuscript and the piles of research work and documents I accumulated into the book it is now. She provided guidance and coaching that was instrumental in realizing my father's dream.

To my publishing consultant, designer, and director, Jeniffer Thompson, an excellent consultant and book designer who possesses keen eyes for art and marketing appeal. She navigated complicated publishing tasks with ease and mastery; I will always be grateful to her and the Monkey C Media team she commands.

To members of the MCM team for the art work (maps, photos, and other resources) including Chad Thompson, Julio Pompa, Anastasia Hipkins, and the organizing and office work of Kat Endries. Thank you for an excellent, well executed project.

To my copy editor; Adrienne Moch; thank you for a job well done.

PHOTO CREDITS

Page 2: From the collection of the author's late father, AbdulAziz Ar Alsuhami.

Page 3: From the collection of the author's late father, AbdulAziz Ar Alsuhami.

Page 6: From the collection of the author's late father, AbdulAziz Ar Alsuhami.

Page 10: Slide courtesy of the author.

Page 12: Courtesy of the Saudi Aramco Media Department.

Page 16: Copyright, Solent News.

Page 21: Map created by BMR Williams.

Page 36: From Pitt Rivers Museum, Oxford, UK/Bridgeman.

Page 40: Farhat Art Museum Collections.

Page 45: From Art Directors & TRIP / Alaauthor's Stock Photo.

Page 49: Courtesy of the author.

Page 51: Courtesy of King Abdul Aziz Foundation.

Page 56: Map created by BMR Williams.

Page 59: Map created by BMR Williams.

Page 60: Courtesy of the Saudi Aramco Media Department.

Page 61: Courtesy of the Saudi Aramco Media Department.

Page 64: Courtesy of the Saudi Aramco Media Department.

Page 71: Map created by BMR Williams.

Page 87: Purchased from the Imperial War Museum.

Page 94: Map created by BMR Williams.

Page 96: Public Domain.

Page 102: Map data ©2021 Google, Mapa GISrael Saudi Arabia.

Page 103: Courtesy of King Abdulaziz Library & Archives photos.

Page 104: Courtesy of King Abdulaziz Library & Archives photos.

Page 105: Photo by Max Steineke; courtesy of the Saudi Aramco Media Department.

Page 108: Courtesy of Farquad Family.

Page 113: Map created by BMR Williams.

Page 116: Courtesy of the Saudi Aramco Media Department.

Page 117: Courtesy of the Saudi Aramco Media Department.

Page 118: Courtesy of the Saudi Aramco Media Department.

Page 120: Top image from the collection of the author's late father, AbdulAziz Ar Alsuhami.

Page 120: Bottom image from the collection of the author's late father, AbdulAziz Ar Alsuhami.

Page 125: Deposit Photos, copyright, Mido Semsem (Mohamed Osama).

Page 126: iStock Photos, copyright Waeel Quttene.

Page 131: Courtesy of the Saudi Aramco Media Department.

Page 133: Courtesy of Mr. Bashar Alhady.

Page 135: Courtesy of the Saudi Aramco Media Department.

Page 136: Alamy.

Page 137: Alamy.

Page 140: Courtesy of the Saudi Aramco Media Department.

Page 141: Courtesy of the author.

Page 145: Courtesy of the Saudi Aramco Media Department.

Page 146: Top and bottom images from the collection of the author's uncle, Abdulrahman Alkadi.

Page 147: From the collection of the author's late father, AbdulAziz Ar Alsuhami.

Page 148: From the collection of the author's late father, AbdulAziz Ar Alsuhami.

Page 150: From the collection of the author's late father, AbdulAziz Ar Alsuhami.
Page 153: Courtesy of the Saudi Aramco Media Department.
Page 158: Map created by BMR Williams.
Page 161: Map created by BMR Williams.
Page 163: Map created by BMR Williams.
Page 164: Map created by BMR Williams.
Page 173: Photo by Karl S. Twitchell, courtesy of the Saudi Aramco Media Department.
Page 174: Courtesy of the Saudi Aramco Media Department.
Page 175: Courtesy of the Saudi Aramco Media Department.
Page 178: Top image courtesy of the Saudi Aramco Media Department.
Page 178: Bottom image courtesy of the Saudi Aramco Media Department.
Page 179: Courtesy of the Saudi Aramco Media Department.
Page 180: Courtesy of the Saudi Aramco Media Department.
Page 182, Courtesy of the Saudi Aramco Media Department.
Page 183: Courtesy of the Saudi Aramco Media Department.
Page 188: Map created by BMR Williams.
Page 190: From the collection of the author's late father, AbdulAziz Ar Alsuhami.
Page 193: From the collection of the author's late father, AbdulAziz Ar Alsuhami.
Page 197: Courtesy of the Saudi Aramco Media Department.
Page 198: Courtesy of the Saudi Aramco Media Department.
Page 199: Courtesy of the Saudi Aramco Media Department.
Page 202: Photo by E.E. Seal and T.F. Walters, courtesy of the Saudi Aramco Media Department.
Page 205: Courtesy of the Saudi Aramco Media Department.
Page 207: Courtesy of the Saudi Aramco Media Department.
Page 208: Courtesy of the Saudi Aramco Media Department.
Page 210: Courtesy of the Saudi Aramco Media Department.
Page 211: From the collection of the author's late father, AbdulAziz Ar Alsuhami.

Page 213: From the collection of the author's late father, AbdulAziz Ar Alsuhami.

Page 215: From the collection of the author's late father, AbdulAziz Ar Alsuhami.

Page 216: From the collection of the author's late father, AbdulAziz Ar Alsuhami.

Page 218: From the collection of the author's late father, AbdulAziz Ar Alsuhami.

Page 220: From the collection of the author's late father, AbdulAziz Ar Alsuhami.

Page 221: Courtesy of the Saudi Aramco Media Department.

Page 222: Photo by A.M. Al Khalifa, courtesy of the Saudi Aramco Media Department.

Page 223: Photo by Ahmed Mentakh, courtesy of the Saudi Aramco Media Department.

Page 225: Top image. Photo by Ali A. Al Khalifa, courtesy of the Saudi Aramco Media Department.

Page 225: Bottom image. Photo by B.H. Moody, courtesy of the Saudi Aramco Media Department.

Page 226: Photo by S. Ghamidi, courtesy of the Saudi Aramco Media Department.

Page 227: From the collection of the author's late father, AbdulAziz Ar Alsuhami.

Page 230: From the collection of the author's late father, AbdulAziz Ar Alsuhami.

Page 231: From the author's collection.

Page 233: From the author's collection.

Page 243: From the author's collection.

www.ingramcontent.com/pod-product-compliance
Lightning Source LLC
Chambersburg PA
CBHW032039150426
43194CB00006B/340